THE CHILTE...
INCLUDING THE EX...
BERKSHIRE LOOP

The Complete Official Guide to this circular Long-Distance Path through Bedfordshire, Berkshire, Buckinghamshire, Hertfordshire & Oxfordshire.

Nick Moon

The Chiltern Way was established by the Chiltern Society to mark the Millennium by providing walkers in the twenty-first century with a new way of exploring the diverse, beautiful countryside which the Chilterns have to offer. Based on the idea of the late Jimmy Parsons' Chiltern Hundred but expanded at the suggestion of Rob Bethell to cover the whole Chilterns, the route was largely devised by the author, while Rob Bethell masterminded the signposting, waymarking and improvement of the route on the Society's Rights of Way Group's behalf in preparation for the Way's formal launch in October 2000. In 2003, following the success of the original route, further loops were added extending the Way to both extremities of the Chilterns including the beautiful Oxfordshire section of the Thames Valley and the spectacular downland of the Barton Hills and in 2010, to mark its tenth anniversary, a further alternative loop has been created to take in the scenic Berkshire hills between Cookham and Henley.

In addition to a description of the route and points of interest along the way, this guide includes 47 specially drawn maps of the route indicating local pubs, car parks, railway stations and a skeleton road network and details are provided of the Ordnance Survey and Chiltern Society maps covering the route.

The author, Nick Moon, has lived in or regularly visited the Chilterns all his life and has, for over 30 years, been an active member of the Chiltern Society's Rights of Way Group, which seeks to protect and improve the area's path and bridleway network. Thanks to the help and encouragement of the late Don Gresswell MBE, he was introduced to the writing of books of walks and has since written or contributed to a number of publications in this field.

OTHER PUBLICATIONS BY NICK MOON

Circular Walks along the Chiltern Way
Volume 1:   Buckinghamshire and Oxfordshire:
                     Book Castle (new edition) 2010
Volume 2:   Hertfordshire and Bedfordshire:
                     Book Castle 2005

Chiltern Walks Trilogy
Chiltern Walks 1:   Hertfordshire, Bedfordshire and
                     North Buckinghamshire:
                     Book Castle (new edition) 2007
Chiltern Walks 2:   Buckinghamshire:
                     Book Castle (new edition) 2010
Chiltern Walks 3:   Oxfordshire and West Buckinghamshire:
                     Book Castle (new edition) 2001

Family Walks
Family Walks 1:   Chilterns - South : Book Castle 1997
Family Walks 2:   Chilterns - North : Book Castle 1998

Oxfordshire Walks
Oxfordshire Walks 1: Oxford, The Cotswolds and The Cherwell
                     Valley: Book Castle (new edition) 1998
Oxfordshire Walks 2: Oxford, The Downs and The Thames Valley:
                     Book Castle (new edition) 2002

The d'Arcy Dalton Way across the Oxfordshire Cotswolds and
                     Thames Valley : Book Castle 1999

First published October 2010

by Book Castle Publishing, 2a Sycamore Business Park, Copt Hewick,
North Yorkshire HG4 5DF

© Nick Moon

Printed in Great Britain by CPI Antony Rowe, Chippenham, Wilts.

ISBN 978-1-906632-10-6

Contents

Chiltern Way Guide

Section

Cover photograph : Old Place, Harpsden Bottom (Sections 16 & 18)

© Nick Moon

Introduction

The Chiltern Way, which was created by the Chiltern Society as its Millennium project, is based on the idea of the late Jimmy Parsons' 'Chiltern Hundred`, but, whereas Jimmy's route was confined to a 100-mile circuit of the central Chilterns, the original Chiltern Way takes in four Chiltern counties in a 133-mile circuit extending from Ewelme, Oxfordshire in the southwest to Sharpenhoe Clappers, Bedfordshire and Lilley, Hertfordshire in the northeast as well as going as far southeast as Chorleywood West on the Chiltern downslope. The extensions lengthen the route to 172 miles and take it southwards to the Thames at Mapledurham and Goring and eastwards via the Barton Hills almost to Hitchin, while a route via the Berkshire Loop and extensions is of similar length and takes in the scenic hills between Cookham and Henley. While these routes do not attempt to take in every corner of or every parish in the Chilterns, they do offer a good cross-section of the various types of characteristic Chiltern scenery.

Starting from Hemel Hempstead Station in Hertfordshire near the confluence of the Rivers Gade and Bulbourne, (which proved to be the nearest railway station to a route conceived as a circuit without a specific starting point), the Way leads you southwards over the Bovingdon plateau to Sarratt Church, before crossing a scenic section of the Chess valley and reaching the picturesque Buckinghamshire village of Chenies. You then continue southwards skirting Chorleywood to reach Newland Park where you can visit the Chiltern Open Air Museum with its collection of historic buildings and artefacts.

Now turning west, the Way descends into the Misbourne valley at the photogenic village of Chalfont St. Giles, where it briefly joins the South Bucks Way before continuing westwards across quiet upland in the Penn Country, passing north of Hodgemoor Wood to reach the traditional hilltop villages of Coleshill and Winchmore Hill. Turning southwestwards, you now pass through Penn Bottom and Penn itself to reach a wood called Coppice Hoop, where the Berkshire Loop forks off the original Chiltern Way.

From here, the **original Chiltern Way** drops into the Wye valley at Loudwater at a point where the preservation of the ancient common meadow of King's Mead as a recreation ground enables you to cross this otherwise very industrialised valley with a minimum of urban intrusion. You then skirt Flackwell Heath to reach the upper northern slopes of the Thames Valley with wide views across it in places before passing through extensive woodland to skirt Marlow by way of

Burroughs Grove, Marlow Bottom and Bovingdon Green. Here the Way turns west across the quiet wooded hills above the Thames Valley before descending into Hambleden and its valley, one of the jewels of the Chilterns.

Now turning north, the Way leads you up the Hambleden Valley to Skirmett, before crossing a wooded hill which affords some fine views and descending to Fingest and Turville, two more villages whose photogenic character makes them favourite locations for calendar pictures and filming. Turning southwest again, the Way climbs with fine views to a high ridge at Southend Common and entering Oxfordshire, takes one of the most beautiful Chiltern paths, descending through woodland and Stonor Park with its magnificent house of mediæval origin to the estate village of Stonor. Continuing westwards, the Way climbs with more fine views to cross the Oxfordshire Way at Maidensgrove, once described as ´perhaps the most remote hamlet in all the Chilterns` and skirt Russell's Water Common, before dropping into the upper end of the heavily-wooded Bix Bottom with its nature reserve where the Southern Extension forks off the original Chiltern Way.

From here, a short cut to Russell's Water village enables you to cut 10 miles off the original Chiltern Way or take a 10-mile circular walk to and from Ewelme, while the main route of **the original Way** continues westwards, crossing another high ridge at Park Corner, then descending through woodland and crossing the Ridgeway to reach an ancient road from Henley to Oxford. Having crossed Harcourt Hill with its wide views across the Thames Valley and Oxfordshire Plain, the original Chiltern Way then rejoins the Southern Extension at Potter's Lane south of Ewelme.

From Coppice Hoop near Penn, **the Berkshire Loop** first leads you southeastwards to Forty Green with its ancient hostelry, before taking Riding Lane southwards down a remote Chiltern bottom to Holtspur Bank Nature Reserve, through which you climb to reach Holtspur on its hilltop plateau. Having passed through this suburban settlement and crossed the A40 and M40, you continue southwards through beechwoods before descending with superb views to Wooburn in the Wye valley. After crossing a further wooded hill to Hedsor with its hilltop church and folly, the Loop then reaches the banks of the Thames and soon crosses Cookham Bridge into the picturesque Berkshire village of Cookham.

Briefly joining the Thames Path, you then follow the towpath upstream towards Bourne End, before leaving the river and climbing Winter Hill where a series of panoramic views of the southern Chilterns and beyond await you. Eventually turning south over the ridge, you then explore the fascinating higgledy-piggledy village of

Cookham Dean with its maze of steep lanes and paths, before continuing southwards through woodland to the wide open expanse of Pinkneys Green on the edge of Maidenhead. Now turning west, you pass through the heavily-wooded area around Maidenhead Thicket, Ashley Hill and Bowsey Hill, once the haunt and hideout of the highwayman, Dick Turpin, where the woods are now interspersed with fine views. On leaving the woods behind, you turn north to cross and then circle Remenham Hill with some of the finest views on the Chiltern Way, passing the Georgian mansion of Culham Court and later descending to cross Henley Bridge into Oxfordshire.

Rejoining the Thames Path, you then turn south to reach Lower Bolney before leaving the Thames Path, turning westwards and climbing gently over a low ridge to join the Chiltern Way Southern Extension in Harpsden Bottom.

From Upper Bix Bottom, **the Southern Extension of the Way** first takes you southwards to an upland plateau at Crocker End with its royal connections before turning east and descending through woodland into the picturesque lower part of Bix Bottom, site of the lost village of Bixbrand where you briefly rejoin the Oxfordshire Way. Turning south again, you then climb through more woodland to skirt the hilltop village of Bix and continue across an upland plateau to pass the secluded Greys Court, another fascinating manor house which originated as a mediæval castle, before crossing a shallow Chiltern bottom and climbing through woodland to Greys Green with its idyllic cricket green and cherry trees. Continuing southwards across a quiet, but now less wooded upland plateau punctuated by the occasional shallow bottom, the Southern Extension of the Way passes a picturesque ancient farmhouse in Harpsden Bottom, where the **Berkshire Loop** rejoins the earlier route.

The Southern Extension now traverses Crowsley Park with its fine Jacobean manor house and eventually skirts the modern suburban settlement of Sonning Common. Now quite close to Reading, the route continues across the plateau to Chalkhouse Green, Tokers Green and Chazey Heath before descending through woodland to the secluded, picturesque, Thames-side village of Mapledurham with its ancient watermill and manor house at the most southerly point on the Chiltern Way.

Now heading westwards, you climb out of the Thames Valley with fine views and continue across upland interspersed with woodland, passing through Collins End, Path Hill and Whitchurch Hill, before more fine views herald another descent into the Thames Valley at Goring, the most westerly point on the Way. Turning northeastwards, the Chiltern Way Extension now climbs and follows the quiet and, at first heavily-wooded, western escarpment emerging from the woods in places to be greeted with superb views, passing through Woodcote and reaching Hailey where the landscape becomes less hilly and wooded and you continue northwards crossing the Ridgeway to rejoin the original Chiltern Way in the gently rolling hills south of Ewelme.

The reunited Chiltern Way now takes you to the picturesque, historic village of Ewelme with its ancient buildings and watercress beds before turning eastwards, crossing another open ridge with superb views and climbing to the top of Swyncombe Down, one of the most spectacular projections of the Chiltern escarpment. The Way then continues along the ridge before turning south onto the Ridgeway to reach Swyncombe with its 1000-year-old church. Leaving the Ridgeway, the Way then turns east to cross the main escarpment ridge at Cookley Green, before turning northeast across the upper reaches of a series of typical heavily-wooded ridges and bottoms at the back of the escarpment, passing through Russell's Water, Pishill Bottom and Northend and recrossing the Oxfordshire Way at Hollandridge. From Northend, descending steeply through woodland to reenter Buckinghamshire, you reach the beautiful Wormsley Valley, where an ancient estate succeeded in excluding public roads, before crossing another high ridge at Ibstone to reach Stokenchurch, one of the highest villages in the Chilterns, which, despite its unfortunate reputation as the ´ugly duckling of the Chilterns`, is a superb centre for walking in the surrounding hills.

Continuing northeastwards with fine views, a series of ridges and bottoms in the Radnage area are crossed before you climb up Bledlow Ridge. Turning northwards, the Way then descends, crossing the Ridgeway west of Lodge Hill and several low ridges to reach Bledlow at the foot of the escarpment, then turns east across the Risborough gap in the escarpment, visiting Saunderton, recrossing the Ridgeway and climbing to Lacey Green with its restored seventeenth-century windmill. From here, the Way leads you northeastwards across the heavily-wooded uplands of the Hampden Country, following parts of Grim's Ditch, visiting Great Hampden, home of the leading Parliamentarian soldier, crossing Hampden Bottom and reaching the remote upland hamlet of Little Hampden, where you once again join the South Bucks Way.

Leaving the South Bucks Way again at Cobblers Hill, the Chiltern Way continues northeastwards, crossing the dry upper reaches of the Misbourne valley and another somewhat less wooded range of quiet uplands by way of Lee Gate, Buckland Common, a further section of Grim's Ditch and Wigginton to reach the Bulbourne valley and Grand Union Canal at Cow Roast. Now back in Hertfordshire, the Way heads for Aldbury with some fine views across the Tring Gap, before climbing to cross the heavily-wooded Ashridge Estate to reach

Little Gaddesden, then descends into the Gade valley, entering Bedfordshire. Turning north, the Way now crosses another range of uplands, passing through Studham and skirting Whipsnade Wild Animal Park and Tree Cathedral, before emerging onto the top of the Dunstable Downs, where the Way reaches its highest point and superb views abound.

From here, the Way begins the circling of the Luton/Dunstable conurbation, which forms its most northerly section, descending to cross the ancient Icknield Way on the edge of Dunstable, then crossing a series of open Chiltern foothills with extensive views in places, passing through Sewell, Bidwell and Chalton. Having crossed the M1, the Way then climbs onto the most northerly ridge of the Chilterns at Upper Sundon and follows it by way of Sundon Hills Country Park to Sharpenhoe Clappers with an abundance of superb views, where the Northern Extension forks off the original Chiltern Way.

Turning south, **the original Way** follows the ridgetop with more fine views before leaving the escarpment, passing through Streatley and heading for the open downs of Galley Hill and Warden Hill, where more panoramic views open out across Luton and the hills to the east. Now turning east, you soon reenter Hertfordshire and pass through the former estate village of Lilley, before turning south through the surprisingly quiet hills east of Luton to rejoin the Northern Extension at Peters Green.

From Sharpenhoe Clappers **the Northern Extension** descends to Sharpenhoe village before crossing lowland fields with superb views of the escarpment to reach Barton-le-Clay. You then climb the Barton Hills with more panoramic views and circle the rim of a spectacular deep coombe before leaving the escarpment and turning east onto the Icknield Way to reach Telegraph Hill. From here you once again descend past a deep coombe to reach Pegsdon and then round the northeastern end of the escarpment crossing Knocking Hoe and High Down. You now head south across an upland plateau to Great Offley before turning east again and descending towards Hitchin. Finally leaving the escarpment, you head south by way of Preston with its picturesque village green, Chapelfoot, the ruins of Minsden Chapel and St. Paul's Walden, alleged birthplace of the late Queen Mother, to reach Whitwell in the Mimram valley before heading southwest across low rolling Hertfordshire hills to rejoin the original Chiltern Way at Peters Green.

The reunited Chiltern Way then crosses the southeastern tip of Bedfordshire and the Lea valley at East Hyde to reenter Hertfordshire on the edge of the dormitory town of Harpenden. Its final 12 miles then lead you westwards through quiet hills to recross the M1 and reach the hilltop village of Flamstead, before turning southwestwards through remote hill country to cross the Gade valley at the picturesque hamlet of Water End. You now cross one final ridge at Potten End to enter Hemel Hempstead by way of one of its 'green lungs' and return to your starting point.

While the full 133-mile or 172-mile routes can be completed by the more energetic in a week or so or, in a more leisurely fashion, in up to a fortnight or can be split into a series of one-day walks, a whole range of shorter variations are also possible. For example, the 10-mile Ewelme loop can be omitted from the original Chiltern Way or the South Bucks Way or Grand Union Canal towpath or both can be used to cut across from the northbound to the southbound section of the Way or vice versa or the Chiltern Way Extensions or the Berkshire Loop can be combined with the part of the original Way to which they form an alternative to create shorter circular routes at either end of the Chilterns, while parts of the western section can be walked together with the parallel part of the Ridgeway. These and other alternative options can be identified by consulting the overview map on pages 14/15.

As the availability of overnight accommodation varies from year to year, it is advisable to contact a local tourist information centre for up-to-date information and bookings. These are as follows:-

Dunstable : 01582-890270
http://www.dunstable.gov.uk
Harpenden : 01582-768278
Hemel Hempstead : 01442-234222
http://www.dacorum.gov.uk/
Henley-on-Thames : 01491-578034
High Wycombe : 01494-421892
Hitchin/Stevenage : 01438-737333
Luton : 01582-401579
Maidenhead : 01628-796502 or 01753-743907 (booking line)
http://www.maidenhead.gov.uk
Marlow : 01628-483597
Princes Risborough : 01844-274795
Rickmansworth : 01923-776611
St. Albans : 01727-864511
http://www.stalbans.gov.uk/
Thame : 01844-212833
Tring : 01442-823347
http://www.tring.gov.uk/
Wallingford : 01491-826972

Wendover   : 01296-696759
http://www.wendover-pc.gov.uk/tourism

Throughout its length, the Chiltern Way follows public rights of way, uses recognised permissive paths or crosses public open space. As the majority of paths used cross land used for economic purposes such as agriculture, forestry or the rearing of game, walkers are urged to follow the Country Code at all times:-

- Be **safe** - plan ahead and follow any signs.
- **Leave** gates and property as you find them.
- **Protect** plants and animals, and take your litter home.
- Keep dogs under close **control**.
- **Consider** other people.

Observing these rules helps prevent financial loss to landowners and damage to the environment, as well as the all-too-frequent and sometimes justified bad feeling towards walkers in the countryside.

Details of possible parking places are given in the introductory information to each section and any convenient railway stations are shown on the accompanying plan. For up-to-date information on bus services consult the Traveline website at <www.traveline.org.uk> or call their telephone hotline on 0871-200 22 33.

While it is hoped that the special maps provided will assist the user to avoid going astray and skeleton details of the surrounding road network are given to enable walkers to vary the route in emergency, it is always advisable to take an Ordnance Survey or Chiltern Society map with you to enable you to vary the route without using roads or get your bearings if you do become seriously lost. Details of the appropriate maps are given in the introductory information for each section.

As for other equipment, readers are advised that some mud will normally be encountered particularly in woodland except in the driest weather. However proper walking boots are to be recommended at all times as, even when there are no mud problems, hard ruts or rough surfaces make the protection given by boots to the ankles desirable. In addition, in some places overgrowth is prevalent around stiles and hedge gaps and in woodland particularly in summer. To avoid resultant discomfort, it is therefore always advisable to carry a stick to clear the way or wear protective clothing.

In order to assist in coordinating the plans and the texts, all the numbers of paths used have been shown on the plans and incorporated into the texts. These numbers, which are also shown on the

Chiltern Society's Footpath Maps, consist of the official County Council footpath number with prefix letters used to indicate the parish concerned. It is therefore most helpful to use these when reporting any path problems you may find, together, if possible, with the national grid reference for the precise location of the trouble spot, as, in this way, the problem can be identified on the ground with a minimum of time loss in looking for it. National grid references can, however, only be calculated with the help of Ordnance Survey Landranger or Explorer maps and an explanation of how this is done can be found in the Key to all current Ordnance Survey maps.

The length of time required for any particular section of the Way depends on a number of factors such as your personal walking speed, the number of hills, stiles, etc. to be negotiated, whether or not you stop to rest, eat or drink, investigate places of interest etc. and the number of impediments such as mud, crops, overgrowth, ploughing, etc. which you encounter, but generally an average speed of between two and two and a half miles per hour is about right. It is, however, always advisable to allow extra time if you are limited by the daylight or catching a particular bus or train home in order to avoid your walk developing into a race against the clock.

Should you have problems with any of the paths used or find that the description given is no longer correct, the author would be most grateful if you could let him have details (c/o Book Castle Publications or the Chiltern Society), so that attempts can be made to rectify the problem or the text can be corrected at the next reprint. Nevertheless, the author hopes that you will not encounter any serious problems and have pleasure from following the Way.

TheChiltern
Society
We care for the Chilterns

The Chiltern Society

The Chiltern Society aims to conserve and protect the natural beauty, environment and heritage of the Chilterns. The Society's Rights of Way Group actively protects and restores open access land and public rights of way in the Chilterns — some 5,000 paths. It has surveyed every individual path and takes up irregularities with parish, district or county councils to preserve and enhance public rights. The charity has over 6,500 members and organises weekly walks and cycle rides, as well as volunteer work parties to carry out footpath maintenance and other conservation projects.

We welcome new members - come and join people like you who love the Chilterns. For more details please contact:

The Chiltern Society,
The White Hill Centre,
White Hill,
Chesham,
Buckinghamshire HP5 1AG.

Tel. : 01494-771250.
Email : office@chilternsociety.org.uk
Website : www.chilternsociety.org.uk

CHILTERN WAY &
Linking Long-Distance Paths

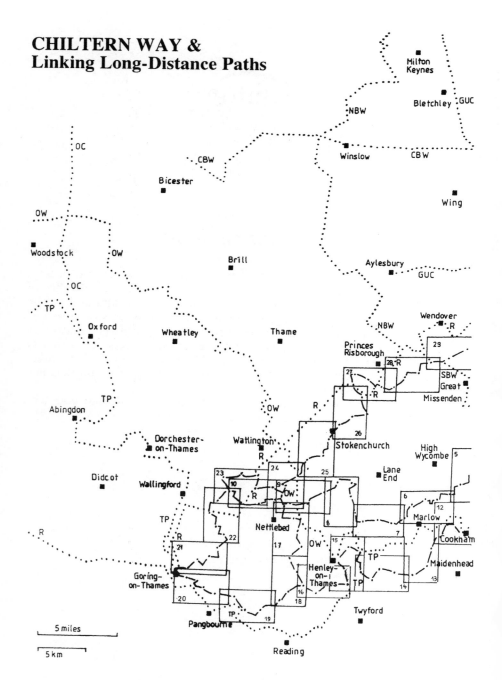

5 miles

5 km

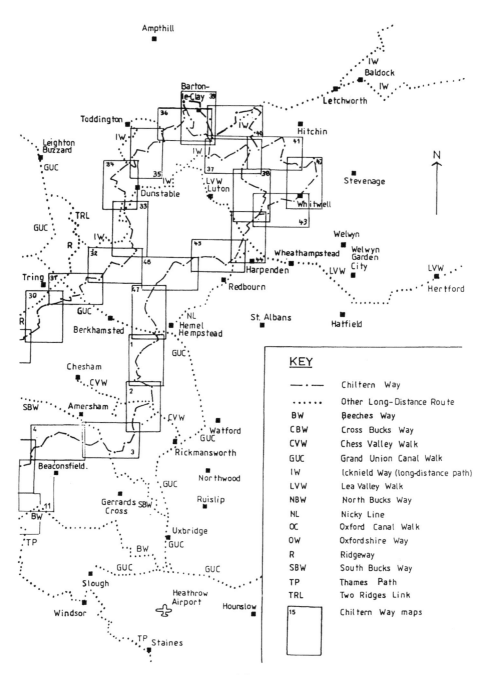

KEY

—·—	Chiltern Way
••••••	Other Long-Distance Route
BW	Beeches Way
CBW	Cross Bucks Way
CVW	Chess Valley Walk
GUC	Grand Union Canal Walk
IW	Icknield Way (long-distance path)
LVW	Lea Valley Walk
NBW	North Bucks Way
NL	Nicky Line
OC	Oxford Canal Walk
OW	Oxfordshire Way
R	Ridgeway
SBW	South Bucks Way
TP	Thames Path
TRL	Two Ridges Link
15	Chiltern Way maps

Distance Table

Height (m.) (ft.)	Place	Distance miles	km	Original Chiltern Way Cumulative miles	km	Chiltern Way via Extensions Cumulative miles	km	Chiltern Way via Berkshire Loop/Extensions Cumulative miles	km
85 280	Hemel Hempstead Station	0.0	0.0	0.0	0.0	0.0	0.0	0.0	0.0
85 280	A4251 (A41 Flyover)	0.2	0.3	0.2	0.3	0.2	0.3	0.2	0.3
155 510	Bovingdon (Chipperfield Rd)	2.4	3.9	2.6	4.2	2.6	4.2	2.6	4.2
135 440	Flaunden	2.0	3.3	4.6	7.5	4.6	7.5	4.6	7.5
115 380	Sarratt Church	2.5	4.0	7.1	11.5	7.1	11.5	7.1	11.5
125 410	Chenies (A404)	1.5	2.4	8.6	13.9	8.6	13.9	8.6	13.9
110 360	Chorleywood West	1.3	2.1	9.9	16.0	9.9	16.0	9.9	16.0
120 390	Chorleywood (Heronsgate Rd)	0.4	0.6	10.3	16.6	10.3	16.6	10.3	16.6
105 340	Chalfont Park (Gorelands La)	1.6	2.5	11.9	19.1	11.9	19.1	11.9	19.1
75 250	Chalfont St. Giles (A413)	0.8	1.3	12.7	20.4	12.7	20.4	12.7	20.4
70 230	Chalfont St. Giles (High St)	0.3	0.5	13.0	20.9	13.0	20.9	13.0	20.9
80 260	South Bucks Way (CG29/30)	0.8	1.3	13.8	22.2	13.8	22.2	13.8	22.2
135 440	Bottrells Lane	0.8	1.3	14.6	23.5	14.6	23.5	14.6	23.5
125 410	A355	1.4	2.2	16.0	25.7	16.0	25.7	16.0	25.7
165 540	Coleshill ('Red Lion')	0.6	1.0	16.6	26.7	16.6	26.7	16.6	26.7
155 510	Winchmore Hill Crossroads	1.0	1.6	17.6	28.3	17.6	28.3	17.6	28.3
110 360	Penn Bottom (Car Park)	1.1	1.8	18.7	30.1	18.7	30.1	18.7	30.1
165 540	Penn (B474)	0.8	1.3	19.5	31.4	19.5	31.4	19.5	31.4

170	560	Penn (Beacon Hill)	0.4	0.7	19.9	32.1	19.9	32.1	19.9	32.1
130	430	Penn (Coppice Hoop)	0.8	1.2	20.7	33.3	20.7	33.3	20.7	33.3
55	180	Loudwater (A40)	1.3	2.1	22.0	35.4	22.0	35.4	----	----
55	180	Loudwater (Kingsmead Rd)	0.4	0.7	22.4	36.1	22.4	36.1	----	----
115	380	Flackwell Heath (Heath End Rd)	0.6	1.0	23.0	37.1	23.0	37.1	----	----
60	200	Sheepridge ('Crooked Billet')	0.9	1.4	23.9	38.5	23.9	38.5	----	----
90	300	Burroughs Grove (official)	2.6	4.1	26.5	42.6	26.5	42.6	----	----
		„ „ (short cut)	2.1	3.4						
55	180	Marlow Bottom	0.9	1.5	27.4	44.1	27.4	44.1	----	----
100	330	Seymour Court (B482)	0.5	0.9	27.9	45.0	27.9	45.0	----	----
85	280	Bovingdon Green (Bucks)	1.1	1.8	29.0	46.8	29.0	46.8	----	----
95	310	Marlow Common	0.9	1.4	29.9	48.2	29.9	48.2	----	----
120	390	Rotten Row	1.8	2.8	31.7	51.0	31.7	51.0	----	----
45	150	Hambleden Church	1.0	1.7	32.7	52.7	32.7	52.7	----	----
50	160	Pheasant's Hill	0.6	1.0	33.3	53.7	33.3	53.7	----	----
55	180	Colstrope	0.4	0.7	33.7	54.4	33.7	54.4	----	----
70	230	Skirmett (Shogmoor Lane)	1.2	1.9	34.9	56.3	34.9	56.3	----	----
80	260	Fingest ('Chequers Inn')	1.7	2.6	36.6	58.9	36.6	58.9	----	----
80	260	Turville (Village Green)	0.6	1.0	37.2	59.9	37.2	59.9	----	----
105	340	Dolesden	0.6	0.9	37.8	60.8	37.8	60.8	----	----
195	640	Southend Common	0.9	1.5	38.7	62.3	38.7	62.3	----	----
90	300	Stonor (village)	1.4	2.3	40.1	64.6	40.1	64.6	----	----
180	590	Maidensgrove (Ox. Way)	0.9	1.5	41.0	66.1	41.0	66.1	----	----
190	620	Maidensgrove Common	0.4	0.7	41.4	66.8	41.4	66.8	----	----
120	390	Upper Bix Bottom	0.6	0.9	42.0	67.7	42.0	67.7	----	----
135	440	Start of Ewelme Loop	0.4	0.6	42.4	68.3	----	----	----	----
165	540	End of Loop (via short cut)	0.5	0.8	(42.9)	(69.1)	----	----	----	----
205	670	Park Corner (B481)	1.1	1.7	43.5	70.0	----	----	----	----

Height (m.) (ft.)	Place	Distance (miles / km)		Original Chiltern Way Cumulative (miles / km)		Chiltern Way via Extensions Cumulative (miles / km)		Chiltern Way via Berkshire Loop/Extensions Cumulative (miles / km)	
		miles	km	miles	km	miles	km	miles	km
160 520	Ridgeway (N. of Nuffield)	1.4	2.2	44.9	72.2	----	----	----	----
125 410	End of Southern Extension	1.9	3.0	46.8	75.3	----	----	----	----
100 330	Forty Green	0.9	1.4	----	----	----	----	21.6	34.7
100 330	Holtspur (Holtspur Top Lane)	1.2	1.9	----	----	----	----	22.8	36.6
100 330	Holtspur (A40)	0.5	0.9	----	----	----	----	23.3	37.5
100 330	Windsor Hill	1.3	2.1	----	----	----	----	24.6	39.6
100 330	Berghers Hill	0.2	0.4	----	----	----	----	24.8	40.0
45 150	Wooburn (Wash Hill)	0.5	0.8	----	----	----	----	25.3	40.8
95 310	Hedsor (Kiln Lane)	0.4	0.7	----	----	----	----	25.7	41.5
65 210	Hedsor Hill	0.9	1.4	----	----	----	----	26.6	42.9
25 80	Cookham Bridge	0.7	1.0	----	----	----	----	27.3	43.9
70 230	Winter Hill	2.3	3.8	----	----	----	----	29.6	47.7
90 300	Cookham Dean (Inn-on-the-Green)	0.8	1.3	----	----	----	----	30.4	49.0
75 250	Bigfrith Common	0.6	1.0	----	----	----	----	31.0	50.0
80 260	Pinkneys Green (A308)	1.5	2.4	----	----	----	----	32.5	52.4
65 210	Stubbings (Henley Road)	1.2	2.0	----	----	----	----	33.7	54.4
75 250	Burchett's Green School	0.9	1.4	----	----	----	----	34.6	55.8
145 480	Ashley Hill	0.9	1.4	----	----	----	----	35.5	57.2
80 260	Warren Row	1.5	2.5	----	----	----	----	37.0	59.7
140 460	Bowsey Hill	0.6	0.8	----	----	----	----	37.6	60.5

90	300	Crazies Hill	0.9	1.4	----	----	----	38.5	61.9
90	300	Cockpole Green	0.4	0.7	----	----	----	38.9	62.6
100	330	Remenham Hill (A4130)	1.3	2.2	----	----	----	40.2	64.8
35	110	Aston ('Flower Pot Hotel')	1.3	2.1	----	----	----	41.5	66.9
30	100	Henley Bridge	1.9	3.1	----	----	----	43.4	70.0
30	100	Henley (Mill Lane)	0.9	1.4	----	----	----	44.3	71.4
40	130	Lower Bolney (A4155)	1.5	2.4	----	----	----	45.8	73.8
85	280	Binfield Heath ('Bottle & Glass')	1.8	2.8	----	----	----	47.6	76.6
60	200	Harpsden Bottom (end of Berks Loop)	1.0	1.7	----	----	----	48.6	78.3
175	570	Crocker End Green	0.9	1.5	----	43.0	69.2	----	----
85	280	Bix Bottom Church (Oxf.Way)	1.2	1.9	----	44.2	71.1	----	----
80	260	Valley Farm, Bix (Oxf.Way)	0.1	0.2	----	44.3	71.4	----	----
130	430	Bix (A4130)	1.0	1.6	----	45.3	73.0	----	----
105	340	Greys Court	1.5	2.4	----	46.8	75.4	----	----
110	360	Greys Green	0.6	0.9	----	47.4	76.3	----	----
60	200	Harpsden Bottom	2.2	3.5	----	49.5	79.8	48.6	78.3
75	250	Crowsley Turn	0.8	1.2	----	50.3	81.0	49.4	79.5
80	260	Sonning Common (B481)	0.8	1.3	----	51.1	82.3	50.2	80.8
80	260	Chalkhouse Green	0.7	1.1	----	51.8	83.4	50.9	81.9
80	260	Tokers Green Pond	1.2	2.0	----	53.0	85.4	52.1	83.9
95	310	Chazey Heath (A4074)	0.5	0.7	----	53.5	86.1	52.6	84.6
45	150	Mapledurham	1.9	3.1	----	55.4	89.2	54.5	87.7
105	340	Collins End	1.3	2.0	----	56.7	91.2	55.8	89.7
110	360	Path Hill	0.6	1.0	----	57.3	92.2	56.4	90.7
130	430	Whitchurch Hill Church (B471)	1.0	1.6	----	58.3	93.8	57.4	92.3
145	480	Coombe End Crossroads	0.7	1.1	----	59.0	94.9	58.1	93.4
55	180	Goring Railway Bridge	2.9	4.8	----	61.9	99.7	61.0	98.2
70	230	Cleeve (Battle Road)	0.9	1.4	----	62.8	101.1	61.9	99.6

Height (m.) (ft.)	Place	Distance miles	km	Original Chiltern Way Cumulative miles	km	Chiltern Way via Extensions Cumulative miles	km	Chiltern Way via Berkshire Loop/Extensions Cumulative miles	km
110 360	Wroxhills Wood (Beech La.)	0.5	0.9	----	----	63.3	102.0	62.4	100.5
160 520	Woodcote (B471)	2.4	3.9	----	----	65.7	105.9	64.8	104.4
165 540	Woodcote (A4074)	0.4	0.6	----	----	66.1	106.5	65.2	105.0
170 560	Garsons Hill	1.5	2.4	----	----	67.6	108.9	66.7	107.4
90 300	Well Place	1.0	1.6	----	----	68.6	110.5	67.7	109.0
120 390	Hailey ('King William')	0.6	1.0	----	----	69.2	111.5	68.3	110.0
85 280	Ridgeway (Grim's Ditch)	1.5	2.4	----	----	70.7	113.9	69.8	112.4
105 340	Oakley Wood (A4130)	1.3	2.0	----	----	72.0	115.9	71.1	114.4
125 410	Gould's Grove	0.7	1.2	----	----	72.7	117.1	71.8	115.6
125 410	End of Southern Extension	0.6	0.9	----	----	73.3	118.0	72.4	116.5
90 300	Ewelme (Recreation Ground)	1.1	1.7	47.9	77.0	74.4	119.7	73.5	118.2
110 360	Icknieldbank Plantation	1.4	2.3	49.3	79.3	75.8	122.0	74.9	120.5
190 620	Swyncombe Down (Ridgeway)	1.1	1.7	50.4	81.0	76.9	123.7	76.0	122.2
165 540	Swyncombe Church	0.7	1.3	51.1	82.3	77.6	125.0	76.7	123.5
220 720	Cookley Green (B481)	1.0	1.6	52.1	83.9	78.6	126.6	77.7	125.1
165 540	End of Ewelme Loop	0.7	1.1	52.8	85.0	79.3	127.7	78.4	126.2
195 640	Russell's Water Pond	0.3	0.5	53.1	85.5	79.6	128.2	78.7	126.7
170 560	Pishill Bottom (B480/Grove Fm)	0.7	1.1	53.8	86.6	80.3	129.3	79.4	127.8
180 590	Oxfordshire Way (College Wd)	1.3	2.1	55.1	88.7	81.6	131.4	80.7	129.9
165 540	Oxfordshire Way (Fire Wood)	0.3	0.5	55.4	89.2	81.9	131.9	81.0	130.4

220	720	Northend Common	0.6	1.0	56.0	90.2	82.5	132.9	81.6	131.4
225	740	Ibstone (N. end of village)	1.8	2.9	57.8	93.1	84.3	135.8	83.4	134.3
225	740	Stokenchurch (A40)	1.7	2.7	59.5	95.8	86.0	138.5	85.1	137.0
150	490	Radnage Church	2.2	3.5	61.7	99.3	88.2	142.0	87.3	140.5
210	690	Bledlow Ridge	0.6	1.0	62.3	100.3	88.8	143.0	87.9	141.5
215	710	Rout's Green	0.7	1.1	63.0	101.4	89.5	144.1	88.6	142.6
185	610	Ridgeway (W. of Wigan's La)	1.2	2.0	64.2	103.4	90.7	146.1	89.8	144.6
115	380	Bledlow (W. of Church)	1.0	1.5	65.2	104.9	91.7	147.6	90.8	146.1
105	340	Saunderton Church	1.3	2.1	66.5	107.0	93.0	149.7	92.1	148.2
125	410	Ridgeway (S. of Saunderton)	0.7	1.1	67.2	108.1	93.7	150.8	92.8	149.3
140	460	A4010	0.6	1.0	67.8	109.1	94.3	151.8	93.4	150.3
225	740	Lacey Green ('Whip')	0.8	1.2	68.6	110.3	95.1	153.0	94.2	151.5
210	690	Lily Bottom	0.9	1.5	69.5	111.8	96.0	154.5	95.1	153.0
230	750	Redland End	0.5	0.8	70.0	112.6	96.5	155.3	95.6	153.8
215	710	Hampden House	0.9	1.5	70.9	114.1	97.4	156.8	96.5	155.3
165	540	Hampden Bottom	0.6	0.9	71.5	115.0	98.0	157.7	97.1	156.2
210	690	Little Hampden (S. Bucks Way)	0.9	1.5	72.4	116.5	98.9	159.2	98.0	157.7
220	720	Cobblers Hill (S. Bucks Way)	0.7	1.1	73.1	117.6	99.6	160.3	98.7	158.8
145	480	Wendover Dean (A413)	0.9	1.5	74.0	119.1	100.5	161.8	99.6	160.3
205	670	Lee Gate	1.2	2.0	75.2	121.1	101.7	163.8	100.8	162.3
200	660	Kingswood ('Old Swan')	0.4	0.6	75.6	121.7	102.1	164.4	101.2	162.9
200	660	St. Leonard's ('White Lion')	1.7	2.7	77.3	124.4	103.8	167.1	102.9	165.6
195	640	Wigginton (Chesham Road)	2.6	4.2	79.9	128.6	106.4	171.3	105.5	169.8
120	390	Cow Roast (A4251)	1.6	2.5	81.5	131.1	108.0	173.8	107.1	172.3
120	390	Cow Roast Lock (GUC)	0.1	0.1	81.6	131.2	108.1	173.9	107.2	172.4
160	520	Aldbury (Malting Lane)	1.6	2.7	83.2	133.9	109.7	176.6	108.8	175.1
190	620	B4506	0.7	1.2	83.9	135.1	110.4	177.8	109.5	176.3
190	620	Little Gaddesden (P.H.)	1.6	2.6	85.5	137.7	112.0	180.4	111.1	178.9

Height		Place	Distance		Original Chiltern Way Cumulative		Chiltern Way via Extensions Cumulative		Chiltern Way via Berkshire Loop/Extensions Cumulative	
(m.)	(ft.)		miles	km	miles	km	miles	km	miles	km
120	390	A4146	1.3	2.1	86.8	139.8	113.3	182.5	112.4	181.0
185	610	Studham (Common Road)	1.0	1.5	87.8	141.3	114.3	184.0	113.4	182.5
215	710	Whipsnade (B4540)	2.3	3.7	90.1	145.0	116.6	187.7	115.7	186.2
230	750	Dunstable Downs (Car Park)	1.4	2.2	91.5	147.2	118.0	189.9	117.1	188.4
165	540	Dunstable (B489/B4541)	1.0	1.6	92.5	148.8	119.0	191.5	118.1	190.0
110	360	Sewell (bend in road)	1.4	2.4	93.9	151.2	120.4	193.9	119.5	192.4
125	410	A5 ('Chalk Hill')	1.1	1.7	95.0	152.9	121.5	195.6	120.6	194.1
115	380	Bidwell (A5120/'Old Red Lion')	1.1	1.7	96.1	154.6	122.6	197.3	121.7	195.8
105	340	Chalton (B579/'Star')	2.8	4.6	98.9	159.2	125.4	201.9	124.5	200.4
160	520	Upper Sundon ('Red Lion')	1.4	2.3	100.3	161.5	126.8	204.2	125.9	202.7
155	510	Sundon Hills Country Park	0.9	1.4	101.2	162.9	127.7	205.6	126.8	204.1
150	490	Sharpenhoe Clappers (car park)	1.8	2.9	103.0	165.8	129.5	208.5	128.6	207.0
140	460	Sharpenhoe Clappers (CW fork)	0.6	0.9	103.6	166.7	130.1	209.4	129.2	207.9
135	440	Streatley (Allotments Car Park)	1.7	2.8	105.3	169.5	-----	-----	-----	-----
150	490	Streatley Church	0.3	0.4	105.5	169.9	-----	-----	-----	-----
130	430	A6 (Swedish Cottages)	0.7	1.1	106.2	171.0	-----	-----	-----	-----
150	490	Icknield Way (Maulden Firs)	1.3	2.1	107.5	173.1	-----	-----	-----	-----
185	610	Galley Hill	0.1	0.2	107.6	173.3	-----	-----	-----	-----
195	640	Warden Hill	0.8	1.3	108.4	174.6	-----	-----	-----	-----
180	590	Stopsley (Whitehill Farm)	1.4	2.3	109.8	176.9	-----	-----	-----	-----

140	460	Lilley Church	1.2	1.8	111.0	178.7	----	----	----
135	440	Hollybush Hill (Glebe Farm)	0.9	1.5	111.9	180.2	----	----	----
120	390	Lilley Bottom	0.8	1.3	112.7	181.5	----	----	----
165	540	Mangrove Green	1.1	1.8	113.8	183.3	----	----	----
155	510	Cockernhoe Green	0.3	0.5	114.1	183.8	----	----	----
150	490	Wandon End Farm	1.0	1.5	115.1	185.3	----	----	----
145	480	Breachwood Green	1.2	2.0	116.3	187.3	----	----	----
145	480	Peter's Green (End of N.Extens.)	2.1	3.3	118.4	190.6	----	----	----
80	260	Sharpenhoe ('The Lynmore')	0.2	0.4	----	130.3	209.8	129.4	208.3
65	210	A6 (Barton Mill)	1.4	2.3	----	131.7	212.1	130.8	210.6
70	230	Barton-le-Clay ('Royal Oak')	0.5	0.8	----	132.2	212.9	131.3	211.4
80	260	Barton-le-Clay Church	0.5	0.7	----	132.7	213.6	131.8	212.1
165	540	Barton Hills (summit)	0.9	1.4	----	133.6	215.0	132.7	213.5
155	510	Icknield Way (Maulden Firs)	1.5	2.5	----	135.1	217.5	134.2	216.0
180	590	Telegraph Hill	1.6	2.6	----	136.7	220.1	135.8	218.6
85	280	Pegsdon (B655)	0.9	1.5	----	137.6	221.6	136.7	220.1
125	410	Knocking Hoe	1.3	2.0	----	138.9	223.6	138.0	222.1
115	380	B655 (nr. Old Wellbury)	1.1	1.8	----	140.0	225.4	139.1	223.9
165	540	Little Offley	1.2	2.0	----	141.2	227.4	140.3	225.9
155	510	A505 (Clouds Hill)	1.2	2.0	----	142.4	229.4	141.5	227.9
155	510	Great Offley ('Red Lion')	1.4	2.2	----	143.8	231.6	142.9	230.1
80	260	Temple End	1.8	2.9	----	145.6	234.5	144.7	233.0
100	330	Offley Holes	0.5	0.8	----	146.1	235.3	145.2	233.8
150	490	Austage End	1.0	1.6	----	147.1	236.9	146.2	235.4
140	460	Preston ('Red Lion')	1.4	2.2	----	148.5	239.1	147.6	237.6
80	260	Chapelfoot ('Royal Oak')	1.7	2.7	----	150.2	241.8	149.3	240.3
130	430	Minsden Chapel	0.5	0.7	----	150.7	242.5	149.8	241.0
110	360	Langley End	0.5	0.8	----	151.2	243.3	150.3	241.8

Height		Place	Distance		Original Chiltern Way Cumulative		Chiltern Way via Extensions Cumulative		Chiltern Way via Berkshire Loop/Extensions Cumulative	
(m.)	(ft.)		miles	km	miles	km	miles	km	miles	km
150	490	Stagenhoe Lodge (B651)	0.8	1.3	-----	-----	152.0	244.6	151.1	243.1
135	440	St. Paul's Walden Church	0.4	0.7	-----	-----	152.4	245.3	151.5	243.8
90	300	Whitwell (High St./B651)	0.9	1.4	-----	-----	153.3	246.7	152.4	245.2
130	430	Whitwell (Water Tower/B651)	0.7	1.2	-----	-----	154.0	247.9	153.1	246.4
105	340	Whiteway Bottom	1.4	2.3	-----	-----	155.4	250.2	154.5	248.7
145	480	Peter's Green (End of N.Extens.)	1.8	3.0	-----	-----	157.2	253.2	156.3	251.7
95	310	East Hyde (B653)	1.6	2.6	120.0	193.2	158.8	255.8	157.9	254.3
110	360	Harpenden (A1081)	1.4	2.2	121.4	195.4	160.2	258.0	159.3	256.5
110	360	M1 (Junction 9)	3.0	4.8	124.4	200.2	163.2	262.8	162.3	261.3
145	480	Flamstead Church	1.0	1.7	125.4	201.9	164.2	264.5	163.3	263.0
165	540	Gaddesden Row School	2.4	3.8	127.8	205.7	166.6	268.3	165.7	266.8
105	340	Water End (A4146)	1.8	3.0	129.6	208.7	168.4	271.3	167.5	269.8
160	520	Potten End (Water End Rd)	1.1	1.7	130.7	210.4	169.5	273.0	168.6	271.5
160	520	Fields End	0.9	1.5	131.6	211.9	170.4	274.5	169.5	273.0
85	280	Boxmoor (Grand Union Canal)	1.5	2.5	133.1	214.4	171.9	277.0	171.0	275.5
85	280	A4251 (A41 Flyover)	0.2	0.3	133.3	214.7	172.1	277.3	171.2	275.8
85	280	Hemel Hempstead Station	0.2	0.3	133.5	215.0	172.3	277.6	171.4	276.1

GUIDE TO THE CHILTERN WAY

Hemel Hempstead Station - Bovingdon (Herts.) (Map 1)

Maps
OS Landranger Sheet 166
OS Explorer Sheet 182
Chiltern Society FP Maps Nos. 5 & 20

Parking
Hemel Hempstead Station car park.

To unfamiliar readers, Hemel Hempstead Station may seem an unlikely starting point for the Chiltern Way, as the town as a post-war ´new town` may conjure up visions of endless housing estates rather than beechwoods and bluebells, but its location is hilly so that it is surrounded by good walking country and ´green lungs` have been left between the estates so that parts of the town can be traversed by walkers with only a minimum of intrusion by urban development. In fact, as the Way was conceived as a continuous circular route and a starting point was only needed for the purposes of this guide, the reason for its choice was that it happened to be the point on the existing proposed route with the best public transport access being only 300 yards from the circular route.

Despite the post-war ´new town` designation, Hemel Hempstead, in fact, has a long history as the A4251, on which the station is situated, is part of a Roman road known as Akeman Street and remains of Roman villas have been found not only here but also in Gadebridge Park to the north of the town centre. In the Middle Ages, Hemel Hempstead must already have been a wealthy market town as is attested by its magnificent twelfth-century church and in the eighteenth and nineteenth centuries the construction of the Grand Junction Canal, the London & North Western Railway main line from London (Euston) to the Midlands and North and several paper mills, where modern paper-making methods were pioneered, all to the south of the mediæval town, caused its expansion southwards and the absorption of neighbouring villages such as Boxmoor, where the railway station is situated.

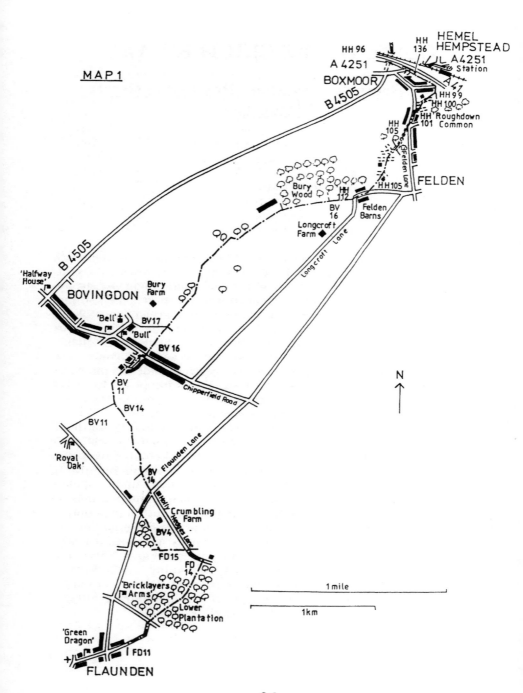

MAP 1

Starting from the main entrance to Hemel Hempstead Station, turn left down the station approach to reach a roundabout. Here cross the A4251 left of the roundabout and turn left onto its footway passing under three bridges carrying the railway and the A41.

Now recross the main road and, **joining the main route of the Chiltern Way**, take fenced path HH136 off the end of a short cul-de-sac. On reaching the entrance to a subway to your left, bear half right onto path HH99, ignoring a gravel lane to your right and passing through a kissing-gate frame, then take an enclosed path uphill to a kissing-gate into woodland on Roughdown Common. Here fork right onto path HH100, climbing gently through the wood and soon passing between bollards to join a flinty drive. Soon after the drive bears right, fork left onto a woodland path, climbing gently to reach another flinty track (byway HH101), then turn right onto this, soon reaching Felden Lane.

Turn left onto this road, then, just past its junction with Roefields Close, fork right onto path HH105, taking the macadam drive to Felden Lodge through woodland onto a golf course. By a single ash tree to your right, leave the drive and bear half left across a fairway to a kissing-gate in the top hedge. Here cross a bridleway and go through a kissing-gate opposite, then bear slightly right across a meadow, passing the corner of a garden hedge to your right to reach a kissing-gate by a garage. Now cross a drive to a bungalow and follow a left-hand hedge straight on to a stile, then follow a right-hand hedge straight on across a field to a squeeze-stile leading to Longcroft Lane.

Turn right onto this road, passing Felden Barns, then, at a left-hand bend, fork right through a kissing-gate onto path HH112, taking what is normally a crop-break straight on across a field (soon on path BV16) to reach a gap in the next hedge. Now bear slightly right across the next field to join the edge of Bury Wood to your right, level with a large clump of bushes to your left concealing a pond. Here ignore a branching path into the wood and follow its outside edge, disregarding all further paths into the wood, then continuing beside a right-hand hedge to the far end of the field. Now go through a small gate and, ignoring a gate to your right, bear slightly left and follow a fenced path past a copse to another small gate, then turn right and follow the right-hand hedge to a field corner. Here turn left and continue beside the right-hand hedge for over half a mile to pass through a kissing-gate at the far end of the field. Now with views to your right of Bovingdon Church and still on path BV16, follow a left-hand hedge straight on to a kissing-gate into a path between gardens, which eventually leads you out to Chipperfield Road in Bovingdon, onto which you turn right.

Bovingdon (Herts.) - Flaunden (Map 1)

Maps
OS Landranger Sheet 166
OS Explorer Sheet 182
Chiltern Society FP Map No.5

Parking
On-street parking is possible in Bovingdon.

Much of Bovingdon today with its housing estates, 'infill' development, shops etc. has a very suburban appearance, but quiet corners remain and the village can boast a number of attractive houses and cottages, some of which date back to the sixteenth or seventeenth century. The picturesque well in the village centre was built in 1881 in memory of a Lord of the Manor, Granville Dudley Ryder from a nearby manor house known as Westbrook Hay, who died in 1879, while the church, set in one of the largest churchyards in Hertfordshire, was rebuilt in 1845 on the site of a thirteenth-century predecessor, from which part of the tower and the effigy of a knight dating from around 1400 are preserved. Until 1833, the then small village of Bovingdon was merely a hamlet of Hemel Hempstead and it is said that services were only held in the ruinous old church once a month if bad weather did not discourage the curate from coming from Hemel to take them!

After 30 yards, by a footpath sign to your left, turn left across the grass verge and take a road called Austins Mead straight on. Where the road turns right, just past a small car park on your left, fork left onto path BV11, an alleyway between houses nos. 51 and 52 leading to a kissing-gate. Now take a fenced path straight on to another gate, then bear half left and follow a left-hand fence across a field to a small gate in the far corner. Here take fenced path BV14, bearing half left across the next field to a kissing-gate at a corner of a hedge hidden by a holly tree, then follow a left-hand hedge straight on. Where the hedge turns left, leave it and bear half right across the field to a corner of another hedge, then bear half left and follow this hedge to the kissing-gate of a crossing path to your right. Here bear slightly left and follow a right-hand hedge to a gap by a gate leading to a road junction.

Turn right onto the priority road (Flaunden Lane), then, just before another road junction, turn left through a kissing-gate onto path BV4, following the edge of a wood through three fields. On passing through a hedge gap into a fourth field, turn left onto path FD15, following a left-hand line of trees to a kissing-gate in a field corner, then go straight on across the next field, passing right of two oak trees to reach a squeeze-stile by metal gates into Holly Hedges Lane, into which you turn right. After 170 yards, where woodland commences to your right, turn right over a stile by a disused gate onto path FD14, following the edge of the wood to the far side of a right-hand field, then keeping straight on through the wood to a road junction. Here cross the priority road and take the Flaunden road straight on gently uphill to reach the Flaunden village nameboard.

Flaunden - Sarratt Church (Map 2)

Maps
OS Landranger Sheet 166
OS Explorer Sheets 172 & 182
Chiltern Society FP Maps Nos. 5 & 28

Parking
Limited on-street parking in Flaunden village. Take care not to obstruct or park opposite driveways in the narrow village streets.

Flaunden, locally pronounced 'Flarnden', is an unspoilt secluded village clustered around a crossroads of narrow lanes on a hilltop north of the Chess valley. The village church, built in 1838 to replace a thirteenth-century predecessor over a mile away in the Chess valley, is notable for being the first to be designed by the celebrated architect, Sir George Gilbert Scott, who was later responsible for the Midland Grand Hotel in London which forms the façade of St. Pancras Station. This church incorporates several items from its predecessor including its fifteenth-century font, three ancient bells and the one-handed church clock.

Just past the Flaunden village nameboard, where the road widens, turn left over a stile by a gate onto path FD11 following a right-hand hedge gently uphill to cross a stile. Now bear half left across the next field, heading for a gap between trees to cross another stile and take a fenced path beside a left-hand hedge to reach a narrow lane. Turn right onto this road, passing Newhouse Farm, then turn left through a hedge gap onto path SA51, following a left-hand hedge to a stile. Cross this and bear slightly right across the field to a stile and steps leading down into a narrow lane. Turn left onto this road, then, after some 350 yards at the entrance to Great Bragman's Farm, fork right over a stile onto path SA25 bearing slightly right across a field to cross a concealed stile at the far end of a weatherboarded barn, where the timber-framed farmhouse can be seen to your right. Now take a hedged path straight on, crossing another stile and continuing to Rosehall Farm.

By an entrance to the farm bear slightly right along the concrete road, bearing slightly left at one fork and slightly right at a second and continuing along a rough road, soon passing Rosehall Wood to your left and a belt of trees to your right. Now ignore a gate to your right and where the farm road turns left, leave it, crossing a stile by a gate under an oak tree and taking path SA24 beside a right-hand fence to a kissing-gate in a field corner. Now bear slightly right across the next field to cross a stile by a gate in the far corner. Here cross a fenced track, go through another gate opposite and bear half right across the next field aiming for a junction of hedges to a kissing-gate into Moor Lane, then go through a kissing-gate opposite and follow a left-hand hedge to another kissing-gate. Now bear half right across the next field to a kissing-gate into the corner of a wood where you take the obvious path beside a row of cypress trees to your right to reach a kissing-gate. Here disregard a branching path to your right, then at a crossways turn right onto a gravelly track and follow it through woodland on Dawes Common, ignoring all branching and crossing paths, to reach Dawes Lane.

Cross this narrow road and take path SA24 through a kissing-gate by a disused gate opposite, following a right-hand fence straight on through woodland. At a waymarked junction take a fenced track straight on, eventually reaching the end of a private macadam road by the entrance to The Old Rectory. Now take this road straight on, then, at a left-hand bend, fork right through a kissing-gate and over a stile. Now follow a left-hand fence along the outside edge of a wood with views of the Chess valley to your right, then, where the fence turns left, leave it and go straight on, heading just right of Sarratt church tower to reach a stile and kissing-gate into the churchyard.

Sarratt Church - Chenies (Map 2)

Maps
OS Landranger Sheets 166 or 176
OS Explorer Sheet 172
Chiltern Society FP Map No.28

Parking
On-street parking is possible at Sarratt Green two-thirds of a mile north of the church. Do not use the 'Cock Inn' car park without the landlord's permission.

Sarratt Church, situated in the old village known as Church End, is a cruciform twelfth-century building appropriately dedicated to the Holy Cross. It is of particular interest as its tower was rebuilt in the fifteenth century in part with Roman bricks (presumably from the ruins of a Roman villa discovered in the vicinity) and it is also the only church tower in Hertfordshire with a saddleback roof. The church, restored by Sir George Gilbert Scott in 1865, also contains a Norman font, a fragment of a thirteenth-century wall painting and a carved Jacobean pulpit, from which the renowned Nonconformist Richard Baxter preached in the seventeenth century. Also at Church End are a pub, a nineteenth-century manor house and some almshouses rebuilt in 1821, but the bulk of the modern village is situated around Sarratt's extensive village green two-thirds of a mile to the north.

If wishing to visit the church or the 'Cock Inn', take path SA53 straight on into the churchyard then, for the pub, bear half left, passing left of the church to reach the lychgate leading to Church Lane where the 'Cock Inn' is to your left.

Otherwise, do **not** enter the churchyard but turn sharp right onto path SA39, following a left-hand hedge to a gate and stile into a tree belt. Cross this stile, then turn left onto path SA32 following a left-hand hedge downhill with superb views to your right up the Chess valley. In the bottom corner of the field cross a stile, descend some steps and follow a fenced path downhill to a path junction by a kissing-gate. Go through the kissing-gate and now in Bucks, turn right onto path CN15 following a right-hand fence to cross a stile and a footbridge over the River Chess. Here go straight on through marshland to cross another footbridge. Now, at a three-way fork, take the central option straight on, passing left of a large holly bush, ignoring a crossing path and crossing a stile into Turvey Lane Wood.

Go straight on through this wood disregarding the kissing-gate of a branching path to your right and continuing along a track up a valley bottom for over a third of a mile, eventually emerging through a gap by an overgrown stile into a field. Here turn left and follow the edge of the wood to an outcrop, then bear half right uphill to the right-hand corner of Wyburn Wood. Now cross a stile into this wood and go straight on through it to a stile into the corner of a field, then take a fenced path leading to a gate onto a road in Chenies.

Chenies - Chorleywood West (Map 2)

Maps
OS Landranger Sheets 166 or 176
OS Explorer Sheet 172
Chiltern Society FP Map No.28

Parking
There are laybys near Chenies on the A404 and on-street parking is possible in the village.

Chenies, which belonged to the Earls and Dukes of Bedford and their predecessors by marriage, the Cheyne family, from the thirteenth century till 1954, is today a picturesque model village largely rebuilt by the Estate in the nineteenth century. Its fine Manor, once known as Chenies Palace as both Henry VIII and Elizabeth I stayed there, is in part fifteenth-century but mainly dates from 1530 when it was extended by the 1st Earl of Bedford while the fifteenth-century church is noted for the Bedford Chapel with its superb monuments dating from 1556. Originally known as Isenhampstead, the village name evolved in the thirteenth century to Isenhampstead Cheynes and only contracted to its present form in the nineteenth century.

Now cross the village street and turn right onto its footway passing the Old Rectory. After 100 yards, where the village inns are straight ahead, turn left through a kissing-gate onto path CN25. Now follow a right-hand hedge across the cricket field then pass through a kissing-gate and continue beside the right-hand hedge. Where the hedge bears right, leave it and go straight on across the field to a climb-through stile, then keep straight on to a kissing-gate. Now continue between a hedge and a fence to a kissing-gate onto a road where the Manor is to your right. Turn left onto this road to reach the A404, then cross this main road carefully and take bridleway CN3 straight on, entering a sunken green lane and following it gently downhill for half a mile, passing through Halsey's Wood and reaching a tunnel under the Metropolitan Line built in 1889 and now jointly used by Chiltern Railways.

At the far end of the tunnel go past a gate into Whitelands Wood reentering Hertfordshire. Now ignoring a branching path to your left, take bridleway CW38 straight on along a woodland track beside a right-hand hedge disregarding branching paths to your left. Where the hedge bears away to the right, take the track straight on downhill and up again ignoring all branching or crossing paths or tracks to reach a gate at the edge of the wood. Here disregard a crossing path and a path forking right through a squeeze-stile into a plantation and walk round the right-hand end of a gate then take a fenced track along the outside edge of Hillas Wood with Chorleywood West coming into view ahead, later leaving the wood behind and taking a fenced track straight on, passing Newhouse Farm with its tall cedar to your right. On reaching its drive (bridleway CN3a), turn left onto it (briefly reentering Bucks) and follow it to a road junction in Chorleywood West.

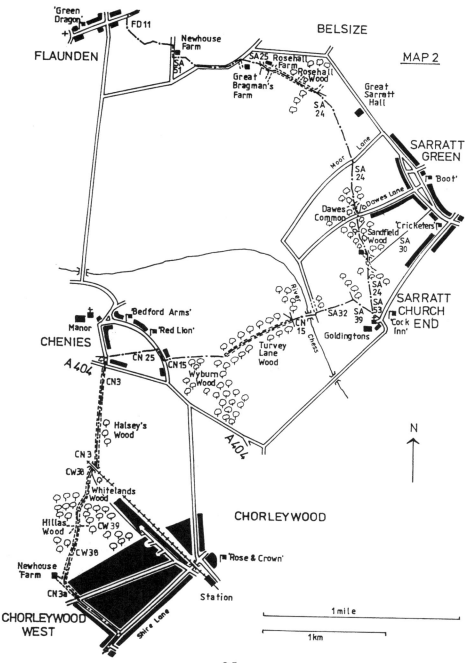

'Green Dragon'

FD 11

BELSIZE

Newhouse Farm

MAP 2

FLAUNDEN

SA 51

SA25 Rosehall Farm

Rosehall Wood

Great Bragman's Farm

SA 24

Great Sarratt Hall

SARRATT GREEN

Moor Lane

SA 24

'Boot'

Dawes Lane

Dawes Common

Cricketers

Sandfield Wood

SA 30

SA 24

SA 53

SARRATT CHURCH END

Manor

Bedford Arms'

'Red Lion'

CHENIES

River Chess

CN 15

SA32

SA 39

'Cock Inn'

Goldingtons

A 404

CN 25

CN15

Turvey Lane Wood

CN3

Wyburn Wood

N

Halsey's Wood

A 404

CN 3

CW38

Whitelands Wood

CHORLEYWOOD

Hillas Wood

CW 39

CW38

Newhouse Farm

'Rose & Crown'

CN 3a

Station

CHORLEYWOOD WEST

Shire Lane

1 mile

1km

35

Chorleywood West - Chalfont St. Giles (Map 3)

Maps
OS Landranger Sheet 176
OS Explorer Sheet 172
Chiltern Society FP Maps Nos. 6, 22 & 28

Parking
On-street parking is possible at Chorleywood West.

Chorleywood West is the name given to the part of Chorleywood which till 1992 was in Buckinghamshire, originally a distant outpost of Chalfont St. Peter parish and more recently part of Chenies. The Hertfordshire village of Chorleywood, of which it is now part, was till the arrival of the Metropolitan Railway in 1889 a tiny village surrounding its Victorian church on the A404 with a scattering of farms and cottages around its 200-acre common to the south including the farmhouse where the Quaker, William Penn (1644 - 1718), founder of the American state of Pennsylvania, was married in 1672. The coming of the railway, however, led to the establishment of built-up areas to the east and west of the common which spilled over the border into Buckinghamshire creating the curious mixture of countryside and suburbia known as 'Metroland', which, amongst others, became home to the conductor, Sir Henry Wood, founder of the Proms.

Now in Hertfordshire again, cross Blacketts Wood Drive and take Chalfont Lane straight on towards The Swillett for a quarter mile to reach a T-junction. Here turn right into Shire Lane, so called because it follows the ancient county boundary. Where the priority road bears left into Heronsgate Road, leave it, forking right into Old Shire Lane (bridleway CW33). Soon reaching an unchanged section of county boundary, follow this access road (bridleway CN52/CW33) for a third of a mile. Where its macadam surface ends, ignore a branching path to your left and take a stony lane straight on soon with Philipshill Wood to your right. Now keep straight on for a further half mile ignoring all branching paths into the wood and later descending (now on bridleway CP44/CW33) into a slight valley. At the bottom of the hill, where the bridleway bears sharp left, turn right through the left-hand of two squeeze-stiles onto path CP6 entering the wood, finally leaving the Hertfordshire boundary behind and following a chestnut-paling fence. After 300 yards you bear left and climb, now with a barbed-wire fence to your right which you follow when the chestnut-paling fence ends, eventually crossing a stile into Newland Park where the Chiltern Open Air Museum can be seen to your left.

The Open Air Museum, which can be reached by turning left onto the Newland Park drive 700 yards ahead, was conceived by the Chiltern Society as a project for European Architectural Heritage Year 1975 and was founded on County Council-owned land in Newland Park the following year. Opened to the public in 1981, the constantly-expanding museum consists largely of buildings of architectural interest which would otherwise have been lost through demolition but have instead been painstakingly taken down and rebuilt at Newland Park. It is open daily from April to October from 10 a.m. to 5 p.m.

Follow the right-hand hedge then the edge of Shrubs Wood straight on through the park. At the far side of the wood bear slightly right across a field to cross a stile by a chestnut tree left of a lodge. Now turn right onto the Newland Park drive and follow it to its T-junction with Gorelands Lane. Bear slightly right across this road and take bridleway CP8 through a gap by an overgrown gate opposite, then continue for a third of a mile through a strip of woodland to reach a gap by a gate into Chesham Lane. Cross this road and before crossing the stile opposite, take a few steps to your left for a view of Ashwell´s Farm with its fine seventeenth-century timber-framed brick farmhouse and weatherboarded barn.

Now cross the stile and take fenced path CP9 beside a left-hand hedge. On reaching two kissing-gates, go through both, ignoring a branching path to your right, then bear slightly right across a field to a kissing-gate in the next hedge. Now keep straight on across the next field to a kissing-gate in its far corner, then continue between fences to a path junction. Here bear right onto fenced path CG32 and follow it gently downhill for 350 yards to reach the A413 at Chalfont St. Giles. Cross this main road carefully and take the continuation of path CG32 down an alleyway opposite to a gate into the Misbourne meadows where a fine view of St. Giles's Church opens out ahead. Now bear slightly right, passing through a kissing-gate then ignoring a stile to your right and continuing beside a right-hand fence to a former kissing-gate and a footbridge over the River Misbourne. Joining the South Bucks Way, disregard a fence gap to your left, then take a fenced macadam path bearing right then left along the edge of the churchyard, eventually reaching an archway leading into the High Street opposite the ´Crown`.

Chalfont St. Giles - Bottom House Farm Lane (Map 3)

Maps
OS Landranger Sheets 175 or 176
OS Explorer Sheet 172 (or old Sheet 3)
Chiltern Society FP Map No.6

Parking
Signposted car park in Chalfont St. Giles village.

Chalfont St. Giles, despite considerable modern expansion, can still boast a picturesque village centre with its small village green surrounded by attractive little shops, cottages and inns. The church, which is of twelfth-century origin but was remodelled in the fifteenth century and restored by George Street in 1861 - 1863, is linked to the green by an archway beneath part of a sixteenth-century cottage and is famous for its mediæval wall paintings, while in the churchyard is buried the circus proprietor Bertram Mills. The most notable building in the village, however, is Milton´s Cottage, where the poet took refuge from the plague in 1665. Built in about 1600, this cottage was where John Milton completed his ´Paradise Lost´ and it was while he was staying here that Thomas Ellwood, who had secured it for Milton, is said to have inspired Milton to write his ´Paradise Regained ´.

Cross the High Street and turn right crossing the entrance to a road called Up Corner, then turn left onto path CG30 following a tarmacked private road called Stratton Chase Drive, soon passing along an avenue of fine chestnut and lime trees. On reaching a gate, take the gravel continuation of the private road straight on, then, at a left-hand bend, fork right off the private road, soon joining a right-hand fence, leaving the trees and continuing between fences to some bungalows where the path becomes a rough road and continues to a bend in Mill Lane where the timber-framed Chalfont Mill to your right, reputed to be the oldest watermill in the county, is well worth a detour.

Now go straight on along Mill Lane, then, at a left-hand bend, leave it and take path CG30 straight on along a fenced track. Where the track ends, ignore a gate to your right and take a narrow path straight on through scrubland into Bycroft Plantation. Here continue within the right-hand edge of this wood ignoring branching paths to

MAP 3

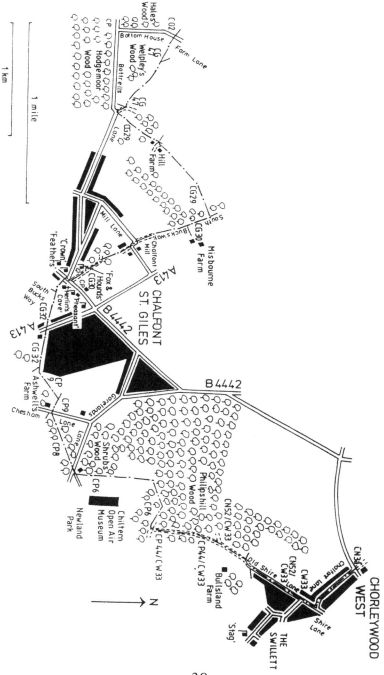

your left. Having passed the stile of a branching path in the right-hand fence, continue for a further 230 yards, then, just past a gap to your right by the corner of a field, leaving the South Bucks Way, turn left onto waymarked branching path CG29 passing through the wood and soon emerging over a stile into a field. Here go straight on up the bottom of a slight dip to pass through a large gap in a line of trees, then join a right-hand hedge and follow it to cross a stile by a wired-up gate. Now take the fenced path straight on uphill for 350 yards to cross a stile. Here continue between a hedge and a fence, later hedges, to reach a gravel drive. Take this straight on past Hill Farm to a T-junction where you turn right then immediately left through gates on path CG29 signposted to Froghall, taking a gravel drive straight on. Just before a gate, fork right over a concealed stile into a fenced path with wide views through gaps in the trees to the east and south over Chalfont St. Giles towards London and the distant North Downs, eventually reaching a bend in Bottrells Lane.

Do not join this road, but turn right onto path CG47 taking a gravel lane gently uphill. Where the lane bears right, leave it and go straight on through a kissing-gate left of some gates then bear slightly left across a field to a stile left of an ash tree where fine views open out towards Coleshill ahead and Amersham to your right. Here keep straight on, heading towards Coleshill House, the right-hand of two white houses at Coleshill, passing just right of an outcrop of Welpley's Wood and through a dip then crossing one rise to reach a redundant stile at the top of a second which acts as a waymark. Now go straight on downhill to a hedge gap and steps leading down into Bottom House Farm Lane.

Bottom House Farm Lane - Coleshill (Map 4)

Maps

OS Landranger Sheets 165 & 175 or 176
OS Explorer Sheet 172 (or old Sheet 3)
Chiltern Society FP Map No.6

Parking

Picnic area and car parks in Bottrells Lane with access to or from the
Chiltern Way via Bottom House Farm Lane, path CO3 (at Brentford
Grange Farm) or the A355.

Cross Bottom House Farm Lane and take path CO2 straight on
through a fence gap opposite, following a left-hand hedge over a rise,
then continuing through a hedge gap into a fenced path. Where the
fence blocks your way ahead, turn left over a stile and follow the
other side of the hedge straight on through three fields. In the third
field, where the hedge bears right, leave it and go straight on across
the field to cross a stile under an oak tree in the next hedge, then
follow a right-hand hedge straight on to a stile onto the drive of a
weather-boarded cottage. Here go straight on over another stile
opposite and across a field passing Brentford Grange Farm to your
right to cross a stile under a small oak tree in the next hedge. Now
continue through a plantation, ignoring branching path CO3 to your
left, crossing a macadam drive and joining a right-hand fence. Just
past a gateway in this fence, turn right over a stile then turn left and
take a fenced path along the other side of the hedge. On entering a
field, follow the left-hand hedge straight on to the A355.
   Cross this road carefully bearing slightly left and taking the
continuation of path CO2 down a steep flight of steps to cross a
footbridge. Now go straight on through a hedge gap, then keep right
of a hedge and follow it straight on for a third of a mile with views of
the eighteenth-century Coleshill House on the ridge to your right in
places, ignoring a crossing path and eventually reaching the edge of
Herts Wood. Here turn right along its outside edge, gradually bearing
left and becoming enclosed by a fence, then take a shady green lane
straight on, eventually emerging at the side of the 'Red Lion' in
Coleshill and continuing through its car park to the village street near
the church and duckpond.

Coleshill - Winchmore Hill (Map 4)

Maps

OS Landranger Sheet 165
OS Explorer Sheet 172 (or old Sheet 3)
Chiltern Society FP Map No.6

Parking

On-street parking is possible in Coleshill village and there is a picnic area in Whielden Lane with access to or from the Chiltern Way via path P83.

Coleshill, on its high ridge above Amersham, was till 1832 a detached enclave of Hertfordshire surrounded by Bucks. As such, in the seventeenth century it afforded a refuge to local Quakers persecuted by the authorities as they were safe here from the Buckinghamshire magistrates and when their Hertfordshire colleagues did make the long trip to Coleshill, the Quakers could quickly flee across the border into Bucks. One notable Quaker to live in Coleshill at this time was Thomas Ellwood, a friend of the poet John Milton, who lived for many years at Hunger Hill Farm (now Ongar Hill Farm) to the south of the village, but the farm you see today is not that of Thomas Ellwood as it was rebuilt in 1873. This is, however, not the village's only literary association as Coleshill, which, with its windmill, common and attractive duckpond, remains a rural oasis within 25 miles of Central London, was in 1606 the birthplace of the poet Edmund Waller, whose sixteenth-century home known as Stock Place still stands in the centre of the village near the 'Red Lion' and Victorian church, designed by George Street in 1861.

Now cross the village street and take path CO6 straight on between safety barriers and along a hedged macadam path, passing the church to your right to reach Manor Way. Bear slightly left across this road and take the continuation of path CO6 along the gravel drive to Lands Farm. Where the drive forks at the farm entrance, keep right, then ignore branching drives to your right to reach a gate and stile. Cross the stile and take a concrete road straight on, continuing along a wide fenced grassy track by a left-hand hedge to a fieldgate. Here fork left onto path CO7 passing through a pedestrian gate left of the fieldgate and taking a fenced path beside the left-hand hedge to reach a stile into the next field. Now turn left and head for the left-hand end of a small copse where you bear half right down the field to reach a hedge gap in the bottom corner into West Wood. Here take a woodland track straight on, ignoring branching tracks and paths to left and right. On emerging into another field, take path P82, keeping right of a hedge ahead and following it straight on through two fields with fine views towards Winchmore Hill ahead and across the woods to your right, above which rises the spire of Penn Street Church built by the first Earl Howe in 1849. At the far side of the second field go straight on into an old green lane which leads you to a village street in Winchmore Hill called The Hill opposite the Methodist Church, onto which you turn left.

Winchmore Hill - Penn (Map 4)

Maps
OS Landranger Sheet 175
OS Explorer Sheet 172 (or old Sheet 3)
Chiltern Society FP Map No.6

Parking
On-street parking is possible in Winchmore Hill village and there is a small parking area in Crown Lane, Penn Bottom near the entrance to path P25.

Winchmore Hill, with its large green by a crossroads with two pubs and one (formerly two) Methodist chapels, though no parish church, may seem the epitome of a Bucks Chiltern village. It is now a hamlet of Penn parish, but till 1955 it was largely in Coleshill (and consequently till 1832 in Hertfordshire) with smaller parts in Amersham and Penn. The fact that the three parishes and two counties met at its crossroads also gave rise to its name deriving from the Old English ´wincel` (meaning angle) and ´mær` (meaning boundary) thus combining as ´angled boundary hill`.

43

Now go gently up The Hill to a crossroads by the ´Plough Inn`. Here cross the priority road and turn right onto path P8 across the green, heading for the right-hand end of a garden hedge protruding onto the green, then continuing past it to reach a hedge gap leading to a stile. Having crossed this stile, take a raised path beside a left-hand fence straight on to cross a stile by gates leading to Horsemoor Lane near a very old pond called Gawde Water. Cross this road and a stile by a gate opposite, then ignore the stile of a branching path ahead and take path P11 bearing left into a strip of woodland. Follow this obvious path straight on through the strip of woodland for nearly a quarter mile, eventually ignoring a branching path to your left and reaching a macadam drive to Penn House. This mile-long banked track was built in the 1930s by the fifth Earl Howe to practise racing his fleet of cars. Bear left onto this and follow it for 250 yards, then, at a left-hand bend, fork right onto a track following the edge of Branches Wood, soon joining another track which merges from your left and leaving the wood. Here bear slightly left, following a grassy track beside a right-hand hedge downhill passing Round Wood to your right then bearing right to reach a road in Penn Bottom.

Turn right onto this road, then at a right-hand bend fork left into Noaks Lane passing a copse to your right and reaching Church Knoll with its sarsen stones and small car park. The knoll to your right, on which a house now stands, is thought to be the site of a Saxon church, which would have been more central to Penn parish than the present fourteenth-century building on the ridge to the south.

Now turn right onto path P25 following a gravel track. At a fork take a path between hedges just right of the left-hand option straight on. On entering a field, follow its left-hand hedge straight on, soon joining a grassy track, then ignore a crossing path and continue beside a left-hand hedge to the far end of the field. Now on path P71, go straight on through a hedge gap and follow a grassy track beside a left-hand hedge straight on to a corner of Twichels Wood. About 25 yards further on, turn left over a concealed stile into the wood, then bear right and follow an obvious, if sometimes overgrown, path through the wood, eventually emerging over a stile onto a grassy track. Here turn left, passing through a bridlegate, then take a worn track gradually bearing right and passing left of a copse. Now bear half right uphill across the field to a kissing-gate at the left-hand corner of a second copse where you continue to a stile onto the B474 at Penn and turn sharp left onto its footway.

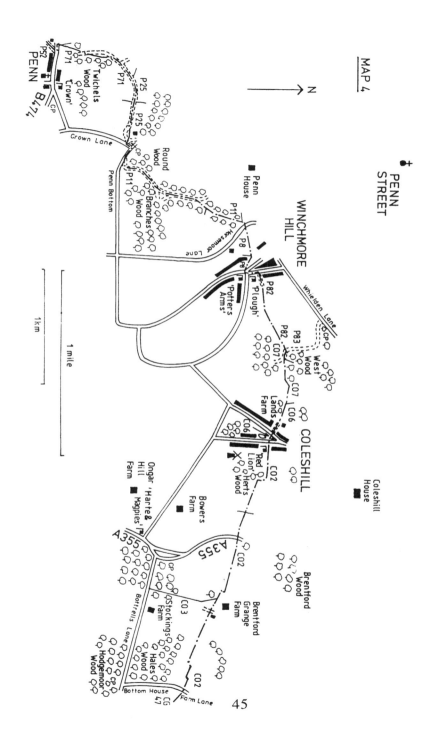

MAP 4

⟶ N

⚓ PENN STREET

45

Penn - Coppice Hoop (Map 5)

Maps
OS Landranger Sheet 175
OS Explorer Sheet 172 (or old Sheet 3)
Chiltern Society FP Map No.13

Parking
On-street parking is possible around the green at Tylers Green or at Beacon Hill.

Penn on its high ridge to the east of High Wycombe is potentially quite a vantage point as locals claim that between ten and twelve counties can be seen on a clear day from the church tower which was used in wartime as a Home Guard look-out post. At ground level buildings and trees largely conceal these views but those who walk the local paths are soon rewarded with vistas largely unseen and unsuspected by those driving through on the B474. Despite its close proximity to High Wycombe, with which it is almost joined by continuous development, Penn, with its picturesque seventeenth-century inn and cottages clustered around its fine fourteenth-century church, has preserved a remarkably rural atmosphere. Though relatively small in size, Penn also attracts visitors from across the Atlantic as the village gave its name to an important Bucks family, from whom William Penn, the leading Quaker and founder of Pennsylvania claimed to be descended and it is indeed after his father, Admiral Penn, that Charles II named the state.

By the entrance to Wellbank and Grove's Barn cross the B474 and take bridleway P52 bearing half right and passing right of the gates of Wellbank to enter a green lane called Stumpwell Lane. Follow this gently downhill for 350 yards to enter a copse then at a fork by a woodland pond called Stump Well, bear right onto bridleway P57, also known as Stumpwell Lane. After 70 yards turn left over a stile onto path P58, bearing slightly right to pass through a gap in the bushes. Now bear slightly left across a meadow, passing right of an oak tree to cross a stile by a gate at the corner of a garden hedge, then follow this right-hand hedge straight on to reach a gravel drive at Beacon Hill (path P50). Beacon Hill, Penn, like other Chiltern hills with the same name, was one of a chain of beacon sites spanning the country which were used in 1588 to give warning of the approach of the Spanish armada.

Turn sharp left onto this drive, then, by the entrance to

'Whitecroft`, bear right and take a path between hedges straight on to a stile into a field. Now follow a right-hand fence straight on across the field with a view of Penn Church to your left to cross another stile where fine views open out to the south across Burnham Beeches towards the distant North Downs. Here fork right onto path P51 along the outside edge of a wood ignoring a gate into it. In a corner of the field go straight on over a stile into and through the wood to a stile into another field. Now follow a left-hand hedge straight on to a stile into a wood called Coppice Hoop, through which you continue ahead for 300 yards to a fork near a corner of a field to your left. Here fork right, soon reaching the far corner of the wood, then turn right over a stile to reach the junction of the original Chiltern Way with its Berkshire Loop, where **the Berkshire Loop** immediately turns left over a second stile onto path CW64 (now see Map 11), while **the original Chiltern Way** takes path P51 straight on beside a left-hand hedge (see below).

Coppice Hoop - Loudwater (Bucks.) (Map 5)

Maps
OS Landranger Sheet 175
OS Explorer Sheet 172 (or old Sheet 3)
Chiltern Society FP Map No.13

The original Chiltern Way now takes path P51 straight on beside the left-hand hedge through two fields to cross a stile by a gate where a fine view opens out to your left towards the Wye Valley and Flackwell Heath. Here take path P92 downhill bearing right and heading for the right-hand end of Sniggs Wood to cross a stile in the bottom hedge leading to a crossing bridleway. Cross this ancient lane marking the parish boundary between Penn and Chepping Wycombe, bearing slightly left and taking path CW22c straight on uphill soon in a sunken way. On crossing a stile, bear left along the inside edge of the wood, soon bearing right and emerging onto the edge of a golf course. Now follow the left-hand hedge, soon bearing right then left, then, by a disused gate, ignore a branching path to your left into a strip of woodland and take a gravel track straight on along the edge of the wood to a junction of tracks on a rise where a fine view opens out to your left across the Wye Valley around Loudwater including the high brick viaduct built as part of the Great Western and Great Central Joint Railway in 1906.

Here bear slightly left and take the gravel track downhill beside a right-hand hedge. At a fork bear right into scrub concealing a disused tip. By a corner of the tip, fork left onto bridleway CW22b, a gravel track downhill out of the scrub with views towards Loudwater, joining a macadam drive and following it downhill to reach a crossing drive (bridleway CW27) near the golf course car park. Turn left onto this, then, at the car park entrance, take bridleway CW27 straight on behind a right-hand fence. At the far end of the fence take a macadam bridleway straight on into bushes passing a gate. Ignoring a branching drive to your right, take the macadam drive straight on, later disregarding a branching bridleway to your right and rejoining the golf course drive. Here continue along its footway to its junction with Robinson Road where you bear half right, crossing Robinson Road and taking fenced bridleway CW27 straight on through woodland and under a railway arch. Now take a concrete road straight on downhill to a service road beside the A40 at Loudwater by a green with cherry trees which are a magnificent sight when in blossom.

 # Loudwater (Bucks.) - Flackwell Heath (Map 5)

Maps
OS Landranger Sheet 175
OS Explorer Sheet 172 (or old Sheet 3)
Chiltern Society FP Map No.13

Parking
Car park at King's Mead recreation ground off Kingsmead Road, Loudwater.

Loudwater on the River Wye, as its name suggests, was once a village with watermills, but with its close proximity to High Wycombe with its furniture industry, the industrial revolution harnessed its water-power to drive papermills and other factories and workers' housing followed so that, by the early twentieth century, Loudwater had virtually become a suburb of the town with only the open expanse of King's Mead, an ancient common meadow, and the enclosing steep hills preserving the semblance of a gap between them.

Turn left onto the footway of the service road, joining the A40 then at traffic lights cross the main road and take Frederick Place over a bridge over one arm of the River Wye, immediately turning right onto macadamed path CW68 following a factory fence beside the River Wye onto King's Mead recreation ground. Here turn left and follow a macadam path round two sides of a floodlit rugby pitch, then bear left and follow a line of chestnut trees to a red-surfaced foot and cycle path. Turn right onto this, ignoring the first foot-bridge to your left and continuing (now on path HW53) until you reach a branching path leading to a second footbridge. Turn left onto this, crossing the other arm of the River Wye and reaching Kingsmead Road, till the 1770s part of an ancient road from High Wycombe to Windsor.

Cross this road and take path CW30 up a concrete drive opposite crossing the course of the old GWR Maidenhead - High Wycombe branch line (opened in 1847 to link High Wycombe to London, but largely superseded by the more direct GWR & GCR Joint Railway in 1906 and closed in 1970) and entering Fennell's Wood, named after the mediæval Fitz Neels who owned land in the Wycombe area. Now continue uphill along the inside edge of the wood ignoring all branching paths to your left. On approaching a tunnel under the M40, disregard a branching path to your right and take path CW53 straight on through the tunnel and up a flight of steps into the southern part of Fennell's Wood. Here ignore a branching path to your left and follow the M40 fence until you emerge into a field. Now turn left and follow the outside edge of the wood uphill, ignoring a branching path back into the wood, then continuing to a gate and stile. Cross this stile and follow the left-hand fence joining a macadam path where there are fine views behind you across the Wye Valley towards the High Wycombe suburbs of Terriers, Totteridge and Micklefield. Take this path straight on, then, where it bears left and becomes fenced on both sides, fork right following a left-hand fence then passing through a kissing-gate into Oak Wood. Now ignore a path merging from your left, then take a winding path through this wood, later keeping left at a fork and staying as close as possible to its left-hand edge, but disregarding a path into the housing estate, eventually reaching the far left-hand corner of the wood where you take the enclosed path straight on between garden fences and a hedge to reach a kissing-gate onto Heath End Road at Flackwell Heath.

Flackwell Heath - Sheepridge (Map 5)

Maps
OS Landranger Sheet 175
OS Explorer Sheet 172 (or old Sheet 3)
Chiltern Society FP Map No.13

Parking
On-street parking is possible in estate roads off Heath End Road,
Flackwell Heath.

**Flackwell Heath, (locally pronounced ´Flack'el'Eath`) on its hilltop
plateau separating the Wye Valley and High Wycombe from the
Thames Valley to the south, was till the eighteenth century largely
uninhabited. In the nineteenth and early twentieth centuries,
however, a scattering of cottages and later ribbons of villas and
bungalows gradually lined the Heath's network of lanes while, in
between, there remained green fields and the vast cherry orchards,
for which Flackwell Heath became famous. It was not, however, till
after the Second World War that the close proximity of High
Wycombe and London and the scattered nature of the village's
development made it a prime target for in-filling and expansion and
the green fields and cherry orchards gave way to the large housing
estates which characterise this suburban satellite of High Wycombe
today.**

Cross Heath End Road, turn right onto its far footway and follow it
for 300 yards. Just past the junction with Spring Lane, by the
entrance to no.159, turn left onto path CW38 along a narrow
concealed alleyway between a hedge and a fence to enter a field. Now
follow the right-hand hedge straight on downhill, soon on path
LM24, with views ahead towards the Thames Valley around Cookham
and Maidenhead. At the bottom end of the field go straight on
through a hedge gap and enter a sunken way, continuing downhill to
gates into New Farm at Sheepridge. Do **not** go through these, but turn
left to a kissing-gate into Sheepridge Lane, then turn right and follow
it to the ´Crooked Billet`.

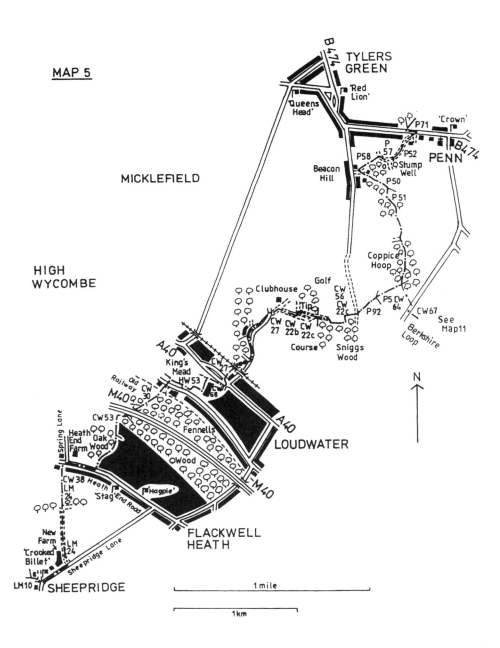

MAP 5

TYLERS GREEN

B474

'Red Lion'

'Queens Head'

'Crown'

P71

PENN

B474

P57

P58   P52

Stump Well

Beacon Hill

P50

P51

MICKLEFIELD

Coppice Hoop

HIGH WYCOMBE

Golf

CW 56

CW 22c

Clubhouse

P5 CW 64

CW67

See Map 11

Tip

P92

Berkshire Loop

CW 27   CW 22b   CW 22c

Course

Sniggs Wood

N

A40

King's Mead

CW 27

Old Railway   CW 30

HW53

CW 68

M40

A40

LOUDWATER

M40

CW53

Spring Lane

Heath End Farm   Oak Wood

Fennells

Wood

CW 38 Heath

LM 24

'Hagpie'

'Stag End Road'

New Farm

'Crooked Billet'

LM 24

Sheepridge Lane

FLACKWELL HEATH

LM10   SHEEPRIDGE

1 mile

1km

51

Sheepridge - Marlow Bottom (Map 6)

Maps
OS Landranger Sheet 175
OS Explorer Sheet 172 (or old Sheet 3)
Chiltern Society FP Maps Nos. 1 & 13

Parking
Parking is possible near the ´Crooked Billet` at Sheepridge, in Monkton Lane and in Pump Lane North at Burroughs Grove.

Now turn right onto path LM10 up a drive left of the ´Crooked Billet`, immediately forking left up a macadam drive, then forking left again into a narrow hedged path. Take this straight on for 100 yards ignoring a branching path to your right. On entering a field, bear half right across its corner to join a right-hand hedge by an oak tree, then follow the hedge uphill to enter Bloom Wood. Here keep straight on, ignoring a crossing track and now on a wide woodland track, continuing gently uphill. On reaching a second crossing track, take a narrow path straight on through the trees. At a clearing bear half right onto a crossing path then immediately fork left and continue through heathy, predominantly birch woods for a quarter mile, ignoring a crossing track and eventually emerging at a junction of wide tracks on the edge of mature woodland. Here cross the major track, bearing slightly right and taking another wide track. At the top of a rise, where there are mediæval earthworks with an interpretation board to your right, ignore branching tracks, then continue downhill, soon disregarding a major branching track to your right and descending steeply to reach a junction of tracks in the valley bottom. Now go straight on through a gap by an old gate into Winchbottom Lane.
Turn left onto this road and after a third of a mile, at a left-hand bend where the woodland to your right gives way to a field, turn right through a gap by a green gate onto path LM15 taking the left-hand of two tracks steeply uphill through Horton Wood, then disregard a branching track to your left and continue over a rise into a dip. Here ignore a crossing track, then at a fork bear left, disregarding a branching track to your right into the corner of a field and keeping straight on through the woods, ignoring all branching tracks and paths. At the far side of the wood, disregard a crossing track and go straight on over a stile by a disused gate to reach Monkton Lane.
Here the **official route** turns left into Monkton Lane and follows it for over a quarter mile, passing under the A404, then, at a left-hand bend, turns right onto the old route of the lane and follows it for 300

yards past Woodbarn Farmhouse (where its tarmac surface now ends) then uphill to reach a crossing concrete drive. Here turn sharp left rejoining path LM15, passing the left-hand corner of a gas compound. If willing to risk crossing the A404 dual-carriageway, you can, however, save about 700 yards by taking **an alternative route**, crossing Monkton Lane and continuing over a stile and up some steps to reach the A404 (Marlow Bypass). Here turn left, then level with a gap in the central-reservation crash-barrier, cross this fast dual-carriageway carefully and take the continuation of path LM15 straight on over a stile by a gate opposite, following a concrete drive to a gas installation crossing the old course of Monkton Lane. Now bear half left passing the left-hand corner of the gas compound. **Both routes** now follow a fenced path by a sporadic left-hand hedge with views through gaps in the hedge across the Thames Valley towards Cliveden, Winter Hill and Ashley Hill to reach a gate into Pump Lane North. Turn right onto this road and follow it to a T-junction with the former A404 near the 'Three Horseshoes' at Burroughs Grove.

Cross this busy road carefully and take path GM38a over a stile opposite, bearing slightly left across a field to a gap in the next hedge by an old stile just right of a copse with taller trees at Juniper Hill. Go through this gap and descend some steps into bridleway GM39. Turn left onto this, then immediately fork right onto bridleway GM38, passing through the copse and emerging at the end of a stony lane by a cottage called 'Juniper'. Take this lane straight on downhill and up again to reach Hill Farm Road on the edge of Marlow Bottom.

Marlow Bottom - Bovingdon Green (Bucks.) (Map 6)

Maps

OS Landranger Sheet 175
OS Explorer Sheet 172 (or old Sheet 3)
Chiltern Society FP Map No.1

Parking

On-street parking is possible in various roads in Marlow Bottom.

Though not planned like the new towns of Hertfordshire, Ordnance Survey maps from the 1920s show that Marlow Bottom is a new village which did not exist 100 years ago. In the 1920s and 1930s, however, the ribbon development, so deplored by the noted local writer, H.J. Massingham in his 'Chiltern Country' published in 1940, spread along its lanes and tracks to such an extent that post-war planners were unable to resist the pressure for 'in-filling' and now a village of some 5,000 inhabitants fills this once remote and reputedly picturesque winding Chiltern 'bottom'.

Bear half right across Hill Farm Road and take bridleway MB7 to the right of the entrance to no.65 along a narrow green lane which bears left. Now ignore a branching alleyway to your left and soon after the left-hand hedge gives way to a fence, fork right onto fenced path MB8. On reaching New Road, cross it and take path MB9 straight on along another alleyway passing the end of a residential cul-de-sac to reach Beechtree Avenue. Turn left onto this road and after some 30 yards, just past house no.43, turn right onto path MB10, a macadamed alleyway into and through woodland then steeply downhill between gardens to the road in the original Marlow Bottom which still bears this name.

Turn left onto this road, then, at a left-hand bend, turn right onto path MB6 up a narrow alleyway, ignoring a crossing track and continuing along the edge of a recreation ground. Some 30 yards short of the top hedge, turn right onto path MB3, following the bottom of a steep bank across the recreation ground to a gap into a corner of Whitehill Wood. In the wood keep straight on, following a slight sunken way along its right-hand edge. On reaching a crossing boundary bank, turn left then right and follow another slight sunken way straight on to reach a gravel track (bridleway GM47) by the ornamental gates to a house called 'Woodlands'. Turn sharp left onto this track, ignoring branching paths to your left, leaving the wood and continuing along a hedged lane to the B482.

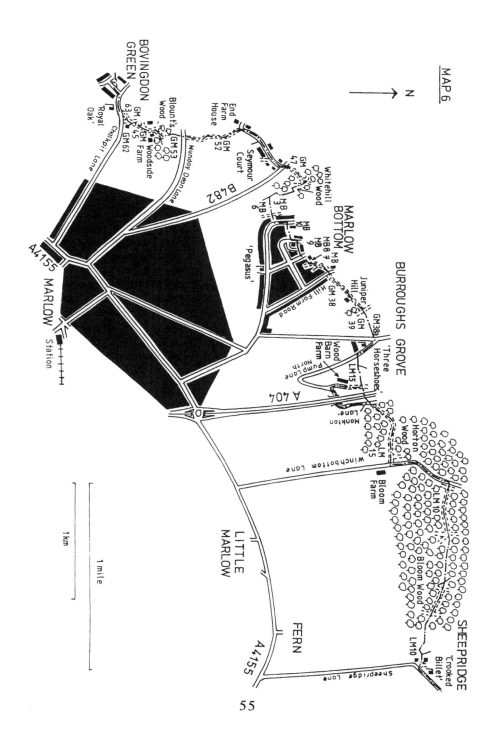

MAP 6

55

Turn left onto its nearside verge, then, after 60 yards, turn right crossing this busy road carefully and taking Seymour Court Lane for over a quarter mile, passing the entrance to Seymour Court, built on the site of an earlier house reputed to have been the birthplace of Lady Jane Seymour, one of Henry VIII's wives and mother of Edward VI, and some enormous ancient oak and ash trees, later with fine views to your left across Marlow towards Winter Hill. Now, at a sharp right-hand bend by End Farm House, turn left onto bridleway GM52, following a narrow sunken lane downhill, later with more views to your left across Marlow towards Winter Hill. On reaching Munday Dean Lane, take path GM53 straight on between bollards, then uphill between hedges to the edge of Blount's Wood where the path bears left and continues between fences along the edge of the wood. By a gate to your left, turn right onto path GM45 following a track uphill through the wood. Near the top edge of the wood keep left at a fork, soon joining a macadam drive by Woodside Farm. Follow it straight on, passing through a gate and continuing on byway GM62 past Blount's Lodge. Now fork right onto byway GM63 to reach Chalkpit Lane opposite the 'Royal Oak` at Bovingdon Green.

Bovingdon Green (Bucks.) - Hambleden (Map 7)

Maps
OS Landranger Sheet 175
OS Explorer Sheets 171 & 172 (or old Sheet 3)
Chiltern Society FP Maps Nos. 1 & 11

Parking
Limited roadside parking is available at Marlow Common.

Bovingdon Green, on a hilltop above Marlow, whose Saxon name means 'green on the hill', is a pleasant hamlet with most of its cottages clustered around the village green. Once boasting two pubs, one of which overlooked the green, the village still retains the 'Royal Oak` in Chalkpit Lane by an attractive duckpond.

Now turn right into Chalkpit Lane to reach the village green where you fork left across the green passing between wooden posts, soon crossing a road and continuing along a gravel track to the far right-hand corner of the green. Where this track bears left, leave it and go straight on across the grass and the end of a macadam road and take path GM10 along a gravelly flint lane to the left of the entrance to Cherry Tree Farm ignoring a branching path to your left. At the end of the lane take a fenced path straight on, then, after 150 yards, ignore a stile to your right and take path GM16 straight on for 350 yards, passing through two squeeze-stiles and a kissing-gate, then following the edge of Wolmer Wood to enter Davenport Wood. Now keep straight on through the wood, after 200 yards disregarding a crossing path in a dip, then reaching a waymarked crossways in a second dip. Here, joining Shakespeare's Way, turn right onto path GM15, going straight on through the wood and ignoring all branching tracks and paths, then, after 250 yards, keep right at two forks, soon bearing left to reach a road at Marlow Common.
  Cross this and take path M12 straight on, crossing a boundary bank, ignoring a branching path to your left and bearing slightly left. At a four-way fork bear half right, soon descending steeply, then, at the edge of the wood, disregard a crossing path and go straight on through a fence gap into a fenced path beside a right-hand hedge. Take this for a quarter mile to a stile into a field, then turn left and follow the left-hand fence through two fields to gates and a stile onto a road on the edge of Homefield Wood. Turn right onto this road, then, in a dip, fork left through a gap by gates into the wood, taking the continuation of path M12 along a wide forestry track in the valley

bottom for two-thirds of a mile ignoring all branching or crossing tracks or paths. After the valley and the track commence a long right-hand bend, look out for a track junction where you turn sharp left onto waymarked path M6, climbing through predominantly coniferous woodland to reach a squeeze-stile onto a road west of Bockmer End.

Turn right onto this road, then, after 150 yards turn left over a stile by a gate onto path M18. Having crossed a second stile by a gate into a field, go straight on across it, heading left of a cottage at Rotten Row ahead with fine views towards Bockmer and Ashley Hill to your left, to cross two stiles in the next hedge. Now take path HA26b straight on to cross a stile right of a gate in front of a traditional black weatherboarded barn at Rotten Row, whose name seems likely to be an example of country humour referring to the one-time condition of its cottages.

Here take a concrete farm road straight on to reach a bend in a public road by an attractive duckpond, then take this road straight on, passing a fine half-timbered cottage with flint and brick extensions and ignoring a branching path to your left. At a left-hand bend leave the road, forking right through a gate onto path HA26a which follows a grassy track between fields. On reaching a crossing stone track, take the grassy track straight on to the next hedgeline, then bear slightly right across a field to a corner of Rickoll's Wood. Now follow the outside edge of the wood to a stile in the field corner leading into the wood. Here go straight on, soon joining a grassy track, then, at a T-junction of tracks, bear half right onto a grassy path downhill through the wood, eventually emerging from the wood by a corner of a field where fine views open out across the Thames Valley towards Mill End, Remenham Hill and Henley. Now follow the left-hand fence straight on downhill with Culham Court, a red-brick seventeenth-century Thames-side mansion on the other side of the river, emerging from behind some trees to your left.

On reaching a stony lane (path HA28), turn right onto it. After 100 yards, just before tall trees begin in the left-hand hedge, turn left through a hedge gap and take path HA26 straight on downhill to the corner of a hedge, then continue past it. Near a cottage turn right through a gate into a car park and go straight on through the car park to reach the end of a picturesque village street in Hambleden.

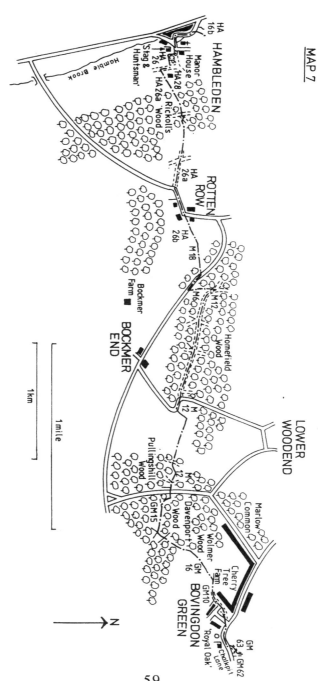

MAP 7

Hambleden - Skirmett (Map 8)

Maps
OS Landranger Sheet 175
OS Explorer Sheet 171 (or old Sheet 3)
Chiltern Society FP Map No.11

Parking
Signposted public car park in Hambleden village.

Hambleden, set in its beautiful valley flanked by beechwoods, remains an unspoilt Chiltern village thanks to the Hambleden Estate which owns much of it and the National Trust, to which most of it is covenanted. This has both largely saved the village from modern development and made it the ideal setting for a number of historical films. Around the village square with its pump and along narrow lanes leading off it are a number of attractive cottages and old-world shops, mostly in characteristic Chiltern brick-and-flint, as well as the manor house built for Emanuel Scrope in 1604 and the parish church. The church, which is believed originally to have been a twelfth-century cruciform building with a central tower, was largely rebuilt in the fourteenth century and given its present tower in 1721 which was then heightened in 1883 when extensive renovations took place. Despite this, it has retained several fine monuments and in its churchyard is the grave of the Victorian bookseller and government minister, W.H. Smith, the first Viscount Hambleden (1825 - 1891), whose descendants lived until recently in the manor house. This house was also the birthplace of Lord Cardigan, who led the Charge of the Light Brigade in the Crimean War, while another famous son of the village was St. Thomas de Cantelupe, a thirteenth-century Bishop of Hereford and advisor of Edward I, who was canonised in 1320 following a series of miracles which took place at his tomb in Hereford Cathedral.

Now go straight on down the village street, passing the ´Stag & Huntsman`, ignoring a road to your right and reaching the village square. Here fork right, passing the entrance to the churchyard and taking a narrow lane straight on past some picturesque cottages, soon bearing right and passing the Old Bakery to your left and the church to your right. Just before a bridge over Hamble Brook, leaving Shakespeare's Way, fork right through a kissing-gate onto path HA16b, bearing slightly left across a meadow, heading for the last cottage on a parallel road to your right to reach another kissing-gate, then go straight on across another meadow to a kissing-gate into a belt of tall trees near its right-hand end. Go through this tree belt and a kissing-gate, then follow a left-hand fence to pass the corner of a garden hedge by a walnut tree at Pheasant's Hill. On reaching a kissing-gate leading into a path between gardens, keep straight on along it until you reach a crossing macadam drive. Here go straight on, soon passing through a kissing-gate into a field and following a right-hand hedge straight on through two fields. At the far end of the second field go straight on through a kissing-gate and follow a left-hand hedge, ignoring the stile of a branching path to your left and eventually reaching a kissing-gate near Colstrope Farm with its traditional Chiltern eighteenth-century brick-and-flint farmhouse. Now keep straight on to reach a kissing-gate onto the road through the hamlet of Colstrope, whose existence was first recorded in 1634.

Turn right onto this road, immediately bearing left, then, at a right-hand bend, take bridleway HA16a straight on along a green lane. On emerging into a right-hand field, continue along a sunken way beside a left-hand hedge, eventually entering a narrow green lane and following it straight on to a cul-de-sac road leading to The Hyde and Bagmoor.

Cross this road, go through gates opposite and take a permissive path straight on across a field to a kissing-gate by the right-hand end of a plantation, with fine views opening out ahead towards Skirmett and Cobstone Mill on a hill beyond. Now take path HA16 straight on across the next field, passing left of a chestnut tree to another kissing-gate in the next hedge. Here follow a right-hand hedge straight on past Flint Hall and Arizona Farm to your left, bearing left near the far end of the field to a kissing-gate into a fenced track. Now cross a stile by a gate opposite and follow a left-hand hedge to cross another stile at the far end of the field. Here bear slightly right, passing right of a hawthorn bush, then follow a sporadic left-hand hedge straight on. Where this hedge peters out, bear slightly left across the field, passing the corner of a right-hand hedge to reach gates into Shogmoor Lane at Skirmett at the right-hand end of a flint wall.

Skirmett - Fingest (Map 8)

Maps
OS Landranger Sheet 175
OS Explorer Sheet 171 (or old Sheet 3)
Chiltern Society FP Map No.11

Parking
Limited on-street parking is available in Skirmett.

Skirmett, which has always been a hamlet of Hambleden parish, like nearby Fingest has the unusual distinction for this part of the country of bearing a Norse name meaning ´Shire meeting-place` although the Vikings only briefly penetrated this far south in the ninth century before being defeated and expelled by King Alfred. The village can boast an inn and some picturesque brick and flint cottages, but, despite its size and distance from the mother church in Hambleden, it did not have its own chapel-of-ease until 1886 and this has since closed and been converted into a private house.

Turn right into Shogmoor Lane and go gently uphill out of the village past some picturesque cottages. Just before a left-hand bend, turn left through a small gate onto path HA14b going straight ahead to the corner of a hedge, then bear slightly left beside a fence to a field corner. Here turn sharp right onto path HA2c beside a left-hand fence to gates, then bear slightly left across a field to a stile into bridleway HA2 by a gate. Turn left onto this bridleway passing this gate and take a flint lane uphill to a fork on the edge of Adam's Wood, then continue uphill through the wood, ignoring a branching path to your left. Where the bridleway levels out, continue for a quarter mile. Soon after it climbs again, at a waymarked junction take path HA2b straight on uphill to a gate and squeeze-stile onto a fenced track (path HA1). Turn left onto this, ignoring a fork to your left and passing through a gap by a gate into a field. Bear slightly right across it to enter Fingest Wood by a wooden Hanger Estate sign. Now continue downhill through the wood to a gate and solid stile erected in memory of the noted walks writer Henry Fearon (1907 - 1995), better known by his pseudonym ´Fieldfare`, who loved the superb view from this point across Fingest towards Turville, Cobstone Mill and Ibstone ahead and Cadmore End and Bolter End on a ridge to your right. Having taken advantage of the nearby seat to admire this view, take the grassy track straight on downhill along the edge of the wood, later bearing right, crossing a stile by a gate and following a left-hand hedge to gates and a stile leading to a road on the edge of Fingest, onto which you turn left.

Fingest - Turville (Map 8)

Maps
OS Landranger Sheet 175
OS Explorer Sheet 171 (or old Sheet 3)
Chiltern Society FP Map No.11

Parking
Limited on-street parking is possible in Fingest.

The name Fingest, like Skirmett, is unusual as it derives from 'Thinghyrst', a Norse name meaning 'meeting place in a spinney' and such names are usually only found in areas in the north and east held for longer by the Vikings. In the village the seventeenth-century 'Chequers Inn' is on your left, but of particular interest is the largely unaltered twelfth-century church with its unusually narrow lofty nave, thick plastered walls and tall Norman tower capped by a double saddleback roof, while in Chequers Lane to your right is the eighteenth-century village pound where stray animals were locked up to be redeemed on payment of a fine.

At a junction by the 'Chequers Inn' continue past the church to your right and at a left-hand bend, leave the road and take path HA61 straight on through a gate and along a fenced path by a flint wall, later continuing between fences to a corner of Mill Hanging Wood. Here, at a three-way fork, bear left onto path I13, soon passing through a gate, crossing a road and continuing within a belt of trees round the contours of Turville Hill to your right. On emerging over a stile into a field, there are superb views of the picturesque village of Turville ahead, familiar to many television viewers as the setting for 'Dibley'. Now bear slightly left across the field with views to your right of Cobstone Mill, an eighteenth-century smock-mill which has featured in many films including 'Chitty Chitty Bang Bang', to join a left-hand fence where it changes from wood to wire and follow it to gates. Here go through a kissing-gate then turn left through a gate onto path T30 down a flinty track between cottages into the centre of the village.

Turville - Southend (Bucks.) (Map 8)

Maps

OS Landranger Sheet 175
OS Explorer Sheet 171 (or old Sheet 3)
Chiltern Society FP Map No.11

Parking

Limited on-street parking is available in Turville, but do not use the pub car park without the landlord's permission.

Although the name Turville has a French ring, it is, in fact, not of Norman origin, but a corruption of the Saxon name 'Thyrifeld' (meaning 'Thyri's field') as the village is documented well before the Norman conquest. Indeed the church, whose fabric is in part eleventh-century but has a sixteenth-century tower and has undergone other substantial alterations over the centuries, is believed to have replaced a Saxon predecessor as it has a Saxon font. It is also associated with a gruesome mystery as, during renovation work in 1900, an old stone coffin was found hidden beneath the floor containing not only the skeleton of a thirteenth-century priest but also the remains of a seventeenth-century woman with a bullet hole in her skull! Apart from the church, the village can also boast a fine selection of sixteenth- to eighteenth-century cottages, some half-timbered and some brick-and-flint, as well as the picturesque timber-framed 'Bull and Butcher'.

Cross the village street and bear half right, passing left of the small green, then turn left into School Lane gently uphill. At the end of the road take bridleway T20 straight on between hedges to a bridlegate into a field, then ignore stiles to right and left and follow a hedge straight on. Disregard a bridlegate to your right and now on bridleway T1, follow the hedge straight on for a third of a mile with fine views to your left towards Fingest and Skirmett and behind you of Cobstone Mill. On reaching gates into Dolesden Lane at Dolesden, cross this road, go through gates opposite and take a fenced track uphill, soon passing through a wood. At the far side of the wood, cross a stile by a gate and take a farm track straight on across a field with more fine views opening out behind you, to cross a stile by a gate at Southend Farm. Here take a macadamed farm road straight on past the farm, then continuing for some 400 yards. Having passed a right-hand cottage, keep left at a fork and take a concrete road across Southend Common to a T-junction.

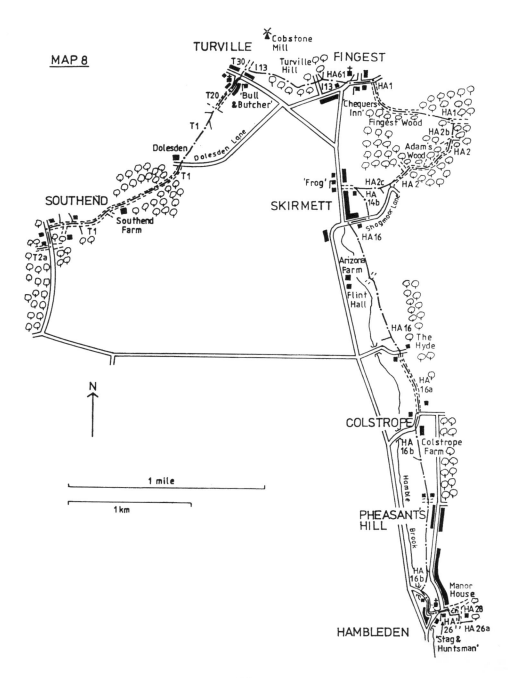

MAP 8

Southend (Bucks.) - Stonor (Map 9)

Maps
OS Landranger Sheet 175
OS Explorer Sheet 171 (or old Sheet 3)
Chiltern Society FP Map No.9

Parking
Parking is possible in places in and around Southend and on the
verge of the B480 north of Stonor village.

**Southend is a scattered hamlet on a plateau on the Bucks-Oxon
boundary with magnificent views to the northeast across the
Turville valley towards Fingest, Turville, Cobstone Mill and
Cadmore End and derives its name from its location at the southern
end of Turville parish. Like many other such hilltop outposts of
southern Chiltern parishes, Southend is built around a common
where hilltop clay was quarried for brickmaking.**

At the T-junction turn left onto the public road. After 160 yards, just
past a cottage to your right, turn right onto path T2a, taking a gravel
track into Kildridge Wood passing through a gate. At a clearing
ignore branching tracks to left and right and now in Oxfordshire on
path PS10, take a flint woodland track straight on downhill. After 350
yards fork left onto a branching path, then keep right at a second
fork and continue through the woods to a large kissing-gate in the
deer fence surrounding Stonor Park. Go through this and follow a
worn waymarked path straight on through the park for over three-
quarters of a mile, for much of the way alongside a deer fence,
passing Stonor House in the valley to your right.

**Stonor House and the adjoining chapel both date from about
1280 and have, for all that time, been the home of the Stonor family
(since 1838 the Barons Camoys). Over the years both house and
chapel have been subject to considerable alterations with the result
that the house now has a Georgian appearance. Despite the
reformation the family have always remained staunch Roman
Catholics and secret hiding places were constructed to conceal such
fugitives as Edmund Campion. Even today the chapel remains a
centre for Roman Catholics over a wide area.**

Eventually path PS10 descends to a kissing-gate onto the B480.
Turn left onto this road and ignoring a branching road to
Maidensgrove and Russell's Water, continue into Stonor village.

Stonor - Maidensgrove (Map 9)

Maps
OS Landranger Sheet 175
OS Explorer Sheet 171 (or old Sheet 3)
Chiltern Society FP Maps Nos. 2 or 9

Parking
Parking is possible on the verge of the B480 north of Stonor.

Stonor, with its picturesque sixteenth- to eighteenth-century cottages and the eighteenth-century ´Stonor Arms`, (currently closed) was, till 1896, called Upper Assendon. As such, it completed the logical trio suggested by Lower and Middle Assendon further down the valley. However, with the establishment of modern local government, this former detached manor of the distant parish of Pyrton, whose main village and parish church are over five miles to the north near Watlington, initially became a separate parish and took the name of the Estate to which most of the parish belonged. Subsequently, in 1922, it was merged with the neighbouring parish of Pishill to form Pishill-with-Stonor. Its former name is, however, still preserved in Upper Assendon Farm with its seventeenth-century farmhouse at the southern end of the village.

At a right-hand bend turn right onto enclosed path PS12 between gardens to a kissing-gate into a field. Now go straight on uphill, passing left of an electricity pole to a kissing-gate in the top hedge. Here bear slightly left with superb views across the village behind you, passing just right of a copse. Now with views of Stonor House over your right shoulder, continue up the field to a kissing-gate into Park Wood, where you should turn round for fine views behind you. Here take the waymarked path straight on through the wood, ignoring all branching paths. At the far side of the wood, bear slightly left across a field heading for a tall conifer right of two cottages at Maidensgrove. By this tree turn left onto bridleway PS17, joining the Oxfordshire Way and taking a short green lane to the entrance to Lodge Farm, then turn right to reach the end of the village lane.

Maidensgrove - Upper Bix Bottom (Map 9)

Maps
OS Landranger Sheet 175
OS Explorer Sheet 171 (or old Sheet 3)
Chiltern Society FP Map No.9

Parking
Parking is possible on roadside verges near the entrance to SW31.

Maidensgrove, referred to in several late mediæval documents as 'Menygrove` (meaning a `common clearing`) and described by the well-known Chiltern writer H.J. Massingham in 1940 as 'perhaps the most remote hamlet in all the Chilterns `, is the collective name for two small hamlets about three-quarters of a mile apart known as Maidensgrove and Upper Maidensgrove. Separated by part of the wide expanse of Russell's Water Common, Maidensgrove is the larger with two farms and a number of cottages as well as several modern properties, while Upper Maidensgrove boasts a farm and a pub. Both the hamlets and the common are situated on a high ridge which affords extensive views over the surrounding hilltops and deep valleys.

Leaving the Oxfordshire Way, follow the village lane for 300 yards. At a right-hand bend fork left onto a gravel track out onto Russell's Water Common. Ignore a branching track to your right, then, at a three-way fork, take the left-hand option and at a further fork go straight on along the back edge of the common to a bend in a macadam road. Here, leaving Shakespeare's Way, turn left into a hedged flint lane (restricted byway SW31), ignoring gates to your left. Where the right-hand hedge ends and views across the woods in Bix Bottom open out ahead, fork right onto path SW22, crossing a field and aiming just left of the corner of a wood called Big Ashes Plantation to reach a waymarked fence gap into it. Take a waymarked path straight on within the top edge of the wood, eventually crossing a stile into a field. Bear half left across it, passing just left of an ash tree to cross a stile into a protruding finger of woodland. Now descend a long flight of steps through the wood to a stile at its bottom edge into a field. Bear half right down this field to a stile by a gate in a corner leading to a junction of green lanes. Here the **original Chiltern Way** turns sharp right onto bridleway SW14 (now see Map 10) while the **Chiltern Way Extension** turns left over a stile onto path SW27 (now see Map 17).

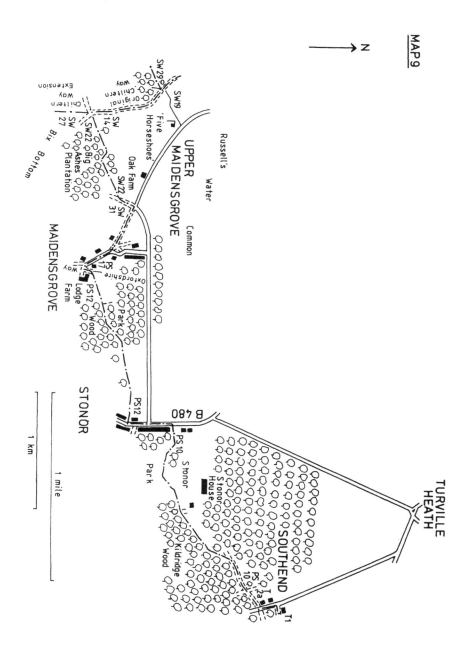

MAP 9

N

UPPER MAIDENSGROVE

MAIDENSGROVE

STONOR

SOUTHEND

TURVILLE HEATH

Russell's Water Common

Five Horseshoes

Oak Farm

Ashes Plantation

Big

Bix Bottom

SW 29

SW9

Original Chiltern Way

Chiltern Way Extension

SW 14

SW

SW 27

SW 22

SW 22

SW 31

PS 17

PS

Lodge Farm

PS12 Wood

Oxfordshire Way

Park

Oxfordshire

PS12

PS10

B 480

Stonor House

Park

Kildridge Wood

PS 12a

T1

1 km

1 mile

69

Upper Bix Bottom - Park Corner (Map 10)

Maps
OS Landranger Sheet 175
OS Explorer Sheet 171 (or old Sheet 3)
Chiltern Society FP Map No.9

Parking
Little parking is available on this section except at Park Corner (see below).

The **original Chiltern Way** now takes bridleway SW14 along a grassy track between a hedge and a fence leading up a valley bottom, eventually entering and passing through a wood.

At the far side of the wood, **if wishing to omit the Ewelme loop**, take bridleway SW14 straight on for another half-mile, ignoring a branching bridleway to your left, then, at a fork, bear right onto bridleway SW30 (Law Lane) rejoining the main Chiltern Way. Now turn to Map 24.

Otherwise, turn left through a kissing-gate onto path SW29, bearing slightly left to the corner of a fence, then bearing slightly right and following the fence to a corner of the wood. Here go through another kissing-gate and follow a right-hand line of trees until reaching an old hedgeline to your left marked by a small grassy bank and a line of ash trees. Now bear half left up the field to pass the left-hand side of a clump of trees shading an old chalkpit and continue to a stile left of a gate in the top hedge. Cross this and a second stile, then turn right and follow a right-hand hedge to a field corner, where you bear left and then right round the edge of a small copse to reach a gate into the next field. Bear half left across this field to the corner of a hedge, then follow this hedge straight on through two fields to cross a stile leading into a green lane called Redpits Lane (bridleway SW15). Turn left into this and follow it to reach a bend in the village lane at Park Corner, then fork right onto this road and follow it straight on to a T-junction with the B481.

Park Corner - Ewelme (Potter's Lane) (Map 10)

Maps
OS Landranger Sheet 175
OS Explorer Sheet 171 (or old Sheet 3)
Chiltern Society FP Map No.10

Parking
Small layby on B481 at Park Corner.

Park Corner, a hamlet at the crossroads of the ridgetop road above the southern Chiltern escarpment, which is sometimes thought to have been an extension of the ancient Ridgeway, and an ancient road from London to Oxford via Henley-on-Thames, Bix Bottom and Benson, is so named as the hamlet is situated by the corner of what used to be Ewelme Park. Despite this, however, the scattered settlement itself does not give the impression of being ancient, but, like its neighbour Cookley Green, would appear to result from a displacement of population caused by the creation of nearby Swyncombe Park.

Here cross the B481 and a stile opposite, then take path SW5 bearing left and following the back of the roadside hedge, eventually diverging away from the road and reaching a hedge gap into a wood called Springalls Plantation. Inside the wood, turn right onto crossing bridleway SW17, part of the ancient road from London via Henley-on-Thames to Oxford, following it through the wood, then along a green lane where you ignore a branching path to your left. On entering a second wood, take bridleway NE17 straight on, keeping right at two forks, then ignoring a crossing track. On reaching a second crossing track, take bridleway NU7 straight on down a valley bottom for over a mile, passing through a bridlegate at one point then continuing along the middle of a belt of trees, crossing the Ridgeway and a grass track which links two fields, then passing a coniferous plantation to your left and eventually emerging at the far end of a tree belt. Here bear half left onto a farm track leading to a T-junction with a macadam road (restricted byway NU29), known as Old London Road as until the 1830s it was part of the London-Henley-Oxford turnpike road.

Turn right onto this road, soon ignoring a branching drive to your right and passing a bungalow to your left. Now on restricted byway EW37, continue past a left-hand copse. On leaving the copse, take the grassy track beside a right-hand bank straight on with wide views

71

opening out ahead towards Wallingford and the Wessex Downs. After half a mile near the top of a rise, turn right through a gap in the grass bank onto bridleway EW29, passing the corner of a hedge. Now follow its right-hand side over Harcourt Hill where gaps in the hedge give views to your left on a clear day towards the Sinodun Hills and distant Oxford and Ewelme Down and Swyncombe Down come into view ahead. Now continue beside the hedge downhill, eventually entering a copse concealing the ruins of Warren Farm. After about 80 yards, at the far end of a large gap in the left-hand hedge, turn left onto bridleway EW36 over a rise. At the top of the rise, where a hedge comes into view ahead, aim for a corner of the hedge where the high hedge with trees to the right gives way to a low hedge to the left. Here turn right onto bridleway EW4, following a grassy track beside the hedge with fine views to your right towards Swyncombe Down and Ewelme Down. At a corner of the field go straight on through a hedge gap and joining the Swan's Way, take a fenced track straight on to meet a farm road by a barn where the Chiltern Way Extension merges from your left and you bear slightly right into a green lane called Potter's Lane (bridleway EW4). Now turn to Map 23.

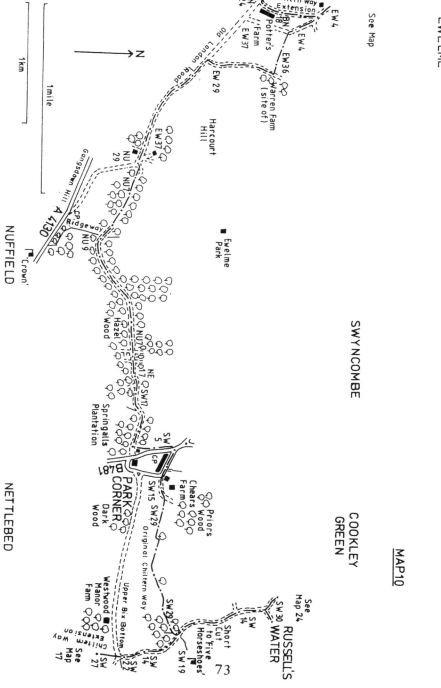

MAP 10

EWELME

SWYNCOMBE

COOKLEY GREEN

NETTLEBED

NUFFIELD

RUSSELL'S WATER

N

1 mile

1 km

See Map

Chiltern Way
Extension

EW 4

BN 18
BN 24

Potter's
Farm

EW 37

EW 4

EW 4

EW 36

Old London Road

EW 29

Warren Farm
(site of)

Harcourt
Hill

EW 37

NU 29

NU 7

NU 29

Gangsdown Hill

A 4130

CP

Ridgeway

NU 9

"Crown"

Ewelme
Park

Hazel
Wood

NU 7

NU 10

NU 17

NE

SW 17

Springalls
Plantation

SW 5

CP

B 481

PARK
CORNER

SW 15

Chears
Farm

Priors
Wood

SW 29

Original Chiltern Way

Dark
Wood

Westwood
Manor
Farm

Chiltern Way
Extension

See Map
17

Upper Bix Bottom

SW 27

SW 29

SW 22

SW 19

SW 14

Short
Cut
to Five
Horseshoes

SW 30

SW 14

See
Map 24

73

Penn (Coppice Hoop) - Forty Green (Map 11)

Maps
OS Landranger Sheet 175
OS Explorer Sheet 172 (or old Sheet 3)
Chiltern Society FP Map No.13

On crossing the stile to leave the southwest corner of a wood called Coppice Hoop, the **Berkshire Loop**, leaving the **original Chiltern Way**, turns immediately left over a concealed second stile onto path CW64, bearing slightly left across a field to a stile left of Lude Farm leading to Whitehouse Lane. Turn right onto this road passing the farm, then, by a converted red-brick farm building, turn left over a stile by a gate onto path CW67 going straight across a field with views ahead towards Holtspur to cross a stile by a gate. Here join a grassy track and follow the right-hand hedge straight on to pass through a hedge gap, then fork left and follow a left-hand hedge downhill to cross a stile in the valley bottom. Now keep straight on uphill (soon on path P60) to cross a stile in the top hedge leading into scrubby woodland. In the wood, ignoring a branching path to your left, keep straight on to reach a grassy track between woods. Here bear half right and follow the edge of Longfield Wood downhill, then a left-hand hedge uphill to cross a stile in the top hedge. Now bear half right across a former orchard to cross a stile behind a leaning cherry tree, then bear slightly left across the next field to cross another stile. Here keep straight on, passing between two pear trees to reach a kissing-gate in the far right-hand corner of the field leading to a road in Forty Green.

Forty Green - Holtspur (Map 11)

Maps
OS Landranger Sheet 175
OS Explorer Sheet 172 (or old Sheet 3)
Chiltern Society FP Map No.13

Parking
On-street parking is limited in Forty Green, but there is plentiful parking on the wide residential roads of Holtspur.

As may be suspected from the remaining vestiges of old orchards, through which you have just passed, Forty Green was once a centre of Buckinghamshire fruit-growing including the cherries needed for the traditional local dish, cherry pie. This small hamlet and childhood home of the author, Sir Terry Pratchett, is, however, principally known for its ancient inn, the ´Royal Standard of England`, (which is 150 yards to your left). Said to be over 900 years old and formerly known as the ´Ship Inn`, it is believed to have been given its present name at the Restoration by King Charles II to mark its use as a refuge and temporary Royalist headquarters during the Civil War by his father, Charles I.

Now turn right onto the road, then, at a road junction, turn right again into an unmade public road known as Riding Lane, keeping right at a fork and following its winding course for two-thirds of a mile uphill and down again, then along a valley bottom to a junction of lanes by Sainfoin Farm. Here ignore Gatemoor Lane to your right and take Riding Lane straight on down the valley, eventually passing under a high railway arch built in 1906 as part of the Great Western and Great Central Joint Railway and now carrying the Chiltern Railways line from London (Marylebone) to Birmingham. Now keep straight on, ignoring a branching path to your right and soon reaching a macadam road. Continue along this, bearing left by Ridings Farm and ignoring gates into Holtspur Bank Nature Reserve, noted for its wide variety of wildflowers and butterflies. Where the tall right-hand hedge gives way to a low hedge, turn right over a concealed stile onto fenced path B33, following the outside edge of the nature reserve uphill to cross another stile. Now continue uphill through scrubland to a kissing-gate, then along a fenced path to emerge at a road junction on the edge of Holtspur.

Holtspur - Wooburn (Map 11)

Maps
OS Landranger Sheet 175
OS Explorer Sheet 172 (or old Sheet 3)
Chiltern Society FP Map No.13

Parking
There is plentiful parking on the wide residential roads of Holtspur as well as a small car park at Holtspur Hill Picnic Area on the B4440 and limited parking at the top of Windsor Hill, near Wooburn Green.

As a study of old Ordnance Survey maps soon reveals, Holtspur in 1945 still comprised little more than an inn on an A40 crossroads and a small ribbon of houses along Holtspur Top Lane. In the 1950s and 1960s, however, it mushroomed into the sprawling suburban settlement we know today and the gap between it and nearby Beaconsfield completely disappeared.

At the road junction cross Holtspur Top Lane and take Cherry Tree Road straight on. After nearly 300 yards by a postbox and telephone box, turn right between metal posts onto tarmacked path B24 and follow it straight on for 250 yards. On reaching a crossing tarmacked path, follow a left-hand hedge straight on across a recreation ground, then continue along an alleyway to emerge onto Mayflower Way by St. Thomas's Church, built in 1961, and a shopping parade. Cross this road and take an alleyway straight on, later continuing along the footway of Kiln Court to North Drive, where you keep straight on across a wide grass verge to the A40 at its junction with Broad Lane.
    Cross this busy road carefully and take the right-hand footway of Broad Lane straight on, soon crossing a bridge over the M40. Some 40 yards beyond this bridge, turn right onto path B25 down a flight of steps, then bearing right along the foot of the embankment. After 25 yards, turn left over a culvert, then keep straight on, crossing the old line of Broad Lane and continuing between the fences of Holtspur Cemetery and the M40. Where gates block your way ahead, turn left and take the fenced path round two sides of a recreation ground to its far corner near Holtspur Hill Picnic Area.
    Here turn left through a kissing-gate frame onto path B37, crossing a stile and keeping straight on across a field to a concealed stile into an outcrop of Mill Wood. Inside the wood, ignoring a branching path to your right, take path WB11a straight on downhill, soon bearing left and levelling out. Now continue for over a third of a

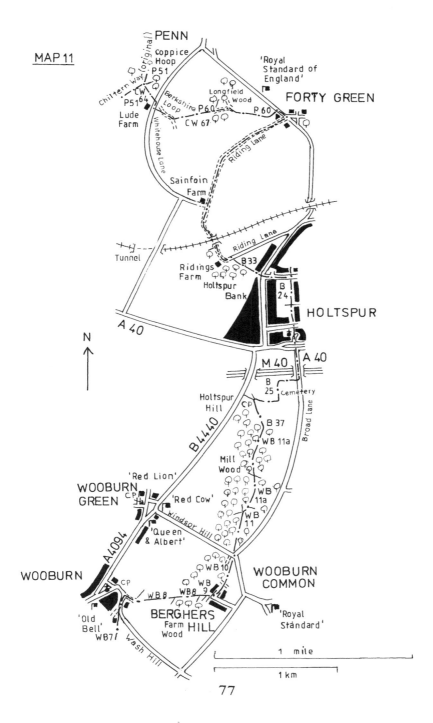

MAP 11

PENN

Coppice Hoop
P 51

'Royal Standard of England'

Chiltern Way (original)

CW
P 51 64
Lude Farm

Berkshire Loop

Longfield Wood
P 60
CW 67

FORTY GREEN

P 60

Whitehouse Lane

Riding Lane

Sainfoin Farm

Tunnel

Riding Lane

Ridings Farm

B 33

Holtspur Bank

B 24

HOLTSPUR

N

A 40

M 40   A 40

B 25   Cemetery

Holtspur Hill

CP

B 37

Broad Lane

WB 11a

Mill Wood

WB 11a

B 4440

'Red Lion'

WOOBURN GREEN

CP

'Red Cow'

Windsor Hill

WB 11

'Queen & Albert'

A 4094

WOOBURN

CP

WB 10

WB 9

WB 8

WOOBURN COMMON

'Old Bell'

WB 7

Wash Hill

BERGHERS HILL

Farm Wood

'Royal Standard'

1 mile

1 km

mile, crossing a clearing beneath a power line, passing a field to your left and disregarding a crossing path. On passing a gate, take bridleway WB11 straight on for a further quarter mile, ignoring branching paths to left and right and eventually emerging by a gate at a road junction at the top of Windsor Hill.

Here go straight on, crossing the top of Windsor Hill and taking fenced bridleway WB10, left of the gated drive to The Chase. After 250 yards ignore a crossing drive and enter the end of the village street of Berghers Hill (formerly known as Beggars Hill). Keep straight on along this street, then, at a sharp left-hand bend, turn right onto bridleway WB9, passing under the protruding upper storey of The Old Cottage, which appears most perilous for horseriders! By the back of its garden at a path junction, take path WB8 straight on through a kissing-gate into Farm Wood, then follow a right-hand hedge and fence straight on downhill through the wood to a stile with superb views to your left over Wooburn with its prominent castellated church tower towards Marlow and to your right up the Wye valley towards Wooburn Green and Penn. Cross this stile and bear half left across a large field to cross the left-hand of two stiles in its far left-hand corner. Now bear right down a green lane to reach Wash Hill on the edge of Wooburn village.

Wooburn - Cookham (Map 12)

Maps
OS Landranger Sheet 175
OS Explorer Sheet 172 (or old Sheet 3)
Chiltern Society FP Maps Nos. 13 & 24

Parking
There is a public car park at the foot of Wash Hill, Wooburn.

Wooburn, locally called 'Wooburn Town' to distinguish it from Wooburn Green half a mile up the valley, was formerly, like its Wye Valley neighbours, a centre of the paper-making industry with a tall factory chimney, but in about 1980 the mill was closed and demolished and replaced by an industrial estate. Despite the close proximity of this industrial site, the village centre boasts a number of picturesque timber-framed sixteenth- to eighteenth-century cottages congregated around its extensively-restored twelfth-century church with a tower dating from 1442.

Turn sharp left onto Wash Hill, passing some attractive cottages and rounding a right-hand bend, then, at a left-hand bend, ignore Wash Hill Lea to your right and just past black metal gates, fork right onto path WB7, following the back of the roadside hedge past a red-brick building and a garden fence to a stile into a field. Go straight on across this field, heading for the middle of a copse called The Swilley with fine views to your right towards Winter Hill, Marlow and Lane End and later behind you over Wooburn towards Penn. Now cross a stile into the wood and take an obvious path bearing right through the wood to cross a stile in its top hedge. Here bear half right across a field to cross a stile by a gate into Kiln Lane left of the 'Chequers Inn'.

Turn left onto this road, then, at a junction, turn right into Harvest Hill. Ignore Kiln Fields to your left, then, at a right-hand bend by the gates to Hedsor Stud, turn left into a narrow lane. After 250 yards, joining the Beeches Way and Shakespeare's Way, turn sharp right through a gap by a gate onto path HD4 taking a fenced track into Woolman's Wood. At a three-way fork, keep right and take a fenced path downhill through the wood, eventually leaving the wood and reaching a kissing-gate onto a private road at Hedsor where there is a fine view of Tower Hill with its eighteenth-century folly known as Hedsor Tower to your right.

Hedsor is a small Thames-side parish east of Bourne End with a church and manor house in parkland but no real village. Hedsor Church, a tiny eleventh-century building with a squat bell-tower almost entirely rebuilt in about 1600, is on the hilltop to your left, while the extensively-restored Victorian manor house hidden by trees beyond is now a conference centre.

If wishing to visit the church with its Russian icon and seat with fine views across the Thames Valley towards Cookham with its prominent church, Winter Hill and Marlow, go through a kissing-gate opposite and climb through a grassy field passing below the churchyard hedge to a corner with a seat, then bear left to reach a kissing-gate into the churchyard. On leaving the churchyard, go back through the kissing-gate and turn right, then go straight on downhill to another kissing-gate onto path HD4, onto which you turn left.

If the first kissing-gate leading to the church is overgrown or you do not wish to climb the hill to the church, turn right onto the private road and follow it, passing the second kissing-gate leading to the church after 150 yards and then continuing to gates onto a road called Hedsor Hill.

Cross this busy road carefully and take path HD6 straight on along the macadam drive to Hedsor Wharf, passing through the left-hand of three gates and soon passing a cattle grid. Where the gates to the large mansion block your way ahead, turn right onto path HD1 along a branching drive, ignoring two branching drives to your right and one to your left, then go through the left-hand of two gates and take a fenced gravel path to a footbridge into a field. Now keep left at a fork following a left-hand fence at first. Where the fence bears away to the left, take path HD1a straight on across the field to an outcrop of trees where you join the bank of the Thames. Now follow this for about 100 yards (soon on path WB1), then, by a large maple tree, where the river bears left and Cookham Church comes into view ahead, bear slightly right across the field to cross a stile by a gate in its far corner onto the A4094. Cross this busy road carefully and turn left onto its footway, soon crossing Cookham Bridge into Cookham.

Cookham - Cookham Dean (Map 12)

Maps
OS Landranger Sheet 175
OS Explorer Sheet 172 (or old Sheet 3)
East Berkshire Ramblers' Association Group FP Map No.2

Parking
There are public car parks in Cookham, at Cookham Station and at Winter Hill.

Cookham, a picturesque Thames-side village with a twelfth-century church which is well worth exploring, has always been important as a point for crossing the Thames. Till the nineteenth century, Cookham was the site of a long-established ferry, which Henry II regularly used in the twelfth century on his way from Windsor Castle to visit his mistress, Fair Rosamund, at Woodstock before Queen Eleanor found out about it and travelled to Woodstock herself to dispose of her rival. In 1839, however, the ferry was finally replaced with a wooden toll-bridge, which, in turn, gave way in 1867 to the present iron bridge carrying the A4094, now totally unsuitable for the amount of traffic it carries. The age of railways also gave Cookham a station in 1854 when the Wycombe Railway was built giving High Wycombe its first railway link to London, branching off the Great Western mainline at Maidenhead, but, while this line was later superseded by the direct modern Chiltern Railways line to Marylebone and the old line north of Bourne End was closed in 1970, Cookham Station has survived as part of the First Great Western Marlow Branch.

At the far end of Cookham Bridge, recross the A4094 and take its left-hand footway, soon turning left down steps onto path C63, then bear right through the car park of 'The Ferry`. At the far end of the car park, turn sharp left into a rough lane (path C72) leading to the river. Here fork left up a ramp onto the terrace of 'The Ferry`, then turn left along its river edge. Now take the Thames towpath (C60) up a ramp and under Cookham Bridge, then keep straight on along the Thames towpath for nearly half a mile, soon joining the Thames Path. Having rounded a right-hand bend in the river and passed the first large willow tree, then a seat, by a fenced disused culvert, leaving the Thames Path and Shakespeare's Way, turn left onto path C38 across the riverside meadow to cross a culvert by another large willow tree. Now turn right onto path C36 between a grass bank marking the edge of the Thames floodplain and a stream, soon with trees to your right.

After about 350 yards turn left up a flight of steps onto path C37, following a right-hand belt of trees, later a hedge concealing the railway, gently uphill along the edge of Winter Hill Golf Course. Having passed through an area of scrub, turn right onto path C33 crossing a railway bridge, then taking a grassy track straight on across the golf course to a gap between a barn and a clump of cypresses. Here go straight on through the golf course maintenance yard, then continue up Winter Hill to reach the corner of a hedge. Now follow the left-hand hedge straight on uphill with fine views to your right towards Bourne End and Wooburn and behind you towards Hedsor Church and House. On passing through a fence gap, at a signposted junction, turn right onto path C34, following a right-hand hedge, soon with a fine view to your right towards Hedsor House and Cliveden House.

Cliveden (pronounced ´Cliv-d'n`), which, as the pronunciation suggests, is situated on the top of a high cliff with superb views, has been the site of three large houses, two of which were destroyed by fire. The first, built in 1666 for Charles II's favourite, George Villiers, Duke of Buckingham, was, at one time, home to Frederick, Prince of Wales, father of George III, and in 1740 was the scene of the first performance of Thomas Arne's ´Rule Britannia`. The present house, built in 1851 for the Duke of Sutherland to a design by Sir Charles Barry, architect of the Houses of Parliament, retains the great brick terrace from the original house and later became home to the Astor family, who made it famous in the inter-war period as the home of a literary and political society known as the Cliveden Set. The house was given to the National Trust by Lord Astor in 1942 and is now a luxury hotel while the attractive grounds are open to the public.

At the far end of the field go through a kissing-gate onto National Trust land at Winter Hill, then turn left onto a permissive path through scrubland, soon emerging onto open downland at the top of the hill. Now follow a worn path straight on along the top of the bank, soon with panoramic views to your right towards Marlow, Flackwell Heath and Bourne End. On entering further scrubland, ignore a gate to your left and keep straight on until you merge with a gravel track (path C57). Turn left onto this, climbing gently and soon passing through gates. About 180 yards further on, ignore a gate to your right and immediately turn right onto a permissive path following the contours of the hill through scrubland to a junction of lanes.

Here turn sharp left to reach a road junction, then take path C25

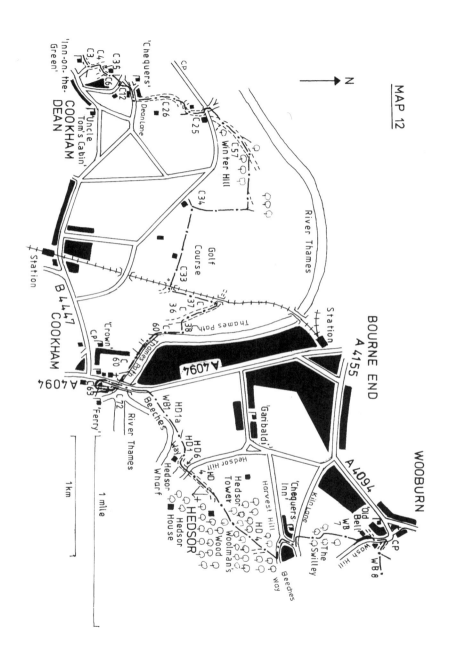

MAP 12

83

straight on along a rough lane. Where the lane turns right, follow it (now on path C26), passing a traditional Chiltern barn, then, where the lane bears right again and becomes a macadam drive, leave it and go straight on through a fence gap, following a right-hand hedge to join a track. Take this track straight on with views of Cookham Dean ahead and later the wooded Cliveden ridge to your left, gradually descending to reach Dean Lane on the edge of Cookham Dean.

Turn right onto this road, then, at a crossroads, turn left into Cookham Dean Bottom. Just before a red-brick cottage on a high bank, turn left onto restricted byway C12, a macadam path between a hedge and a wall leading uphill to a small green. Here bear right, joining Popes Lane and almost immediately turning left past a safety barrier onto hedged concrete path C6, climbing steeply. On reaching a green, follow the concrete path bearing slightly left and joining a gravel track which emerges onto the Old Cricket Common. Here turn right onto path C35 along a gravel track, then, at a junction by a cherry tree, fork left onto path C4, following a gravel track to the sign for the 'Inn on the Green'.

Cookham Dean - Pinkneys Green (Map 13)

Maps
OS Landranger Sheet 175
OS Explorer Sheet 172 (or old Sheet 3)
East Berkshire Ramblers' Association Group FP Map No.2

Parking
There is limited on-street parking in Cookham Dean and a car park on Cookham Dean Common.

The picturesque village of Cookham Dean, with its maze of lanes and footpaths, some very steep, and a plethora of greens and commons of various sizes and inviting pubs, gives a very higgledy-piggledy rural impression and seems worlds away from the modern suburbs of Maidenhead, a mere mile and a half to the south. This layout is probably explained by its cottages being encroachments on a remote upland common on the parish boundary which served to fragment a once continuous expanse of common land and this is also why its church only dates from 1845. In the 1860s and 1870s Cookham Dean was the childhood home of the author Kenneth Grahame and it is thought that the surrounding countryside inspired his masterpiece 'The Wind in the Willows'.

By the sign for the 'Inn on the Green', turn right onto path C3 following the pub drive, then, by its entrance, bear right, passing the right-hand end of the building to enter scrubby woodland. Continue through this, then, at its far side, ignore a branching path to your left and pass through a squeeze-stile into a field. Here follow a right-hand fence straight on over a rise passing a turkey farm to your right. In the valley bottom, turn left onto path C1 following a gravel track up the bottom. Where the gravel track ends, take a fenced grassy track straight on to a kissing-gate leading to a road junction on Bigfrith Common.

Here take Bigfrith Lane, signposted to Pinkneys Green and Maidenhead straight on. At a double-bend fork left onto a road signposted to Coombe End, immediately forking left again onto path C16 along the left-hand edge of a small green to enter a green lane into woodland on Cookham Dean Common. Go straight on through this woodland, then, on passing through a squeeze-stile, take a gravel track straight on. Where it turns left and becomes a macadam road, take bridleway C15 straight on into woodland, immediately bearing right and soon emerging onto open common. Now follow the left-hand edge of the grass common, soon passing through three outcrops of woodland, after which you continue along the left-hand edge of the grass common. At its far left-hand corner take a woodland track straight on to emerge near the road junction at Butler's Gate near Turpin Lodge, named after the notorious eighteenth-century highwayman who frequented these parts.

Here cross Choke Lane and take path M62 straight on along the left-hand verge of Winter Hill Road to enter woodland. In the wood, take the left-hand of two paths straight on through it, passing a left-hand field and then continuing for 350 yards until you reach a wooden shed. Now turn right onto path M63, following a left-hand hedge and ducking under a wooden rail, then, by a large white house, join its gravel drive which bears left then right past the house and continues to Winter Hill Road.

Turn left onto this road, then, after 15 yards, turn right onto a permissive path into woodland, immediately turning left onto a permissive bridleway and following it for 150 yards. On reaching the edge of a grass common, turn right onto a crossing path, passing right of a row of cottages and continuing through woodland. At a T-junction of paths, turn left, soon passing through a squeeze-stile and continuing along a gravel lane to reach Golden Ball Lane by the 'Golden Ball' on the edge of Pinkneys Green.

Pinkneys Green - Stubbings (Map 13)

Maps
OS Landranger Sheet 175
OS Explorer Sheet 172 (or old Sheet 3)
East Berkshire Ramblers' Association Group FP Map No.2

Parking
There are several car parks and possibilities for informal parking around Pinkneys Green.

Pinkneys Green, an extensive, largely open common on the western edge of Maidenhead, is now managed by the National Trust. Its name derives from the de Pinkney family from Northamptonshire, who owned the Elington Manor of Cookham (to which the part of Maidenhead north of the Bath Road formerly belonged) from the twelfth to the fifteenth century and this family is also remembered by the name of the village of Moreton Pinkney in their county of origin.

Cross Golden Ball Lane and keep straight on across the grass verge to cross the A308 opposite a signpost for path M21. Now take this path straight on along a rough track. On reaching a corner of the open common to your left, turn left through a gap in a low grass bund and then turn right along a worn permissive path gradually diverging from the right-hand hedge to pass left of an outcrop of trees. Now follow the edge of Pinkneys Green straight on to reach a group of young trees, where you fork left onto a worn path crossing the green diagonally to its far corner.

Here cross Lee Lane by a large chestnut tree and take path M32 along a gravel track, soon narrowing to a path and passing between bollards. By the far end of the left-hand cottages, turn left between further bollards onto a rough track past a row of cottages leading to Bakers Lane, onto which you turn right. At a road junction take path M35 straight on across the green, passing just left of a much-extended half-timbered cottage, then ignoring a crossing path and continuing through scrub. By Leigh Cottage bear slightly left along a wide grass track beside a right-hand hedge to reach Henley Road (the former A423) at Camley Corner near the hamlet of Stubbings.

Stubbings - Burchett's Green (Map 13)

Maps
OS Landranger Sheet 175
OS Explorer Sheet 172 (or old Sheet 3)
East Berkshire Ramblers' Association Group FP Maps Nos. 1 & 2

Parking
There is a car park on Pinkneys Drive c.350 yards east of Camley Corner.

Stubbings, a hamlet of Bisham parish on the Henley Road just north of Maidenhead Thicket, has its own church built in 1850 and a manor house called Stubbings House on the edge of the Thicket, which sheltered the exiled Queen Wilhelmina of the Netherlands during World War II, while her country was under German occupation. The woods known as Maidenhead Thicket, which were once far more extensive, in the seventeenth and eighteenth centuries were known as a haunt for highwaymen, who preyed on travellers on the Bath and Henley roads, including the notorious Dick Turpin. The woods, which were cut in half by the new A404, also conceal an Iron Age farmstead known as Robin Hood's Arbour, but are probably best known today for the roundabout which used to mark the western end of the first section of the M4.

At Stubbings, cross the Henley Road and take path M67a straight on along a stone track into Maidenhead Thicket. On nearing the new A404, the path bears right and becomes path M67b, descending a steep bank to join the drive to Stubbings House. Now on path B34, share its underpass under the A404, then, at the far end of the underpass, fork right onto fenced path B24 climbing steeply to a kissing-gate. Here bear half left across a field to pass the corner of a fence at the far end of a line of chestnut trees and reach a signposted path junction. Now turn right onto fenced path B23, soon passing through a kissing-gate, then take a grassy track beside a sporadic left-hand hedge straight on for over a third of a mile, eventually becoming a gravel track and passing through Stubbings Farm to reach gates onto Burchett's Green Lane at Burchett's Green.

Turn left onto this road, then, at a slight left-hand bend, turn right onto path HU61, following a gravel drive at first, then keeping straight on through woodland to reach the former A404 by a school.

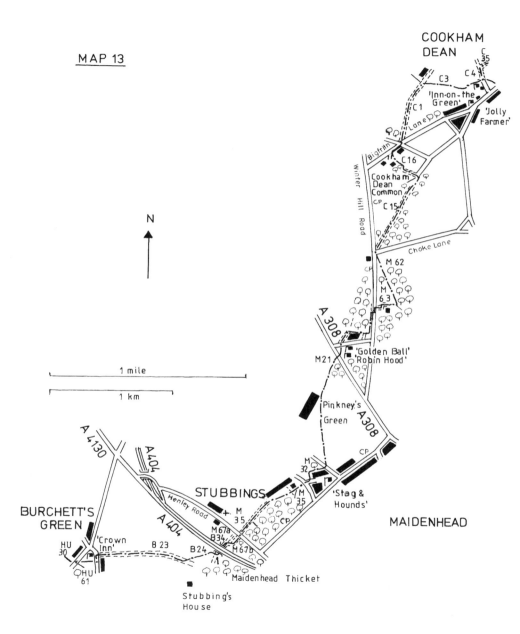

MAP 13

COOKHAM
DEAN

C 35

C3   C 4

'Inn-on-the
Green'

C1   'Jolly
Farmer'

Bigfrith Lane

C16

Cookham
Dean
Common

Winter Hill Road

CP   C 15

Choke Lane

CP   M 62

M
6 3

A 308

'Golden Ball'
'Robin Hood'

M21

Pinkney's

Green

A 308

CP

M
32

STUBBINGS

M
35

'Stag &
Hounds'

MAIDENHEAD

A 4130

A 404

Henley Road

A 404

+ M
35

M67a

B 23

B34

'Crown
Inn'

BURCHETT'S
GREEN

HU
30

B 24   M 67b

HU
61

Maidenhead Thicket

Stubbing's
House

N

1 mile

1 km

Burchett's Green - Warren Row (Map 14)

Maps
OS Landranger Sheet 175
OS Explorer Sheet 172 (or old Sheet 3)
East Berkshire Ramblers' Association Group FP Map No.1

Parking
Limited on-street parking is possible at Burchett's Green.

Burchett's Green, straddling both the parish boundary between the riverside parishes of Bisham and Hurley and an ancient turnpike road from Reading to St. Alban's, is a pleasant leafy village, now much quieter than it once was thanks to the building of the new A404 which has effectively bypassed it. The village, which has no church, but can boast a pub, an infants school and a manor house called Hall Place (now accommodating the Berkshire Agricultural College), built in 1728 on the site of a mediæval predecessor, is, however, still best known for its formerly congested roundabout, which was also bypassed by the new road.

By the school, bear slightly right across the old A404 and take path HU30, passing through a gap by an overgrown gate right of the gates to Burchetts Place and taking a fenced path to a stile. Now go straight on along the edge of a bamboo plantation, keeping left of a hedge ahead and then following a right-hand fence to a crossing track. Here ignore a gate and gap to your right and follow a right-hand fence straight on along the edge of an oak plantation, then a disused field to a kissing-gate into Ashley Hill Forest. In the wood keep right at a fork, soon reaching Honey Lane at Dellars Hill, onto which you turn right. After 200 yards, on rounding a right-hand bend, fork left onto path HU24, taking a disused tarmac drive up Ashley Hill for nearly 200 yards to join the realigned drive. Now follow it straight on uphill, ignoring two branching paths to your right and one to your left. At the top of the tree-covered hill, by the gates to a house called Clifton, fork right onto a woodland path, descending the hill and ignoring a branching path to your left and a crossing track to reach a squeeze-stile at the bottom leading to a crossing bridleway, where the fascinating 'Dewdrop Inn', where the notorious highwayman Dick Turpin used to hide from his pursuers in an underground room, is 200 yards to your right.

Cross this bridleway and take path HU25 straight on down a sunken way, bearing right, leaving the wood and ignoring a lane merging from your left. Now continue past a cottage, disregarding branching paths to your left and right and then following a winding fenced path along the edge of a wood with views to your right of a newly-built mansion on the site of the former Grassland Research Institute. Eventually you cross a footbridge into the wood, then turn right and follow its inside edge. On leaving the wood, turn sharp left onto path HU26, following a concrete road between the wood and a plantation, gradually bearing right, then bearing left with wide views to your right towards the Buckinghamshire and Oxfordshire Chilterns. At the far side of the wood, where the concrete road turns left, leave it and take a fenced grassy track straight on downhill with views to your left towards Warren Row and to your right towards Medmenham. At the bottom of the hill, go straight on through a squeeze-stile and down steps into sunken bridleway HU15 known as Hodgedale Lane, into which you turn right.

After 100 yards, turn left through a squeeze-stile, then left again onto fenced path HU16, passing three right-hand horse paddocks. On reaching the corner of a copse, follow the left-hand fence along its edge, then, by a kissing-gate, turn right, soon crossing a macadam drive and continuing through the copse. At its far side bear left into a fenced path beside a left-hand hedge, later the edge of another copse, eventually reaching a kissing-gate. Now take the fenced path straight on to join a gravel drive, then continue through gates to reach the village street at Warren Row.

Warren Row - Remenham Hill (Map 14)

Maps
OS Landranger Sheet 175
OS Explorer Sheets 171 & 172 (or old Sheet 3)
(pt. only) East Berkshire Ramblers' Association Group FP Map No.1

Parking
Limited on-street parking is possible at Warren Row.

Warren Row, a remote hamlet nestling at the foot of Bowsey Hill, has had a strange recent history as, in 1942, underground chalkpits near the village were used as an underground factory for making parts for aeroplane engines. In the subsequent Cold War, they were then converted into an underground nuclear bunker designed to act as a centre of regional government before becoming surplus to requirements in 1988 and being used for document storage. The village, which once boasted three pubs, now has only one as well as a green corrugated-iron chapel which is said to have been built in 1894 from a mail-order catalogue!

At Warren Row turn right onto the village street, then, at a right-hand bend, turn left onto path HU36, following a macadam, then a gravel lane between gardens, then past garages into woodland known as Cayton Park. In the wood, cross a stile by a gate and take a winding track gently uphill then down again to cross a culvert before climbing more steeply. Near the top of Bowsey Hill the track narrows to a path and you eventually emerge through a gate into the macadamed Hatchgate Lane (restricted byway HU41/WG16).

Turn right onto this road, then almost immediately turn sharp left onto restricted byway WG45, taking a stone track downhill, briefly with a fine view towards Reading. Where the stone track ends by a bungalow, take its unmade continuation straight on downhill through the wood, then, at a T-junction of tracks, turn right onto path WG43, following a woodland track below hillside gardens. On passing through a squeeze-stile, bear left downhill to reach a crossways. Here turn right onto path WG44, ignoring a crossing path, then crossing a rise and continuing through High Knowl Wood for a third of a mile, eventually joining a right-hand fence and reaching a gap by a gate into Rose Lane.

Turn right onto this road and follow it towards Holly Cross for over 250 yards, ignoring a restricted byway and the drive to Thistle House to your left. At the top of a rise turn left through a kissing-gate

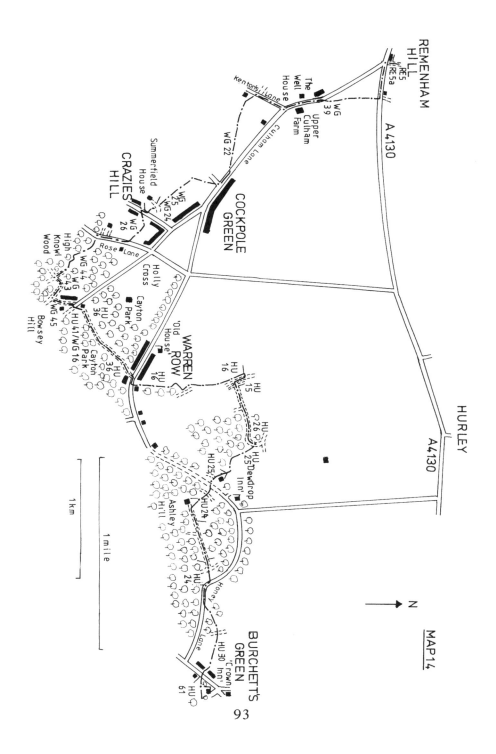

MAP 14

93

by a gate onto fenced path WG26, later bearing left, continuing between hedges and joining a macadam drive leading to the road at Crazies Hill.

Turn right onto this road, then almost immediately turn left onto fenced path WG24, soon passing through a kissing-gate and continuing to the gravel drive to Summerfield House. Originally built as the Town Hall in Henley in 1790, this house was moved to Crazies Hill and extended by Major W.H.M. Willis when the new Town Hall was built in 1898 and was at first named The Crazies before being renamed as Summerfield House. Here fork right onto path WG25, crossing this and a branching drive and taking a fenced path straight on, being sure to turn round for a view of this rather eccentric house. Having passed through an old kissing-gate, take a wider path straight on between a fence and a hedge, then, at the end of the hedge, turn right over a stile and bear half left across a field to cross a stile left of a cottage with three white gables and reach a road junction at Cockpole Green.

Here turn left into Culham Lane, the priority road, then, having passed a line of tall poplars, just before a left-hand bend, turn left over a stile onto path WG22, following a left-hand fence through two fields to a kissing-gate where there is a fine view to your left across the Thames valley towards Reading. Now follow a left-hand hedge straight on to another kissing-gate, then bear half right beside another left-hand hedge to a kissing-gate leading to Kentons Lane opposite the pillars of old lodge gates. Turn right onto this road, then, at a T-junction, turn left into Culham Lane, passing The Well House. At a left-hand bend, fork right onto path WG39, passing between tall lime trees to a concealed kissing-gate under a tall oak tree, then follow a power line straight on to cross a high stile onto the A4130 opposite an entrance to the Culham Court Estate. Cross this busy road carefully and then turn left and follow its footway for over 300 yards to the junction with Culham Lane on the edge of the hamlet of Remenham Hill.

Remenham Hill - Henley-on-Thames (Map 15)

Maps
OS Landranger Sheet 175
OS Explorer Sheet 171 (or old Sheet 3)
(part only) Chiltern Society FP Maps Nos. 2 & 11

Parking
Limited on-street parking is generally possible at Remenham Hill and in Remenham Lane on the edge of Henley, but the area should be avoided during Henley Royal Regatta or other large local events.

Remenham Hill, on the opposite bank of the Thames at Henley, causes the river and its valley to turn in a wide arc around it and so, despite some tree cover, provides some of the most spectacular views in both the Thames Valley and the Chilterns. Motorists, however, may think of it in a less favourable light as the section of the A4130 of the same name, built in 1776 by Humphrey Gainsborough, brother of the artist, is notorious for its traffic jams, particularly at Regatta time!

At the junction of the A4130 and Culham Lane on the edge of the hamlet of Remenham Hill, turn right through a gap by a gate onto path RE5a, following a grassy track beside a sporadic right-hand hedge past a garden to enter a field. Here take path RE5 straight on along the edge of the field with views ahead towards Fawley and the Hambleden Valley. On reaching a bend in a track, follow it straight on beside a right-hand hedge, then, on nearing a wood, turn right through a waymarked hedge gap and gate into a field, where superb views open out towards Medmenham to your left, Danesfield House and Bisham Hill ahead and Ashley Hill and Bowsey Hill to your right. Now bear slightly left down this field, heading for gates on a private road on the far side of the field with Culham Court soon coming into view to your left.

The Thames-side mansion of Culham Court, built in 1771, is thought to have been designed for Robert Michell by Sir William Chamber, architect of Somerset House in London and was visited in 1804 by King George III. It later passed to the Smith family, which founded the booksellers W.H. Smith, and, after further ownership changes, was acquired in 2006 by the Swiss financier, Urs Schwarzenbach, who has subsequently also bought the Smiths' nearby Hambleden Estate.

On reaching the private road, go through a small gate left of a gated cattle grid and turn left onto the road. At a fork keep left, then, on approaching another cattle grid, fork right and follow a left-hand deer fence across the grass verge and along a woodland track. On leaving the wood, follow the fence straight on with a close-up view of the side of Culham Court to your left, then go through gates and keep straight on to a wooden signpost by a disused gate. Here, joining the Thames Path, turn left onto path RE12, soon rejoining the deer fence and following it towards Culham Court, ignoring a branching permissive path to your right and passing through two kissing-gates. Now directly below Culham Court, a narrow gap in a privet hedge to your left provides a good close-up view of its façade. Having passed through two further kissing-gates, go straight on across a large parkland field, heading just left of Culham Farm ahead with views to your right of the River Thames and Hambleden Valley including a glimpse of Hambleden Church. At the far end of the field, keep straight on through gates and past the picturesque farm to your right to join a tarmac drive, along which you continue to Aston Lane at Aston, where you can just see the 'Flower Pot Hotel' to your right.

Leaving the Thames Path, turn left into Aston Lane gently uphill, passing between the abutments of a former bridge carrying a drive over the road. Now, just beyond the far end of a brick-and-flint wall to your right, turn right through gates onto path RE6, following a right-hand wall, then a hedge uphill to cross a stile by a gate, then continue uphill beside a right-hand hedge to a gate and kissing-gate. Here, at a fork, keep left, taking a sunken way straight on beside a right-hand belt of trees. Eventually the mature trees give way to a plantation and wide views open out to your right across the Thames Valley towards the Buckinghamshire hills around Hambleden and Fawley. On reaching a gravel track merging from your left, keep straight on over a rise where views open out ahead towards Henley Park in Oxfordshire, then continue past a left-hand copse to cross a stile by gates into Remenham Church Lane.

Turn left onto this road and after 250 yards, just before a tall oak tree, turn right through a hedge gap onto path RE9, bearing half left across a large field with wide views to your right across the Thames Valley towards Henley Park and Fawley and a brief glimpse at one point of the red-brick façade of Fawley Court hidden in trees on the far bank of the Thames.

Fawley Court, which had been ransacked during the Civil War and completely rebuilt in 1684, during the 'Glorious Revolution' of 1688, played host to King William III of Orange on his way from Brixham to London. In more recent times, the house which is

thought to have been the inspiration for Toad Hall in Kenneth Grahame's 'The Wind in the Willows`, was requisitioned during the Second World War and subsequently sold to the Marian Fathers for use as a Polish school. After this closed, it was controversially put on the market and its future is currently uncertain.

Eventually you drop down into a dip to enter Remenham Wood left of an electricity pole, where you ignore a crossing permissive path and keep straight on through the wood over a rise to cross a stile into a field. Now keep straight on, heading just left of a group of tall elms to join path RE8 by a signpost and take a terraced path within the scrubby edge of woodland to a stile into a field used for golf practice. Here follow a left-hand fence to a signpost, then keep straight on, crossing the field diagonally with views of Matson House over your left shoulder, to cross a stile in the bottom hedge. Now keep straight on across the next field, keeping left of a stone track to reach a kissing-gate into Remenham Lane. Turn left onto this road and follow it round a right-hand bend to reach the A4130 by the 'Little Angel`. Here turn right onto its footway, soon passing the entrance to the Leander Club and joining the Thames Path. Now continue over Henley Bridge with its world-famous views of the town and its riverside to reach the traffic lights at the far end of the bridge.

Henley-on-Thames - Lower Bolney (Map 15)

Maps
OS Landranger Sheet 175
OS Explorer Sheet 171 (or old Sheet 3)
(part only) Chiltern Society FP Maps Nos. 2 & 4

Parking
There are various car parks and possibilities for on-street parking in Henley-on-Thames and there is also a car park off Mill Lane near Marsh Lock.

Henley-on-Thames, home of the world-famous Royal Regatta, has, for at least 150 years, been a fashionable riverside resort. Although this has, to some extent, contributed to the architectural beauty of the town, its former role as a commercial centre is responsible for much of its legacy of picturesque buildings. Prior to the age of railways, the town was of commercial importance, being both a river port and a bridgehead on a main road crossing the Thames. In Hart Street, the street leading from the bridge to Henley Town Hall, are to be found a number of ancient timber-framed houses and inns, some dating back to the fifteenth and sixteenth centuries. The Town Hall around which the street divides, was built in 1901 on the site of the mediæval Guildhall and the imposing Parish Church by the bridge and nearby almshouses date from the fourteenth to sixteenth centuries. Henley Bridge, surely one of the most graceful on the Thames, was built in 1786 to replace a wooden structure swept away by a flood in 1774, while in Mill Meadows to the south of the town centre is the River and Rowing Museum which opened in 1998.

At the traffic lights at the end of Henley Bridge, now in Oxfordshire, turn left across the bridge approach to the ´Angel on the Bridge`, then turn right and immediately left into Thames Side. Just past the pub, turn left along a paved path to the riverbank, then turn right and follow it, briefly diverting round a small building. Where the road to your right turns right away from the river towards Henley Station, take macadam path H27 (later H28) straight on along the picturesque riverside for two-thirds of a mile, passing two islands to your left and the River and Rowing Museum to your right.

On reaching the end of Mill Lane, still on path H28, turn left over a long footbridge to reach Marsh Lock. Briefly back in Berkshire, take path RE13 straight on past the lock onto another long footbridge which bears right back into Oxfordshire (again on path H28). On reaching the Oxfordshire bank, bear left along a fenced path to a gateway into riverside meadows. Here take path HA21 straight on along the riverbank for a third of a mile, later bearing right. Near the start of an island to your left called Ferry Eyot at the site of the former Bolney Ferry where the ancient towpath transfers to the Berkshire bank, take path HA1, following the edge of scrub away from the river to a footbridge. Now continue along a fenced path, then cross a track and pass left of a padlocked gate to enter another fenced path continuing past the grounds of Thamesside Court to your left. Here look out for a scaled model of the legendary Rhætian Railway and St. Moritz Station in the owner's native Switzerland. Eventually you join a private road and follow it straight on, rounding a left-hand, then a right-hand bend to reach a fork, where the Thames Path keeps straight on towards Shiplake Station while the Chiltern Way Berkshire Loop turns right onto byway HA24.

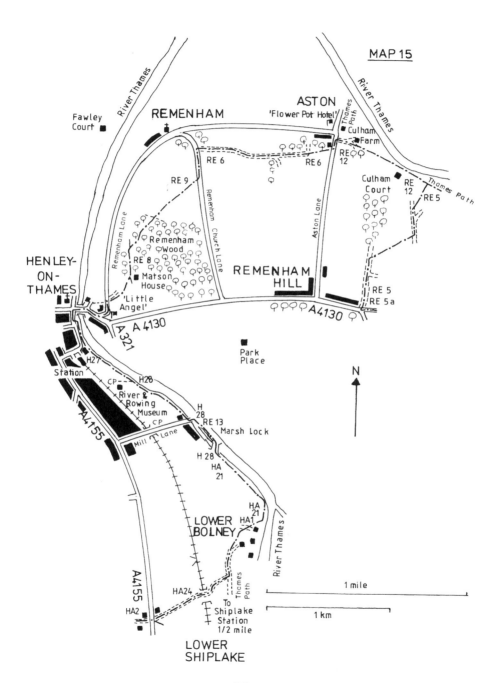

MAP 15

River Thames

River Thames

Fawley
Court ■

REMENHAM

ASTON
'Flower Pot Hotel'

Thames Path

Culham
Farm

RE 6   RE 6

RE 9

RE 12

Culham
Court

RE
12

Thames Path

RE 5

Remenham Lane

Remenham Church Lane

Remenham
Wood

RE 8

Matson
House

Aston Lane

REMENHAM
HILL

HENLEY-
ON-
THAMES

'Little
Angel'

A 4130

RE 5
RE 5a

A 4130

A 321

Park
Place

N

H27

Station

CP

H28

River &
Rowing
Museum

CP

A4155

Mill Lane

H
28
RE 13

H 28

HA
21

Marsh Lock

LOWER
BOLNEY

HA
21
HA1

River Thames

A 4155

HA24

HA2

Thames Path

To
Shiplake
Station
1/2 mile

1 mile

1 km

LOWER
SHIPLAKE

Lower Bolney - Binfield Heath (Map 16)

Maps
OS Landranger Sheet 175
OS Explorer Sheet 171
(part only) Chiltern Society FP Map No.4

Parking
Limited on-street parking is available at Lower Shiplake, Woodlands Road and Binfield Heath, but is forbidden on some private roads.

Bolney was once a separate riverside strip parish between Harpsden and Shiplake stretching westwards for about two miles from the Thames near Bolney Ferry and Bolney Court along the byway and bridleway you are about to walk to Mays Green on the upland Chiltern plateau and beyond. It is thought that its church and main village were located at Lower Bolney near the junction of lanes which you have now reached. For some reason, however, possibly flooding or the Black Death, its population declined sharply in the late Middle Ages so that the church (of which there is now no trace) became ruinous in the fifteenth century and the parish was formally merged with neighbouring Harpsden in 1453. For several centuries Bolney Manor then comprised merely a few scattered farms and cottages, but following the building of the Henley Branch of the Great Western Railway in 1857 with a station in neighbouring Lower Shiplake, development started to mushroom around the station and in about 1900 began to spill over into Lower Bolney, so that now a sizeable proportion of the population of Harpsden parish lives on the edge of Lower Shiplake.

At the junction of lanes, the Chiltern Way (Berkshire Loop) forks right onto byway HA24 and follows it for nearly half a mile, crossing a bridge over the railway, continuing along an avenue of horse chestnut trees with views to your left towards Lower Shiplake and to your right over Henley towards the wooded hills around Hambleden and Remenham and eventually reaching the A4155.

Cross this busy road carefully and take bridleway HA2 straight on along a rough lane for nearly half a mile, climbing steadily. At the top of the hill, cross Woodlands Road and take bridleway HA4 straight on along a private macadam road for nearly half a mile. On nearing the gates to Upper Bolney House, follow the road, bearing right then left, then continue for a further 200 yards ignoring a branching fenced path to your right. By the stile of a second branching path to your right, fork left onto bridleway HA7, following the macadam road until it bears left to the gates of Highwood House. Here take the waymarked bridleway straight on into High Wood, then, at a waymarked fork, keep right and follow a winding woodland track for a third of a mile to gates at the far side of the wood. Now pass right of these gates and take bridleway BH28 straight on along a green lane to Harpsden Road. Turn left onto this road and follow it for nearly a third of a mile to a road junction by the 'Bottle and Glass' on the edge of Binfield Heath.

Binfield Heath - Harpsden Bottom (Map 16)

Maps
OS Landranger Sheet 175
OS Explorer Sheet 171
Chiltern Society FP Map No.4

Parking
Limited on-street parking is available at Binfield Heath, but do not use the pub car park without the landlord's permission.

Binfield Heath, as its name suggests, was originally an upland common of Shiplake parish sharing the name of an ancient Oxfordshire hundred and old maps indicate that in the early nineteenth century it still comprised only a few scattered cottages. It would seem that it was not until after the enclosure of the ancient common in 1867 that development started to take place and that during the following 80 years before the introduction of the modern planning system, the village grew to its present size. This explains its largely modern suburban appearance. It was not, however, till 2003 that Binfield Heath, part of which had been in Eye & Dunsden parish, was united and given separate parish status.

At the road junction by the 'Bottle and Glass', turn right onto bridleway BH6 through its gravel car park, passing the thatched pub to your right, then take a gravel track straight on. Where this track turns right, leave it and take a sunken green lane known ominously as Bones Lane straight on, eventually bearing right to reach a waymarked junction on the edge of Summerhouses Wood. Here, still on bridleway BH6, turn left onto a track into the wood, descending gently. Just past the corner of a field to your left, fork right into a waymarked sunken way dropping more steeply. Near the bottom of the hill, the sunken way bears left and now on bridleway HA12, follow it, soon bearing right along a slight causeway across the valley bottom, then continuing uphill. On reaching an old iron-railing fence surrounding Crowsley Park, bear right and follow it within the edge of the woodland to reach the gravel drive to North Lodge. Here cross the drive and take the waymarked bridleway straight on, descending gently through woodland and eventually entering another sunken way leading you down to the road in Harpsden Bottom, where the timber-framed Old Place can be seen ahead. Now, do **not** join the road, but turn left onto a path along the roadside bank leading to a kissing-gate, through which you turn left onto path HA13 joining the **Chiltern Way Extension.**

Now **turn to Map 18** in **Harpsden Bottom.**

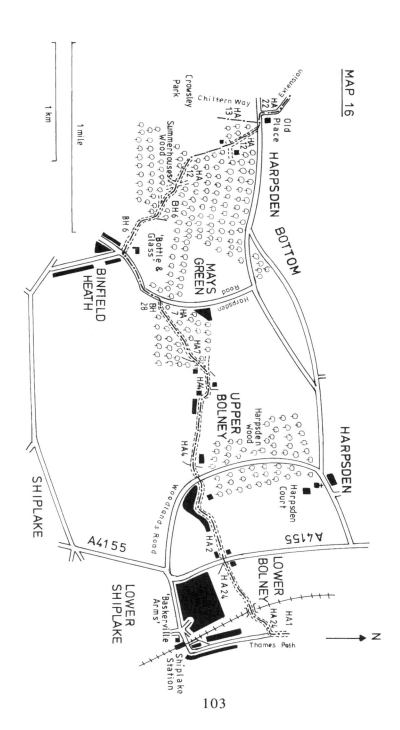

MAP 16

Upper Bix Bottom - Crocker End (Map 17)

Maps
OS Landranger Sheet 175
OS Explorer Sheet 171 (or old Sheet 3)
Chiltern Society FP Map No.2

Parking
The only parking available near this section is at the Warburg Reserve
car park, three-quarters of a mile down Bix Bottom from the fork of
the original Chiltern Way and its extension.

At the junction of green lanes where the **Chiltern Way Extension**
forks off the **original Chiltern Way** (c.f. Map 9), the **Chiltern Way
Extension** takes path SW27 southwards over a stile and bears slightly
right up a field to cross a stile near the tallest tree in woodland ahead.
Now follow a left-hand fence uphill through the trees to cross another
stile, then continue along the outside edge of Stockings Plantation
soon with fine views over your right shoulder towards Redpits Manor
to reach a gate and stile into a lane. Take this lane (path NE7) straight
on along the edge of Home Wood past the former Soundess Farm to
reach the end of a macadam road by Soundess Lodge.
   Turn right onto this road, then, at a right-hand bend, fork left over
a stile by a gate onto the continuation of path NE7 going straight
across a parkland field with views of Soundess House, reputedly the
home of Charles II's mistress, Nell Gwynne, opening out to your left.
Now pass right of three cedars and cross a concealed stile by another
cedar right of a group of cottages at Crocker End. Here take a fenced
path to reach a road at Crocker End Green.

Crocker End - Bix Bottom (Map 17)

Maps
OS Landranger Sheet 175
OS Explorer Sheet 171 (or old Sheet 3)
Chiltern Society FP Map No.2

Parking
Limited parking is available on unmown sections of verge at Crocker End Green but cars should be parked no more than 15 feet from the road.

Crocker End, despite its small size and remote location, has more than one royal connection as not only is Nell Gwynne reputed to have lived at Soundess House, but the village was, until recently, also home to the Duke and Duchess of Kent. If one looks at Crocker End, however, this is not entirely surprising as this scattered hamlet, separated from nearby Nettlebed by a wooded part of the latter's extensive common, has an attractive village green, around which are to be found most of its picturesque old cottages, while the only modern development is hidden away at Catslip on the edge of woodland to the south.

Now turn left onto the road, immediately keeping left at a fork, then, at a right-hand bend by Field House, take bridleway NE11 straight on along the edge of the green to join another road leading to the gates of an attractive timber-framed former farmhouse known as The Leaze. Here cross a stile by a gate onto path NE8, following a right-hand hedge through another parkland field with more fine views of Soundess House to your left to reach a stile into Wellgrove Wood. Take the obvious path straight on through this wood, with an unusual yew plantation to your left at first, then ignore a crossing track, where your path widens into a track, and continue (soon on path B28), ignoring all branching tracks and soon with fine views down Bix Bottom to your right. On leaving the wood, follow a track straight on, descending gently beside a right-hand tree-belt, later a hedge, to reach the road in Bix Bottom (restricted byway B32) by the ruins of Bixbrand Church.

Bix Bottom - Bix (Map 17)

Maps
OS Landranger Sheet 175
OS Explorer Sheet 171 (or old Sheet 3)
Chiltern Society FP Map No.2

Parking
Limited parking is available on the roadside verge opposite the ruined church in Bix Bottom or alternatively there is the Warburg Reserve car park at the end of the road three-quarters of a mile beyond.

Bix Bottom is a long winding characteristic Chiltern dry 'bottom' followed by a lane which is an ancient route of the London - Henley - Oxford road, but, just as the main road has moved to the ridge to the south, so has the ancient village of Bixbrand also virtually disappeared and been replaced by modern Bix just off the A4130. All that remains of Bixbrand today are Valley Farm and the ruins of its Norman church, abandoned in 1875 after a new church was built in Bix. Aerial photographs taken after the harvest, however, reveal the outlines of other buildings which explain there having been a church in this deserted bottom. Since 1967 the woodland further up the valley has been a nature reserve of the Berkshire, Buckinghamshire and Oxfordshire Wildlife Trust named after the Oxford botanist, Dr. E.F. Warburg and is notable for its unusual chalkland flora including rare orchids.

Turn right onto this road (restricted byway B32), briefly rejoining the Oxfordshire Way, then, at Valley Farm, leaving the Oxfordshire Way again, turn right through a gate onto path B7, passing left of the farmhouse and soon leaving the farm through a gate. Now join a flinty track merging from your left, then, after 150 yards, turn left up a bank and over a stile onto path B4, following a left-hand hedge uphill to a stile into Bushy Copse where you should turn round for a fine view across Bix Bottom. In the wood, soon turn right by a gate onto a woodland track. After 120 yards fork left onto a waymarked path along the inside edge of the wood. Eventually you join another track and bear left, soon bearing right and climbing gently between plantations. On entering mature beechwood, at a fork take the left-hand option straight on, eventually bearing left with a field to your right. On leaving the wood, bear slightly right across a field, soon crossing a grassy track and heading for the corner of a garden hedge right of twin-poled and single-poled electricity pylons, then follow this hedge straight on to a stile leading to the A4130 at Bix.

Bix - Greys Green (Map 17)

Maps
OS Landranger Sheet 175
OS Explorer Sheet 171 (or old Sheet 3)
Chiltern Society FP Map No.2

Parking
There are small car parks by Bix Church and at the end of Rocky Lane near Greys Court and limited parking is also available at the entrance to Old London Road off the A4130 at Bix.

Bix, named after the box trees which grow locally, with its large hilltop common, which, until quite recently, was one of the last remaining commons to be cultivated in rotation by local farmers, must have been inhabited since Roman times as the remains of a Roman building have been discovered to the east of the common. It is also thought to occupy the site of the mediæval village of Bixgwybynt, which, at one time, had its own mediæval church. After the demolition of this building, of which there is now no trace, it then shared the church of the deserted village of Bixbrand, a mile to the north in Bix Bottom, until in 1874 the present neo-Gothic dressed-stone and flint church was built by the architect John Gibson (a pupil of Sir Charles Barry, designer of the Houses of Parliament) on the course of the old Bix Hill turnpike road, now superseded by the less steep modern A4130.

Now bear half left, crossing the A4130 dual-carriageway carefully and taking fenced path B8 to the left of the gate to 'Foxhill Meadow' to reach a stile into a field. Here follow the left-hand hedge, later the edge of Drew's Wood, straight on through two fields, ignoring a stile into Drew's Wood, then cross a farm road flanked by stiles and continue to a cattle track flanked by stiles. Now bear slightly left across the next field to cross a stile in its left-hand fence left of an electricity pole, then turn right and follow the fenced cattle track ignoring a stile to your right and reaching a stile into Famous Copse. Just inside the wood, turn left over a second stile onto path B14 and follow a winding path passing an ancient earthwork to your left. At the far side of the wood, on nearing a small gate, turn right onto path B25 following the inside edge of the wood and later becoming path RG34. On reaching a crossing bridleway, take path RG9 straight on through the wood to a stile into a field. Here take path RG8 straight on towards a tall oak tree crossing a private macadam road and passing through a kissing-gate. Now bear slightly left across the next field to cross a stile right of a clump of trees concealing an old pond, then continue across another field to a marker post leading to a fenced path through a copse, soon bearing left and then forking right to a path junction near a pond. Here turn right onto path RG7, crossing a footbridge and following a left-hand fence to a gate, then taking a sunken way to another gate. Now follow a right-hand tree-belt straight on over the next rise passing through a gate and soon reaching the drive to Greys Court by the National Trust information office.

Greys Court has had a chequered history. The mediæval castle, built by the de Grey family, from which the name ´Greys` derives, was fortified by the construction of a surrounding wall in 1348, from which four of the five towers and part of the wall survive. The stables and a donkey-wheel well-house remain from an Elizabethan house built by the Knollys family, to whom Greys Court had been given by Henry VIII after it had been forfeited to the Crown in 1485. This house, where the controversial Earl and Countess of Somerset were placed in their brother-in-law, Sir William Knollys' custody by James I, was then destroyed in the Civil War and replaced by the present house in the style of many large Oxfordshire houses which had to be rebuilt at this time. Greys Court can, however, today boast some fine plasterwork and furnishings acquired when it was renovated in the eighteenth century.

Turn right onto this drive passing Greys Court to your right and ignoring three branching drives to your right, then, at a left-hand bend, leave the drive and keep straight on, disregarding a permissive path branching right and crossing a stile to reach Rocky Lane. Cross this road and a stile opposite onto path RG6, bearing half right across a field to a stile into woodland. Now continue uphill through this, ignoring a crossing permissive path, crossing a stile and soon emerging through an overgrown paddock onto the back of the cricket green at Greys Green. Here turn right and follow the edge of the green past the cricket pavilion to reach a road at the far corner of the green.

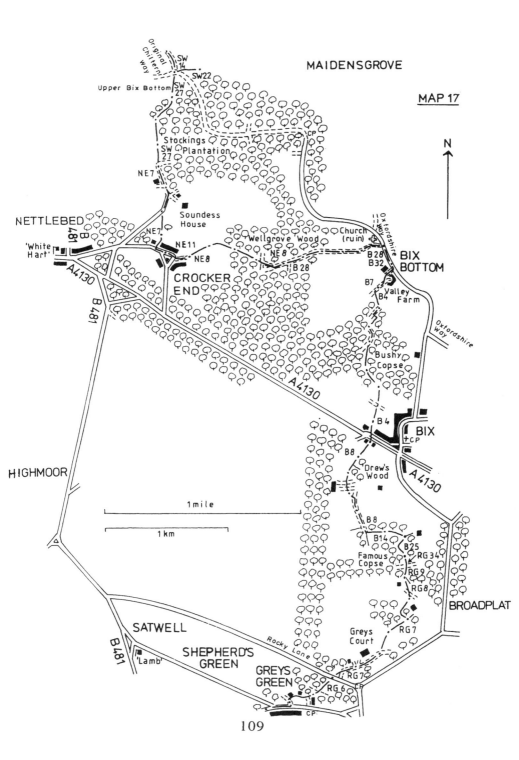

MAIDENSGROVE

MAP 17

N

MAP 17

Original Chiltern Way

SW14

SW22

Upper Bix Bottom

SW27

Stockings Plantation

SW27

CP

NE7

Soundess House

NETTLEBED

B481

B

'White Hart'

A4130

NE7

NE11

NE8

CROCKER END

Wellgrove Wood

Church (ruin)

Oxfordshire Way

NE8

B28

BIX BOTTOM

B32

B7

B4

Valley Farm

Bushy Copse

Oxfordshire Way

B4

BIX

+CP

B8

Drew's Wood

A4130

HIGHMOOR

1 mile

1 km

B8

B14

B25

RG34

Famous Copse

RG9

RG8

BROADPLAT

Greys Court

RG7

SATWELL

B481

'Lamb'

Rocky Lane

SHEPHERD'S GREEN

GREYS GREEN

RG7

RG6

CP

CP

109

Greys Green - Harpsden Bottom (Map 18)

Maps
OS Landranger Sheet 175
OS Explorer Sheet 171 (or old Sheet 3)
Chiltern Society FP Map Nos. 2 & 4

Parking
There is an unmarked gravel parking area in front of the wooden village hall at Greys Green.

Greys Green, with its cottages and cherry trees, which create a spectacular display when in blossom, clustered around a picturesque village green where cricket is played in summer, is, in some ways, the epitome of the English village, but it has no church, pub or manor house as the church and pub are located half a mile to the southeast at Rotherfield Greys while the ancient manor house, Greys Court, which you have just passed, is set in secluded parkland a third of a mile to the northeast.

Turn right onto the road ignoring a branching road to your right. 100 yards beyond this junction, turn left through gates onto fenced bridleway RG14 and follow it past a golf course for over half a mile, passing through a gate, disregarding a crossing track and eventually bearing left and later right to enter a green lane (bridleway P18). Now follow this lane for a further 300 yards, ignoring a branching path to your left, to reach gates at the appropriately-named Cross Lanes.

Here take a disintegrating macadam road (restricted byway RG33) straight on along the edge of a wood. By White Cottage keep straight on along a flinty lane starting to bear left and ignoring branching tracks and paths into the wood. On leaving the wood behind, now on restricted byway HA22, keep straight on to King's Farm where the macadam surface resumes. Now bear right by some red-brick cottages, ignoring a branching path to your left and continuing downhill for a further 700 yards to a T-junction by the attractive, gabled, timber-framed Old Place, formerly known as Bottomhouse Farm, in Harpsden Bottom.

At the T-junction turn left, then, on rounding a left-hand bend and meeting the end of the **Chiltern Way (Berkshire Loop)**, the **continuation of the Chiltern Way Extension** turns right up a steep bank and through a kissing-gate onto path HA13. (NB The reverse direction of the **Berkshire Loop** takes bridleway HA12 a few yards further on to your right).

Harpsden Bottom - Sonning Common (Map 18)

Maps
OS Landranger Sheet 175
OS Explorer Sheet 171
Chiltern Society FP Map No.4

Parking
Little parking is available on this section except at Sonning Common (see below).

Old Place marks the western extremity of a string of scattered hamlets, farms and cottages stretching along a dry Chiltern 'bottom' from the northern boundary of Crowsley Park to the southern edge of Henley collectively known as Harpsden. The original village with its heavily-restored twelfth-century church and Harpsden Court, a predominantly Tudor manor house which incorporates part of a thirteenth-century hall, is some two miles to the east, but John Blagrave's exquisite (and amazingly accurate) coloured map of Harpsden dating from 1586 shows that the parish's fields were already then enclosed and there already existed a similar pattern of settlement to today.

The reunited **Chiltern Way Extension** and **Berkshire Loop** now take path HA13, following a worn path marked by white-topped posts straight on uphill through Crowsley Park, which is home to a radio station. At the top of the rise, on crossing a raised grass track which once formed the main drive to the house, bear half right onto path BH3 (which is also marked with white-topped posts) heading for a tall chestnut tree left of two tall lime trees, passing a smaller chestnut tree and reaching an awkward stile near what is actually a clump of chestnut trees. Now bear slightly left to a gate in green iron railings near the left-hand end of an avenue of chestnut trees with Crowsley Park House, a large red-brick Jacobean house, coming into view to your left. Here continue along a fenced path to another gate then turn left onto a macadamed drive passing the main gates to the house and continuing to lodge gates onto the Shiplake-Sonning Common road.

Go through the left-hand gate then turn left onto the road. After 150 yards, at a road junction, turn right onto a road signposted to Crowsley and follow it for nearly a third of a mile into the scattered hamlet, ignoring branching drives to your left. Just past a half-timbered thatched cottage called Frieze Cottage, turn left onto path BH1 following a rough lane. By the entrance to The Well House (also half-timbered) fork right into a green lane leading to a gate and stile. Here fork right over the stile and take a worn path across a field to cross a stile by the right-hand corner of Morgan's Wood. Now keep straight on following the edge of the wood at first then continuing across another field to cross stiles between two trees in the bottom hedge. Here take path SC9 following a left-hand fence uphill to a stile into Bird Wood, through which you continue to a road. Now turn right to reach a crossroads with the B481 by the 'Bird in Hand' on the edge of Sonning Common (currently boarded up in 2009).

Sonning Common - Chalkhouse Green - Tokers Green (Map 18)

Maps
OS Landranger Sheet 175
OS Explorer Sheets 159 or 171
Chiltern Society FP Map No.4

Parking
On-street parking is possible in residential side streets in Sonning Common.

Sonning Common, which today is a large suburban settlement four miles north of the centre of Reading, was only established about 100 years ago when the rapid expansion of towns and improvements in transport made the idea of commuting to work practicable and attractive but before planning control was introduced to limit the threat this posed to the countryside. Its name is, however, indicative of its origins as the Berkshire parish of Sonning traditionally included a long strip of Oxfordshire countryside stretching from the Thames-side hamlet of Sonning Eye up into the Chilterns to an upland common which was enclosed in 1820 and now forms the site of much of the modern village. Although Sonning's Oxfordshire empire was detached by late nineteenth-century local government reform to form the Oxfordshire parish of Eye and Dunsden, it was not until 1952 that the upper ends of that parish and the neighbouring riverside 'strip parish' of Shiplake were detached and put together to form the separate parish of Sonning Common.

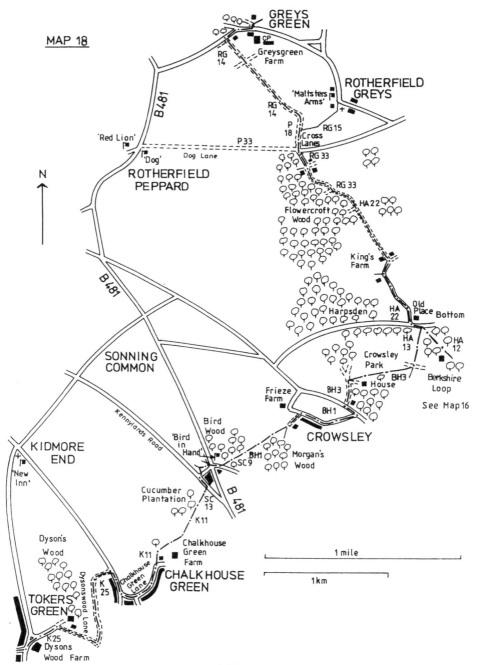

MAP 18

GREYS GREEN

CP

RG 14

Greysgreen Farm

'Maltsters Arms'

ROTHERFIELD GREYS

RG 14

P 18

RG 15

Cross Lanes

RG 33

RG 33

B 481

'Red Lion'

P 33

'Dog'

Dog Lane

ROTHERFIELD PEPPARD

HA 22

Flowercroft Wood

King's Farm

N

B 481

Harpsden

HA 22

Old Place

Bottom

HA 13

HA 12

SONNING COMMON

Crowsley Park

HA 13

Berkshire Loop

BH3

House

BH3

See Map 16

Frieze Farm

BH1

Bird Wood

'Bird in Hand'

BH1

CROWSLEY

KIDMORE END

Kennylands Road

SC9

Morgan's Wood

'New Inn'

B 481

Cucumber Plantation

SC 13

K 11

Dyson's Wood

K 11

Chalkhouse Green Farm

K 25

Dysonswood Lane

Chalkhouse Green Lane

CHALKHOUSE GREEN

TOKERS GREEN

K 25

K 25

Dysons Wood Farm

1 mile

1 km

113

Now cross the B481 and take the continuation of path SC9 straight on through a kissing-gate into Sonning Common's millennium green. At a T-junction of stone paths turn left onto a permissive path, keeping left at a fork by a seat, then turning left through red gates onto a road. Turn right onto this, then, at a T-junction, turn left onto the near verge of Kennylands Road. Where this verge ends, cross the road and take path SC13 over a stile by gates opposite, then bear half left, heading towards the left-hand end of a red-brick building at Chalkhouse Green Farm and passing a copse to your right known as Cucumber Plantation, presumably because of its shape. Now on path K11, continue, crossing a stile at a corner of a hedge, then taking a fenced path straight on past the farm to cross a stile by a gate. Here turn left and take a fenced path through scrub to reach a stile into a garden, then follow a wide grassy track straight on through the garden to a bend in Chalkhouse Green Lane at Chalkhouse Green.

Bear slightly right onto this road and follow it past pre-war ribbon development to a T-junction. Here take the Kidmore End and Stoke Row road straight on, then, at a second junction, ignore Tanners Lane to your left. 200 yards further on, on rounding a left-hand bend, turn left into a rough lane called Dysonswood Lane (restricted byway K25) and follow it downhill into a valley bottom, where it bears left along the bottom for a third of a mile, then turns sharp right and continues uphill. By a cottage to your right, the lane becomes macadamed and continues uphill. Where a private drive merges from your right and the lane widens, you bear left and follow it to a small green at Tokers Green, where you fork left to reach a T-junction.

Tokers Green - Chazey Heath - Mapledurham (Map 19)

Maps
OS Landranger Sheet 175
OS Explorer Sheets 159 or 171
Chiltern Society FP Map No.4

Parking
On-street parking is possible in places at Tokers Green and Chazey Heath.

Tokers Green, on the ancient parish boundary between Mapledurham and the once small former Oxfordshire riverside town of Caversham, in 1900 still comprised a cluster of cottages by a pond and small green at a rural crossroads. However, the rapid expansion of Caversham, which led to its urban area being incorporated into the county borough of Reading in 1911, spilled over into the countryside beyond with ribbon development spreading along the lanes around Tokers Green until modern planning legislation brought it under control. The vicinity of the green, however, remains rural in character.

At the T-junction turn left then almost immediately right into Rokeby Drive and follow it for some 700 yards to a T-junction with the A4074 at Chazey Heath, a hilltop hamlet with a coaching inn on the old main road from Caversham to Oxford named after the Chazey family who once held one of the two manors of Mapledurham.
Turn right onto this busy road, then, after 30 yards, turn left through a hedge gap onto path M10 going straight across a field to a corner of Currs Copse. Now bear left and follow its edge to a fence gap onto the Goring Heath road. Turn left onto this road, passing a copse called Winsley Shaw to your right. After 80 yards, turn right onto path M7 down a sunken green lane called Newell's Lane along the edge of the copse. At the bottom of the hill, continue past a corner of a golf course and take a sunken way straight on uphill. On reaching a crossing track (path M6), turn left onto it, ignoring a crossing gravel track and going through a former gateway, then fork right onto path M8, following a grassy track along the edge of a copse called Noke End Shaw, soon leaving the copse behind and continuing to Rose Farm. Here ignore a branching track to your left and take a concrete road straight on between the buildings, noticing to

your right a fine weatherboarded granary on staddle stones (intended to prevent rats eating the stored grain). On leaving the old farm, follow the road, bearing right with views between woods to your left towards Tilehurst. At a T-junction of concrete roads, take path M5 straight on over a stile, bearing slightly left across a field to a gap in the edge of Park Wood. Here take a wide track straight on through mature woodland. On reaching a plantation, fork left onto a mown grassy path, descending at first, then bearing right and following the contours of the hillside with views to your left in the winter months across the Thames Valley towards Tilehurst and Purley. On passing a folly in the trees to your left, you start to descend again with views ahead towards Mapledurham House and Purley, eventually passing through a fence gap and continuing through scrub to a stile into a field. Here go straight on downhill to a gate and stile onto a concrete road (bridleway M13). Turn right onto this and follow it, soon with views to your left towards Mapledurham House and Church to reach Mapledurham village street by The Lodge and The Mill House.

Mapledurham - Collins End - Path Hill (Map 19)

Maps
OS Landranger Sheet 175
OS Explorer Sheets 159 or 171
Chiltern Society FP Map No.16

Parking
There is a car park at Mapledurham open only during the opening hours of Mapledurham Country Park. At other times, the only parking near this section of the Way is on the roadside verge opposite the former 'King Charles's Head' at Goring Heath.

Mapledurham, the name of which is derived from the Saxon 'Mapledreham', meaning 'homestead by the maple tree', has been described as the prettiest village on the Thames and, with its old-world charm and lack of through-traffic, it has often been used as a film-set, notably in the war film 'The Eagle has Landed'. Along the village street are a number of seventeenth-century cottages includ-ing a row of almshouses from 1613. At its far end on the right is the fifteenth-century mill with its wooden tower which is both the oldest mill on the Thames and the only one still working. To the left is the church built in about 1200 with the tower heightened during extensive renovations by William Butterfield in 1862. An interesting

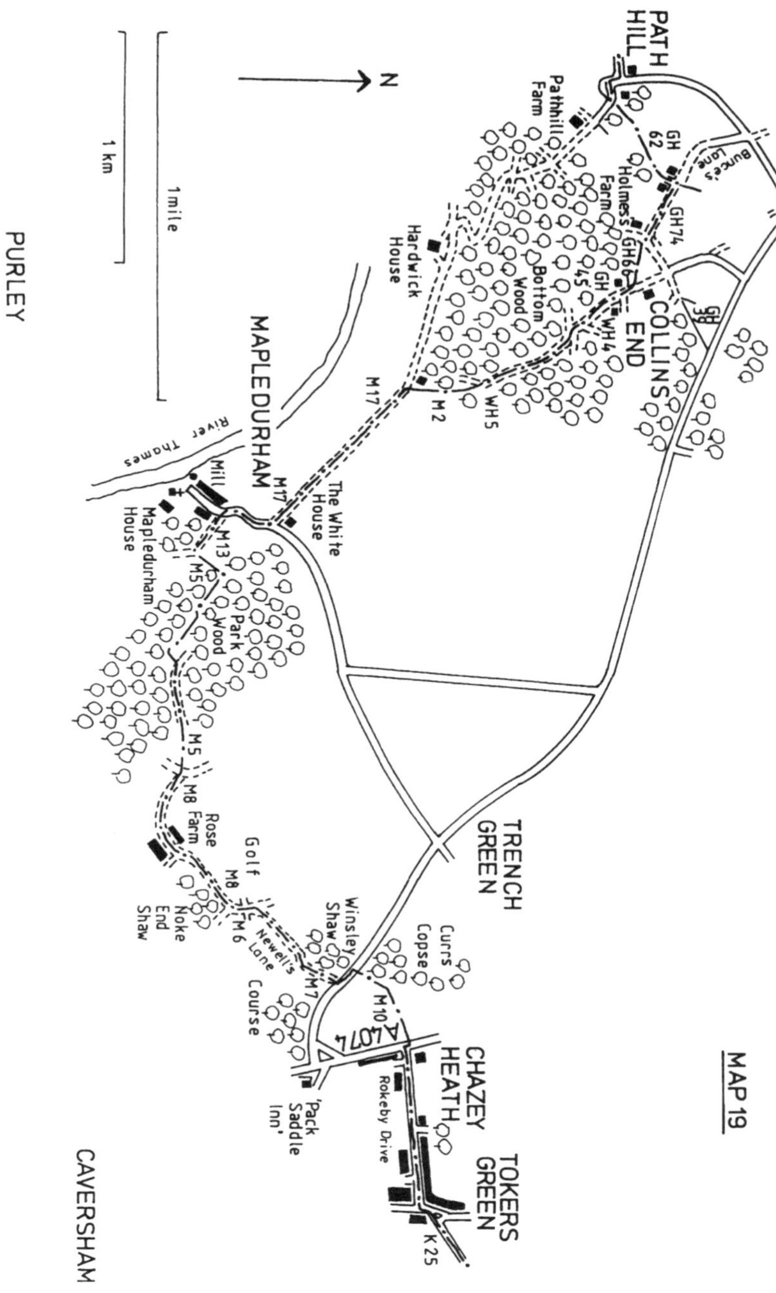

MAP 19

PURLEY

CAVERSHAM

GORING HEATH

PATH HILL

Pathhill Farm

GH 62

Holmes Farm

Bunce's Lane

GH 74

GH 67

GH 45

GH

WH 14

COLLINS END

38

Hardwick House

Bottom Wood

M 17

M 2

WH 5

WH 5

MAPLEDURHAM

River Thames

Mill

M 17

The White House

M 13

M 5

Park Wood

Mapledurham House

M 5

M 8 Farm

Rose

M 8

Noke End Shaw

Golf

Newell's Lane

Course

Winsley Shaw

M 1

M 10

A 4074

TRENCH GREEN

Currs Copse

CHAZEY HEATH

'Pack Saddle Inn'

Rokeby Drive

TOKERS GREEN

K 25

N

1 km

1 mile

117

feature of this otherwise Anglican church is a screened-off Roman Catholic chapel belonging to the Eystons, heirs of the Blount family, the traditionally Roman Catholic owners of the Mapledurham Estate. Behind the church is Mapledurham House, part of which is a timber-framed fifteenth-century building, but much of which was rebuilt in brick by Sir Michael Blount between 1585 and 1588. This house was visited when new by Elizabeth I and made famous by John Galsworthy who names it as the home of Soames in his 'Forsyte Saga'. Alexander Pope, the eighteenth-century satirist, also visited it in 1713 and 1714 and befriended Martha Blount, to whom he left his books, his plate and £1000 in his will.

Now, if wishing to explore the village, turn left. Otherwise, turn right onto this road, then, after over 200 yards by a white house, fork left onto bridleway M17, following this hedged lane for half a mile with wide views across the Thames Valley to your left. On nearing the far end of the left-hand field, fork right through a kissing-gate onto path M2 bearing slightly left and climbing steeply to enter an outcrop of Westfordhill Copse, before which you should take advantage of a new seat and turn round for a superb view down the Thames Valley towards Mapledurham, Purley, Tilehurst and Reading. Just inside the wood, cross a stile and follow a waymarked path straight on, soon becoming path WH5 and joining a wider track. Take this track straight on, eventually descending through regenerating woodland in Bottom Wood where over 80 fallen trees obstructed the path after the hurricane in 1990. At a track junction in the valley bottom bear left onto bridleway WH4, then keep right at the first fork and left at a second to enter a sunken way which climbs through laurel bushes.

On leaving the wood and emerging by the attractive half-timbered thatched Holly Copse Cottage at Collins End, (now on bridleway GH45) join its macadamed drive. At a right-hand bend, leave the drive and go straight on through a wicket-gate right of a stile onto bridleway GH66, following a left-hand fence through a paddock to a gate at its far end. Here go straight on, ignoring a crossing track, joining restricted byway GH74, a macadam road called Bunce's Lane and following it straight on. After 300 yards, turn left into a green lane between cottages (path GH62) and follow it to a gate into a field. Now follow a right-hand hedge, then, at the far end of the field, turn right through gates and follow the outside edge of a copse downhill to a kissing-gate in the field corner. Here continue downhill through scrub to a fence gap, then go straight on downhill passing right of a midfield oak tree, then climbing to a kissing-gate at the bottom edge of a copse. Now keep straight on through the copse to reach a bend in a road at Path Hill.

Path Hill - Whitchurch Hill (Map 20)

Maps

OS Landranger Sheet 175
OS Explorer Sheets 159 or 171
Chiltern Society FP Map No.16

Parking

Little parking is available on this section except at Whitchurch Hill (see below).

Bear slightly right into this lane and follow it round a right-hand bend to a T-junction. Here turn left, then, just before a long left-hand bend where the road starts to descend, fork right onto path WH1 following a fenced gravel track past a pair of cottages, then continuing ahead to a kissing-gate into a field. Here bear slightly right to a kissing-gate in its far right-hand corner, then turn left into a fenced lane (restricted byway WH12). After 30 yards turn right through a fence gap and take the continuation of path WH1 going straight across the field to the corner of a hedge, then follow this hedge straight on. Where the hedge ends, continue along what is normally a crop-break to a gap in a belt of trees at the end of a gravel farm road. Here take path GH60 straight on along this farm road, keeping right at a fork and passing the right-hand end of another tree-belt, then, 120 yards beyond the tree-belt, fork left through a kissing-gate and head for the corner of a fence left of a terrace of cottages at Whitchurch Hill. On reaching the fence, bear slightly right and follow it to a kissing-gate, then continue along a fenced path which widens into a gravel lane and leads you to the Upper Whitchurch Hill road opposite the village green.

Whitchurch Hill - Goring-on-Thames (Map 20)

Maps
OS Landranger Sheet 175
OS Explorer Sheet 171
Chiltern Society FP Map No.16

Parking
There is a roadside parking area by the Whitchurch Hill village green in the Upper Whitchurch Hill road and on-street parking is possible in various places at Whitchurch Hill.

Whitchurch Hill, on the edge of the upland plateau above the Thames Valley, is a village of relatively modern origin. Before 1813, it merely consisted of a few farms and cottages on the edge of a vast upland heath known as Whitchurch Common and Goring Heath, but, following the inclosure of Whitchurch Common in that year and that of Goring Heath the year before, the village grew until, in 1952, it became the principal settlement in the newly-created upland parish of Goring Heath. Since then, substantial 'in-filling' development has taken place to produce the mixture of predominantly Victorian and modern architecture which we find here today.

Now bear slightly left across the Upper Whitchurch Hill road and keep straight on across the village green to a gap by a gate in the far corner leading to the B471. Turn right onto its near verge, passing a lychgate leading to St. John the Baptist Church, then, just past Goring Heath Parish Hall to your left, turn left onto path GH57, following a concrete road towards Beech Farm. Just past the drive to Laundy Cottage, by gates to Beech Farm, fork right through a kissing-gate and follow a right-hand hedge to reach a concealed kissing-gate in a corner of the field leading into Beech Wood. Turn right through this onto path GH27 and follow its winding course through the wood. On reaching a kissing-gate in a right-hand fence, do **not** use it, but take path GH26, following the fence straight on to a kissing-gate into a field. Now keep straight on towards the right-hand end of a Dutch barn at Coombe End Farm, passing through another kissing-gate and reaching a gate into the farmyard. Here turn right through a concealed kissing-gate, then bear half left across the corner of a field to the corner of a fence, where you bear slightly left to a kissing-gate right of a gate leading to a farm road. Turn right onto this road, passing through gates and continuing to a further set of gates at a

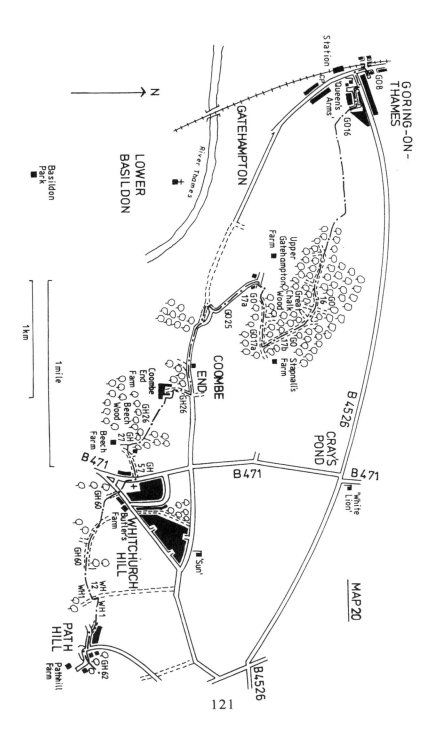

N

GORING-ON-
THAMES

Station

Queen's
Arms'

GO8

GO16

GATEHAMPTON

River Thames

LOWER
BASILDON

Basildon
Park

1km

1mile

Upper
Gatehampton
Farm

Great
Chalk
Wood

GO
16

GO
17a

GO25

GO17b

GO
17a

Stapnall's
Farm

B4526

CRAY'S
POND

B471

B471

'White
Lion'

COOMBE
END

Coombe
End
Farm

Beech
Wood

GH26

GH26

Beech
Farm

GH
27

GH
57

B471

B471

+

GH 60

WHITCHURCH
HILL

Butler's
Farm

'Sun'

GH 60

WH1
12

WH1

WH1

PATH
HILL

GH62

Pathhill
Farm

B4526

MAP 20

121

crossways.

Now turn left onto a macadamed road. After 250 yards, by some cottages, keep right at a fork, then, after a further quarter-mile, having rounded a right-hand bend, where the road wiggles to the right by a large oak tree, fork left into a sunken green lane (an unmade public road). Now follow this lane with fine views across the Thames Valley towards a striking eighteenth-century house called Basildon Park and the Wessex Downs. After nearly 200 yards turn right onto path GO25 following a grassy track then bearing left onto a private macadamed road. On rounding a left-hand bend, superb views open out to your left across the part of the Thames Valley known as the Goring Gap including Brunel's graceful railway viaduct at Gatehampton built in 1840 and later Basildon Park over your left shoulder. At a derelict farm at a left-hand bend fork right onto bridleway GO17a following a left-hand fence round a copse then continuing between fences into Great Chalk Wood.

Now take the obvious winding bridleway straight on through the wood for over a quarter-mile. At the far side of the wood, just before reaching a bridlegate, turn left onto bridleway GO17b following a woodland track along a valley bottom for over a quarter-mile ignoring a branching path to your right. On reaching an old fenceline, turn left onto path GO16 keeping right at a fork. Now disregard a crossing track, keep left at another fork and continue straight on through the wood for a further 750 yards ignoring two branching paths to your left and eventually leaving the wood by a kissing-gate. Here keep straight on through scrub to another kissing-gate then follow a right-hand hedge uphill. At the top corner of the field turn left and follow its top hedge through two fields with fine views ahead across the Goring Gap towards a house called The Grotto and the Wessex Downs. At the far end of the second field, ignore a fence gap to your right and go straight on through a hedge gap following the right-hand fence for 80 yards, then turn right over a stile into a recreation ground on the edge of Goring. Bear slightly left across this to a squeeze-stile and gate in the far hedge. Here continue along an alleyway to reach the end of a road called Whitehills Green. Now take this road, soon bearing left, then at a T-junction turn right to reach the B4526. Here turn left to reach another T-junction by the 'Queen's Arms` near Goring & Streatley Station.

Goring-on-Thames - Woodcote (Map 21)

Maps
OS Landranger Sheet 175
OS Explorer Sheet 171 (or old Sheet 3)
Chiltern Society FP Map No.16

Parking
There are public car parks at Goring & Streatley railway station and behind the ´Catherine Wheel` in Station Road, Goring and on-street parking is generally possible in the housing estates east of the railway if you can find a place where anti-commuter restrictions do not affect the time of your walk.

Goring-on-Thames, at the south-western extremity of the extended Chiltern Way, although, in some ways, resembling other Thames-side Chiltern towns, has a number of unique features arising from its geographical location. Situated in the Goring Gap which separate two ranges of chalk hills, the Chilterns and the Wessex Downs, where these two ranges drop steeply into the Thames Valley, Goring has a scenically spectacular setting. This is enhanced by the wealth of trees on both sides of the river and a number of islands in the river itself. Goring is also of considerable historic interest as, although it has only had a bridge since 1837, it is the point at which the ancient Icknield Way crossed the Thames well before Roman times. It can also boast a substantially unaltered eleventh-century church built by Robert d'Oilly containing a bell cast in 1290 believed to be the oldest in Britain and a number of highly attractive inns and cottages including the sixteenth-century ´Miller of Mansfield`. Excavations in 1892-3 also revealed that a nunnery founded in 1181 was once attached to the church, but this later became ill-disciplined and impoverished and following its dissolution in 1536, it was allowed to fall down. In more modern times, Goring, which the Great Western Railway had made readily accessible from London, became fashionable in the Edwardian era and this has left a legacy of neo-Gothic red-brick riverside villas and ornamental boathouses which characterise the little town to this day.

By the ´Queen's Arms` turn right into Gatehampton Road, then, at a road junction by a railway bridge (where the town centre and river-side are to your left), turn right onto path GO8 along a narrow residential road. Where this road bears right, fork left along an alleyway to reach a road junction, then take Lockstile Way straight on. At the far end of this road, take a macadam path (still GO8) straight on, gradually bearing left. After 40 yards, fork right through a hedge gap onto path GO9 crossing a private road and continuing along an alleyway to cross a stile. Now bear half right across a grassy track, then cross another stile left of some gates and take a worn path straight on, gradually bearing right to cross a further stile. Here take an enclosed path keeping right at a fork and passing an old kissing-gate frame. Now continue with garden fences to your left and a hedge to your right, eventually leaving the gardens behind and following a left-hand fence along the edge of Battle Plantation to reach Battle Road.

Turn right onto this road, then immediately left onto hedged path GO11 left of a drive. Soon the left-hand hedge gives way to a fence and fine views open out to your left across Goring towards the Wessex Downs. By the far end of the left-hand field the path then bears right into Wroxhills Wood and climbs. At the top of the hill turn left onto crossing bridleway GO13, following a right-hand fence through the wood for 250 yards to a gate and gap where superb panoramic views open out towards the Downs to your left, Didcot Power Station, Wittenham Clumps and the Oxford Hills ahead and the Ipsden area to your right.

Here turn right onto an unmade public road called Beech Lane and follow it for half a mile, soon reentering Wroxhills Wood and later ignoring a branching path to your right and leaving the wood behind. On reaching the end of the macadamed section of Beech Lane by the gates to Beech Farm to your left, take Beech Lane straight on for a further 400 yards, then, at a slight left-hand bend, turn left onto path GH69 following a flinty track across a field. On entering High Wood, fork left onto path WD29, leaving the track and keeping straight on downhill into the valley bottom. Here ignore a crossing track and continue uphill, soon bearing left. Now disregard another crossing track and continue through a plantation. On reaching mature beechwoods, you join the inside edge of the wood and follow it closely for a quarter mile gradually bearing right. At the far end of the wood cross a stile and bear left across a field to cross a stile by a gate onto South Stoke Road.

Turn right onto this road passing Broadstreet Farm House to your right. After 200 yards turn left through a hedge gap onto path WD7 with superb views opening out towards the Downs, Didcot Power Station, Wittenham Clumps and the Oxford Hills. Now bear right and follow a right-hand hedge then the outside edge of Dean Wood downhill. On nearing Dean Farm in the valley bottom, bear left and follow its garden fence. At the far side of the garden go through a hedge gap and turn right onto enclosed path WD5 soon passing left of a black weatherboarded barn. Now ignore a gravel drive to your right and pass left of a weatherboarded double garage to emerge onto a macadam road. Turn left onto this ignoring a branching path to your right and taking path WD31 following the road up the valley bottom, passing through Dean Wood then continuing along a sunken lane which eventually meets the B471 on the edge of Woodcote.

Woodcote - Garsons Hill (Map 21)

Maps
OS Landranger Sheet 175
OS Explorer Sheet 171 (or old Sheet 3)
Chiltern Society FP Maps Nos. 15 & 16

Parking
There is a car park by Woodcote Village Hall and on-street parking is possible at various places in the village.

At first sight, Woodcote with its profusion of modern and Victorian red-brick houses gives the impression of being a village of relatively modern origin, but the first recorded reference to it dates from 1109 and a close examination of its church reveals the fact that it was built in Norman times. The reason for this is that the village, the name of which means ´cottage(s) in the woods`, until it was enclosed in 1853, consisted of a few cottages and farms scattered around a large upland common similar to that still to be found at Russell's Water and it is only since then that a considerable expansion has occurred. It is also interesting to note that the church was constructed as a chapel-of-ease for the riverside parish of South Stoke and it was only in 1952 that Woodcote, which had, by then, far outstripped its ´mother village` in size, became a separate civil parish.

Turn right onto the B471, then, at a right-hand bend, turn left into Tidmore Lane (restricted byway WD27). After 250 yards turn left onto path WD1 following a branching lane, then, at a fork, keep right passing an attractive thatched cottage called Massey's Pightle. Where its drive ends, go straight on through a tall wooden gate, cross another drive and a stile opposite and take a narrow fenced path to a stile onto the A4074. Cross this main road and a stile opposite and take path C38 following a right-hand hedge to another stile into Rushmore Lane (restricted byway C31). Turn left onto this little-used road and after 150 yards, turn right through a gap by a gate onto path C39 following a woodland track to a second gate. Here turn left and follow a left-hand fence along the edge of a wood called North Grove, soon bearing right into the wood. Now ignore a track merging from your right and a branching path to your left and continue to a gate and stile into a field, where fine views open out ahead towards Didcot Power Station, Wittenham Clumps and the Oxford Hills beyond. Here bear slightly right down the field to cross a stile by gates, then take a grassy track straight on to reach Bottom Lane, the spine road of the ancient strip parish of Checkendon which, until 1952, extended for over six miles from the wooded uplands near Cane End to the River Thames at Little Stoke.

Turn right onto this quiet road and follow it for a quarter mile, then, by the entrance to Bottom Farm House, turn left over a stile onto path IP27 passing just right of a large pond and continuing to a clump of trees. Here the path becomes fenced and leads you under an arched trellis to a gate into a field. Now follow a right-hand fence straight on. By a cattle trough leave the fence and continue straight on uphill, passing through two kissing-gates to enter woodland at Green Hill at John's Gate where there is a fine view behind you back across Bottom Farm. Now take path C6 up a flight of steps. At the top of the steps, turn left onto path C7 following the contours of the hill through the wood to reach a flint road called Braziers Lane (restricted byway C1). Turn sharp right onto this and follow it for a third of a mile, ignoring two branching paths to your left and a crossing path and (now on restricted byway IP26) continuing to Garsons Lane at the top of Garsons Hill where there is a fine view to your left towards Didcot Power Station and the Downs.

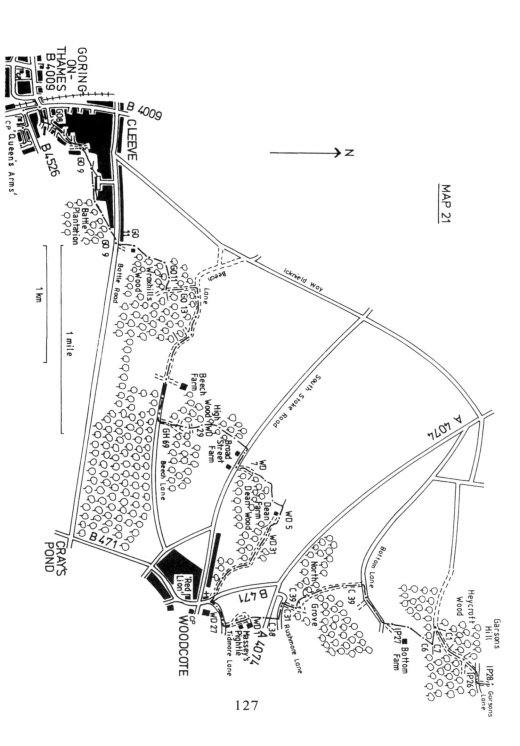

MAP 21

GORING-ON-THAMES

B 4009

B 4009

CLEEVE

B 4526

cp 'Queen's Arms'

GO 8

GO 9

Battle Plantation

GO 11

GO 9

Battle Road

Wood

Wroxhills

GO 11

GO 13

Beech Lane

Icknield Way

South Stoke Road

1 km

1 mile

Beech Farm

High Wood

Street Farm

WD 29

GH 69

Beech Lane

Broad Street

WD 7

Dean Farm

Dean Wood

WD 5

WD 31

CRAY'S POND

B 471

B 471

WOODCOTE

'Red Lion'

cp

WD 27

Tidmore Lane

Massey's Pightle

WD 01

C 38

A 4074

C 31 Rushmore Lane

C 39

Northcourt Grove

C 39

Bottom Lane

IP 27

Bottom Farm

C 6

C 1

C 7

Heycroft Wood

Garsons Hill

IP 28

IP 26

Garsons Lane

127

Garsons Hill - Hailey (Map 22)

Maps
OS Landranger Sheet 175
OS Explorer Sheet 171 (or old Sheet 3)
Chiltern Society FP Map No.15

Parking
There is very limited parking space on or around this section.

Turn right into Garsons Lane, then, after 100 yards, turn left onto path IP28 along the drive to Keepers Cottage. By a gate fork left and continue within a tree belt to the edge of a wood known as Wee Grove. Enter this wood bearing right and following its inside edge. By a corner of the field to your right, ignore a crossing path and a crossing track, then at a waymarked junction turn sharp left onto path IP6, soon bearing right and descending to a stile into a field with fine views ahead towards Didcot Power Station, Wittenham Clumps and the Oxford Hills. Now go straight on downhill to a stile by the end of a hedge, then bear half left across a field to a gap in its bottom hedge 50 yards right of the point where a tall hedge gives way to a low hedge. Go through this and descend a steep bank to a road at the foot of Berins Hill.

Berins Hill is named after St. Birinus, a missionary sent from Rome by Pope Honorius I to spread Christianity among the West Saxons. Having arrived in Dorchester-on-Thames in 634, St. Birinus converted King Cynegils of Wessex and set up the see of Dorchester, of which he became first Bishop. He then proceeded to build churches including one at Berins Hill which had already been inhabited in Roman times as nearby Wellplace derives its name from the fact that a Roman well was discovered near the foot of the hill.

Turn left onto the Berins Hill road, then immediately left again onto path IP1 crossing a rail-stile and following a left-hand hedge. At the far end of the field, go straight on over a concealed stile and continue along a hedged path, eventually bearing right to reach a path junction. Here take fenced path IP2 straight on downhill to a road. Turn right onto this, then, after 120 yards, turn left onto bridleway IP22 following a fenced grassy track uphill, later beside a right-hand hedge, eventually climbing, with fine views to your left towards the Downs, to reach Hailey Lane. Turn left into this and follow it gently downhill through Hailey passing the 'King William`.

Hailey - Ewelme (Potter's Lane) (Map 22)

Maps

OS Landranger Sheet 175
OS Explorer Sheet 171 (or old Sheet 3)
Chiltern Society FP Maps Nos. 10 & 15

Parking

There is very limited parking space on or around this section.

Hailey, formerly spelt 'Hayley`, is thought to mean 'clearing at the foot of the hill'. While this may seem somewhat surprising with the fine views from the village across the Thames Valley to the west, the reason for its name becomes apparent if one walks the lane eastwards out of the village which climbs continuously for about a mile before levelling out! Always a small village without its own church, Hailey, like its neighbour Ipsden, was originally a hamlet of the ancient riverside strip parish of North Stoke which extended for six miles from the River Thames up to and beyond the tellingly-named heavily-wooded hilltop settlement of Stoke Row. In more recent times, however, with the change in the relative importance of Ipsden and North Stoke leading to the former, which had had its own chapel-of-ease since about 1200, becoming a separate parish, Hailey then became part of Ipsden.

By the gate to a bungalow called Paddock End to your left and a tall cedar at Stone Farm to your right (probably the oldest house in the village dating in part from the early sixteenth century and extended in 1677), turn right into Poors Lane (path IP11), a macadam lane which soon changes to gravel, and follow it for a third of a mile with fine views to your left at one point towards the Downs, Didcot Power Station and Wittenham Clumps. In a hollow at Poors Farm (which is so named as it was at one time allotted to the relief of the parish poor), ignore a farm road to your left and take a gravel track straight on uphill. At the top ignore another branching track to your left and continue with more fine views to your left towards the Downs and Didcot Power Station until the track ends at a former gateway into a field. Now go straight on across the field to a corner of Wicks Wood where you enter the wood and take a grassy track straight on through it ignoring branching tracks to right and left and then descending to reach a rough road (restricted byway IP29) at Woodhouse Farm.

Turn left onto what was once the spine road of another ancient riverside strip parish called Mongewell (whose church, which closed

129

in 1932 is now a ruin, and houses were, until recently, part of a large boarding school) and follow it for over a quarter mile. On reaching a crossways by cottages at Forest Row, turn right onto a quiet macadam road, part of the ancient Icknield Way and the Swan's Way long-distance bridleway, and follow it for over three-quarters of a mile crossing the Ridgeway and passing Blenheim Farm. At a crossroads, leaving the ancient Icknield Way and Swan's Way, turn right into Nuffield Lane and follow it for nearly a third of a mile. At the far side of Oakley Little Wood to your left turn left over a stile onto path NU31 following a fenced path along the edge of the wood. At the end of the first right-hand field the path bears right then turns left over a stile. Now continue along the edge of the wood past a second field to a hedge gap then bear left to a stile and steps leading up to the A4130.

Cross this and take path BN19 through a gap left of green gates opposite into Oakley Wood. Now follow a gravel track bearing left and disregarding the first right-hand fork. At a second fork go right then ignore a crossing track and keep straight on through the wood. Near the far side of the wood bear right and then left to reach a three-way fork at the wood edge. Here take the central option bearing half right and walking beside a fenced grassy track to your left, then disregard a crossing track and go straight on through a copse to cross a stile into a field. Now bear half left across the field to cross another stile, then take a fenced path within a tree belt for a third of a mile with views to your left towards Oxford and later the Culham Laboratory (a large white building), eventually bearing right and then left to reach the pre-war route of the Henley-Oxford road which was severed by the building of RAF Benson. Here cross the road and a grass traffic island and turn right onto a rough road (restricted byway BN24) known as the Old London Road as until the 1830s it was part of the London-Henley-Oxford turnpike road. After a quarter mile, just past a large barn, turn left onto path BN18 following a concrete road past Potter's Farm then continuing along a gravel track. Just past a group of farm buildings, ignore a branching track to your left and then **rejoining the original Chiltern Way** and the Swan's Way, bear half left into a green lane (bridleway EW4).

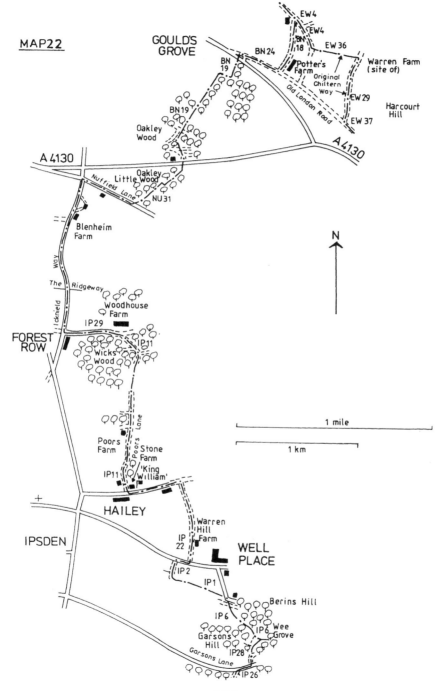

MAP22

GOULD'S GROVE

EW4
EW4
BN 18
BN 24
BN 19
Potter's Farm
EW 36
Warren Farm (site of)
Original Chiltern Way
Old London Road
EW 29
EW 37
Harcourt Hill
A 4130

BN 19
Oakley Wood
Oakley Little Wood
NU 31

A 4130
Nuffield Lane

Blenheim Farm

N

The Ridgeway
Icknield Way
Woodhouse Farm
IP 29

FOREST ROW
IP 11
Wicks Wood

1 mile
1 km

Poors Lane
Poors Farm
Stone Farm
IP 11
'King William'

HAILEY

Warren Hill Farm
IP 22
WELL PLACE
IPSDEN
IP 2
IP 1

Berins Hill
IP 6
Garsons Hill
IP 6
IP 6
Wee Grove
IP 28
Garsons Lane
IP 26

131

Ewelme (Potter's Lane) - Ewelme (Map 23)

Maps
OS Landranger Sheet 175
OS Explorer Sheet 171 (or old Sheet 3)
Chiltern Society FP Map No.10

Parking
Little parking is available on this section except at Ewelme village (see below).

The **reunited Chiltern Way** now keeps straight on for over half a mile along a green lane called Potter's Lane (bridleway EW4), eventually joining a concrete track and reaching a crossing road, part of the ancient Icknield Way. Leaving the Swan's Way, turn right onto this road. After 30 yards, where a left-hand hedge begins, turn left onto bridleway EW17 known as Henley Way, passing the corner of a quarry fence with fine views to your right towards Swyncombe Down, then continuing beside the fence with a deep gravel pit to your left, later with a second fence to your right, eventually reaching Day's Lane. Turn right onto this road with superb views of Ewelme opening out ahead, then immediately turn right again onto fenced path EW18, soon passing through a kissing-gate and following a left-hand hedge downhill to another kissing-gate into a belt of scrub. Continue through this, soon emerging onto a recreation ground, where you follow its left-hand edge straight on past a pavilion to reach Ewelme High Street by an iron gate (where the ´Shepherds Hut` is two-thirds of a mile to your left).

Ewelme - Swyncombe (Map 23)

Maps
OS Landranger Sheets 164 or 175
OS Explorer Sheet 171 (or old Sheet 3)
Chiltern Society FP Map No.10

Parking
Car parks at Ewelme Recreation Ground and Icknieldbank Plantation.

Ewelme today is an idyllic sleepy Oxfordshire village with its cottages and old watercress beds nestling in the folds of the foothills of the southern Chiltern escarpment. The village became prominent in the early fifteenth century when the poet Chaucer's son, Thomas, married the heiress to the manor and its fame was increased by their daughter Alice's marriage in 1430 to William de la Pole, Duke of Suffolk. In the years which followed, the Suffolks completely rebuilt the church except for its recently-constructed tower and in 1437 they added thirteen almshouses built around a cloister in the fashion of Oxford colleges and a grammar school which is still in use as the village primary school and is believed to be the oldest primary school building in the country. The church contains a magnificent fifteenth-century carved oak font cover, an alabaster effigy of Alice Chaucer and her parents' tomb with brasses depicting the poet's son and one-time Speaker of the House of Commons and his wife, while Jerome K. Jerome, author of 'Three Men in a Boat' was buried in the churchyard in 1927. On the Suffolks' downfall, the manor passed to the Crown and this resulted in the construction of a palace by Henry VII. This palace was later used by Henry VIII, whose bathing activities led to the pool at the head of the stream (more recently a watercress bed) being named King's Pool. The palace also served as a childhood home to Elizabeth I but was later sold and allowed to decay so that only fragments of it have survived as part of the present Georgian manor house.

Turn right into Ewelme High Street, then, at a road junction, turn sharp left into Parson's Lane (signposted to Britwell Salome and Watlington). After 150 yards at the top of a rise, turn sharp right onto path EW23 along a flinty drive. At a fork take a grassy path straight on past a garden, soon becoming enclosed by a hedge to your right and a fence to your left. On emerging into a field with fine views ahead towards Swyncombe Down and Ewelme Down, take a grassy track straight on for a third of a mile, following a right-hand fence to the top of a rise where there are superb panoramic views including the Sinodun Hills and Wessex Downs behind you. Now follow the track straight on, eventually dropping to a gate onto a bend in the Icknield Way road in Warren Bottom. Take this road straight on, then, after 350 yards just before the top of a slight rise, fork left through a hedge gap onto restricted byway EW26. Now bear half right, following a grassy track along the edge of a young plantation to a junction of rough roads. Here turn right onto restricted byway EW14 to reach a crossways with an unmade section of the Icknield Way and part of the Swan's Way near a corner of Icknieldbank Plantation.

Now take a rough road straight on for 20 yards, then turn left through a gap into the wood and take waymarked path SW37 bearing slightly right through open mature beechwoods. At the far side of the mature woodland take a worn path straight on uphill through scrubby woodland, eventually emerging through a kissing-gate near the top of Swyncombe Down onto one of the rare remaining areas of open downland in the Chilterns. Here take a grassy path straight on beside an ancient earthwork called the Danish Intrenchment, possibly dating from the abortive Danish attempts to conquer Southern England in the 870s A.D. which were ultimately repelled by King Alfred. On reaching the crest of the ridge, where fine views open out ahead along the Chiltern escarpment towards Watlington Hill, Shirburn Hill and Beacon Hill and to your left towards Britwell House, built for Sir Edward Simeon in about 1728, go through a kissing-gate in another earthwork and at a path junction by a metal gate, bear slightly right onto path SW36, passing through scrubland with a fence to your left and the Danish Intrenchment to your right and with fine views to your left in places. After over a third of a mile, where the fence bears away to your left, take a worn path straight on across open downland, eventually keeping right at a fork and climbing into Dean Wood to reach a T-junction with the Ridgeway (path SW4).

Turn right onto this, soon crossing the Danish Intrenchment and continuing uphill, ignoring branching tracks first to your left, then to your right. Having crossed the top of the ridge, continue downhill disregarding all branching tracks. On leaving the wood, take a fenced track straight on downhill and up again to a gate and kissing-gate leading to the junction of Church Lane and Rectory Hill at Swyncombe.

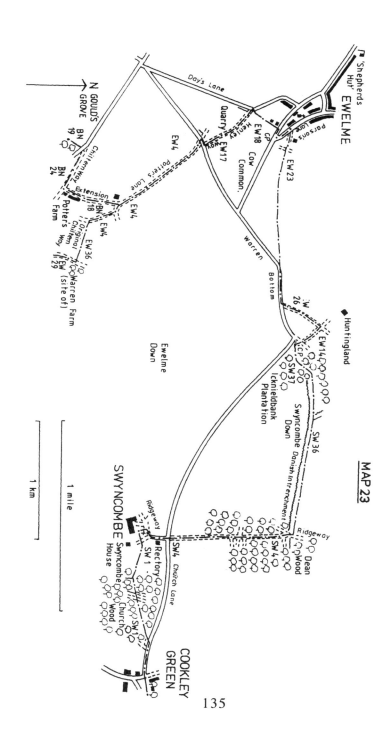

MAP 23

135

Swyncombe - Cookley Green (Map 23)

Maps
OS Landranger Sheet 175
OS Explorer Sheet 171 (or old Sheet 3)
Chiltern Society FP Map No.10

Parking
Limited parking is available opposite Swyncombe Church and by the eastern end of path SW1.

The name Swyncombe means ´valley of the wild boar` suggesting that it was once even more remote than it is today. With little more than a manor house, a farm, a church and a rectory, Swyncombe is a good example of a ´closed village`, where the ordinary villagers were forced by the Lord of the Manor to live around commons on the edge of the parish or driven out entirely. The eleventh-century church of St. Botolph is one of few in the Chilterns which are, in part, Saxon, while Swyncombe House is an Elizabethan manor house extensively rebuilt in the nineteenth century.

At the road junction cross Church Lane and take Rectory Hill straight on downhill, bearing right at a fork and passing the church to your left. By the far end of the church, leaving the Ridgeway, turn left through a gate into the churchyard. Now take a gravel path downhill past the church, bearing right by the church door and leaving the churchyard by another gate. Here turn left onto path SW1, following the right-hand edge of a clearing at first, then keeping left at a fork, crossing the drive to Swyncombe House and following a left-hand fence to a kissing-gate into a parkland field. Now bear slightly right, passing just left of a lime tree, then following a slight depression in the ground marking an old fenceline uphill with views of Swyncombe House over your right shoulder to reach a kissing-gate into Church Wood. Go straight on through the wood for over a quarter mile, ignoring two branching paths to your right and a crossing track and eventually passing through a fence gap into Church Lane. Turn right onto this road and follow it for 300 yards to a road junction on the edge of Cookley Green.

Cookley Green - Russell's Water (Map 24)

Maps
OS Landranger Sheet 175
OS Explorer Sheet 171 (or old Sheet 3)
Chiltern Society FP Map No.9

Parking
Limited parking is possible in Church Lane, Cookley Green.

Cookley Green, with its large triangular green at the point where a number of ancient lanes meet, is today a picturesque village with a spacious feel which has suffered little from modern development. Like many villages with a green as their focal point, Cookley Green is not an ancient parish and has no church of its own, but grew up as a settlement to house the farmworkers and servants of Swyncombe Park, where the manor house, church, rectory and a farm are situated.

At the junction leave the road and go straight on across Cookley Green to its far end, then cross the B481 and turn left along its far verge. After a few yards by a large chestnut tree, turn right into a gravel lane called Law Lane (bridleway SW30), ignoring the drive to Cookley House to your right and soon passing the house and a cottage. Now ignore the stile of a branching path to your left and continue gently downhill for half a mile, passing through a copse and eventually reaching a fork.

Here, **if wishing to take a circular walk on the Ewelme loop,** fork right onto bridleway SW14 and follow it down the valley bottom for half a mile, ignoring a branching bridleway to your right. On reaching the edge of a wood, fork right through a kissing-gate onto path SW21. Now go back to Map 10 for the continuation.

Otherwise, at the fork go left (still on bridleway SW30), soon bearing right and climbing steeply, then bearing left, levelling out and (now on bridleway PS15) reaching a road at Russell's Water, where the 'Five Horseshoes' at Upper Maidensgrove is half a mile to your right.

Russell's Water - Northend (Map 24)

Maps
OS Landranger Sheet 175
OS Explorer Sheet 171 (or old Sheet 3)
Chiltern Society FP Map No.9

Parking
Parking bay west of Russell's Water Pond.

Russell's Water, which is named after a local brickmaker and his picturesque duckpond in the centre of the village, is a scattered community ranged along the edge of its extensive hilltop common on the ancient parish boundary between Pishill and Swyncombe. Its origins are obscure, but it is known to have existed since at least the late seventeenth century and it may occupy the site of a settlement called Pishill Venables which was recorded in the thirteenth century.

Turn left onto the road, rounding a left-hand, then a right-hand bend. Now by a triangular green with an old pub sign serving as a village nameboard, fork right onto a gravel track passing the attractive duckpond to your right, then fork right again. Just past the far side of the pond to your right and Pond Cottage to your left, turn left onto bridleway PS22. By the entrance to Beehive House, formerly the village pub, bear right and, ignoring branching tracks to left and right, continue until you emerge onto open common. Here turn left onto path PS21, following the edge of the common and ignoring gates to your left. After 350 yards at a corner of the open common, bear slightly left onto the right-hand of two paths into woodland and follow a waymarked path, soon entering a slight sunken way. Eventually, by a huge beech tree, you leave the wood and continue down a cottage drive to the B480 in Pishill Bottom, the name of which, though being pronounced ´Pis-hill` with a short ´i` and a soft ´s`, is, in fact, a corruption of ´Peas-hill`.

Turn left onto this road and follow it for 350 yards, then turn right through iron gates onto bridleway W21 entering the farmyard of Grove Farm. Go straight across the farmyard, then, where a wire fence blocks your way ahead, bear right and immediately fork left onto a track beside the left-hand fence climbing into Shambridge Wood. On nearing the top of the rise, bear right and follow the waymarked track for 300 yards, ignoring all branching tracks. At a waymarked fork, take bridleway W21 straight on, descending into a valley where you

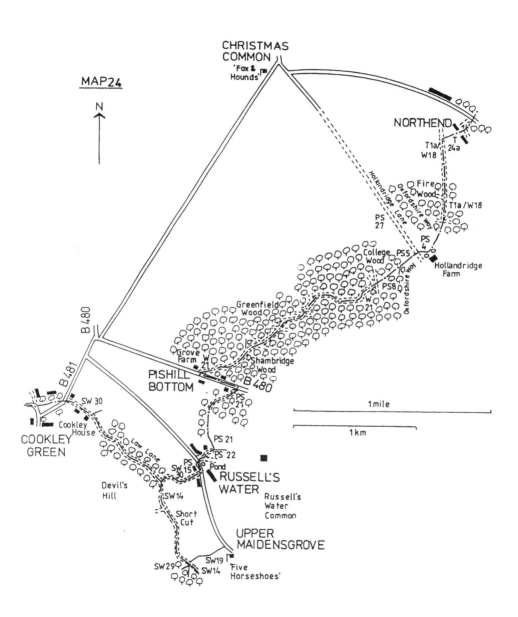

ignore a crossing track, then climb another rise. Now in Greenfield Wood, at a junction of tracks at the top of the rise, bear right, then keep left at two forks, descending again to reach a waymarked junction in the valley bottom. Here take bridleway W21 again, bearing half right, ignoring a crossing track and soon climbing again. At a fork keep right, soon bearing right into a mature plantation and following a winding waymarked track for a third of a mile, which later descends to reach a large clearing in another valley bottom.

Here bear slightly left, crossing the main track, then taking path PS8 straight on, climbing steeply through College Wood. Near the far side of the wood at a path junction, bear half left onto path PS5, joining the Oxfordshire Way and crossing a stile into a field. Now bear slightly right across a corner of the field to a corner of the right-hand hedge, then follow it straight on to a gate and stile into Hollandridge Lane, a road dating from Saxon times which formed part of the spine road of the twelve-mile-long ancient strip parish of Pyrton stretching from Lower Standhill near Little Haseley on the Oxfordshire Plain to south of Stonor in the Chilterns.

Cross this unmade road and take path PS4 straight on along the edge of a copse concealing two ponds, gradually bearing left. At the far end of the copse, keep straight on across the field to a slight kink in the edge of a wood. Here bear left, passing a concealed disused stile, then bear right, descending steeply to a crossways in the valley bottom. Now, leaving the Oxfordshire Way, take bridleway W18 straight on along a woodland track in the valley bottom for 350 yards, soon becoming T1a/W18 and straddling the Oxon/Bucks boundary and eventually entering a field. Here follow the valley bottom straight on for a quarter mile, passing a solitary oak tree. By a marker post some 30 yards short of the corner of a fence, bear half right onto path T24a, entering Buckinghamshire and crossing the corner of a field to cross a stile in the fence. Now bear half right across a corner of the next field, heading just right of two white cottages to enter a narrow enclosed path between gardens. On emerging onto Northend Common, bear slightly left, crossing a gravel track and taking a worn path through scrubland to rejoin the gravel track and reach a road.

Northend - Ibstone (Map 25)

Maps
OS Landranger Sheet 175
OS Explorer Sheet 171 (or old Sheet 3)
Chiltern Society FP Map No.9

Parking
Parking at Northend is now difficult, so that it is probably best to walk this section from Ibstone (see below).

Northend, with its scattered cottages spread unevenly around its extensive heathy and, in parts, wooded common, is justifiably popular with walkers owing to its attractive setting and the superb Chiltern views which can be obtained from surrounding footpaths. Although the village now straddles the Oxfordshire boundary, its name derives from its location at the northern end of the Buckinghamshire parish of Turville.

Cross the road and take an obvious grass path straight on through scrubland. On entering Blackmoor Wood by a Wormsley Estate sign, where you cross back into Oxfordshire, take waymarked path SH8 straight on, descending gently at first and later steeply, then levelling out and continuing on a track along the inside edge of the wood to a waymarked T-junction near New Gardens Farm where you should notice a short ha-ha ahead in front of a magnificent brick-and-flint wall and a large palladian stone ornament recently relocated in the wood to your left. Here turn right onto path SH4 following a green lane past the farm to reach a private road at the county boundary. Turn right onto this, reentering Buckinghamshire. Now on path S21, after 40 yards, fork left through gates and cross the bottom corner of a field diagonally to a kissing-gate leading to another private road where fine views open out up and down the Wormsley Valley with the Stokenchurch telecom tower on the skyline to your left.

Most of the Wormsley Valley belongs to the Wormsley Estate, which, for over 400 years, was in the hands of one family, the Scropes and later, through female succession, the Fanes. It is thanks to them that no public road has ever been established through this beautiful valley and, in consequence, its natural peace and serenity have been preserved. In 1984, however, the Estate was sold to a holding company representing the late Sir Paul Getty and since then, large amounts of money have been spent on renovating the

farms and cottages and not least **Wormsley Park**, its manor house of Palladian, eighteenth-century appearance but concealing some much older fabric, which is half a mile north of your present location. Extensive work has also been carried out on clearing and replanting the Estate's storm-ravaged woodlands, but it will be many years before their former glory has been restored.

Go through another kissing-gate opposite, then bear slightly left across a large field to a kissing-gate by gates onto bridleway S7. Now take path S21 straight on over a stile opposite and follow a left-hand fence uphill, passing through a gate and a clump of trees and bushes. Where the fence bears left, keep straight on along the edge of Commonhill Wood until the worn path bears left into the wood. Here turn round for a fine view back across the valley before entering the wood and climbing steeply to reach a T-junction with a sunken way (bridleway S7a). Turn right into this and follow it uphill. After 200 yards, where the bridleway levels out, go straight on, ignoring a crossing track and following the inside edge of the wood, then a green lane to a T-junction on the edge of a scrubby part of Ibstone Common. Here turn left onto bridleway I18, soon passing a pond to your left. At a fork, **if wishing to visit the 'Fox'**, take bridleway I20 going right, then right again. **Otherwise**, fork left (still on bridleway I18), soon passing a second pond and continuing through scrubland for 200 yards to reach a bend in the road at Ibstone.

Ibstone - Stokenchurch (Map 25)

Maps
OS Landranger Sheets 165 & 175
OS Explorer Sheet 171 (or old Sheet 3)
Chiltern Society FP Map No.14

Parking
There are two parking bays at Ibstone opposite the ´Fox` and cars can also be parked along the western edge of the road to the north of this. Do not use the pub car park without the landlord's permission.

Ibstone, scattered along more than a mile of lofty ridgetop separating the Wormsley and Turville valleys from Penley Bottom, until 1895 straddled the Bucks/Oxon boundary with its church, common and most of its cottages being in Oxfordshire, but, like neighbouring Stokenchurch, the village was then placed entirely within Buckinghamshire. While the origins of its Saxon name (spelt ´Hibestanes` or ´Ybestane` in the eleventh century) are uncertain, it may mean ´yew stone` referring to stones marking the old county boundary and the native Chiltern yew trees which seem to thrive on the shallow local soil. There is, indeed, a particularly fine ancient yew tree in the churchyard of Ibstone's tiny twelfth-century church which also boasts a carved fifteenth-century wooden pulpit believed to be one of the oldest in the country and a Norman tub font. Being close to London, the village has, in modern times, attracted a number of well-known residents including the authoress Dame Rebecca West who lived at the imposing neo-classical eighteenth-century Ibstone House.

Cross the road and turn left along its far verge. On passing the entrance to the last cottage, turn right through a bridlegate onto path S34, following a right-hand fence bearing right into Commonhill Wood to reach another bridlegate. Here turn left, crossing a major woodland track and taking a waymarked path straight on along a lesser track. Follow the inside edge of the wood at first, ignoring branching tracks to right and left before continuing downhill through the wood. In the valley bottom bear right to reach a path junction by the corner of a field. Here take path S28, crossing a stile and turning left to follow the outside edge of the wood uphill. Just before the top corner of the field, turn left through a waymarked fence gap and take a winding waymarked path generally uphill through scrubby woodland. On emerging into a plantation, turn left at a path junction (still on path S28) and follow a left-hand hedge uphill through the plantation and two fields to Studdridge Farm, with fine views over your right shoulder in places down Penley Bottom and the Hambleden Valley towards the distant Thames and Ashley and Bowsey Hills in Berkshire.

At Studdridge Farm, go through a kissing-gate and take the macadam drive straight on, passing left of most of the buildings and continuing to the far end of a line of trained fruit trees enclosing the garden. On passing through gates, turn right over a stile by a gate with views towards Stokenchurch and the M40 ahead, then bear half left across the field to pass the right-hand end of a copse concealing two ponds. Now bear slightly left and follow the edge of this copse to its far end where you bear slightly right across the field, aiming to the left of three trees, to reach the far corner of the field. Here cross a stile by a gate and take path S27, following a left-hand hedge gently downhill to gates into Bissomhill Shaw. Now take a fenced track downhill through this wood to cross a culvert in the valley bottom, then take a fenced track beside a left-hand hedge straight on uphill, soon levelling out and continuing to a gate leading to a junction of tracks by Coopers Court Farm. Here go straight on through a pair of gates, then turn right across a field to a small gate leading in 25 yards to a junction of farm roads. Now turn left and take the fenced path through the left-hand side of the M40 underpass, then bear left up a macadam farm road to reach a road junction. Here take Coopers Court Road straight on uphill to Stokenchurch village green where you go straight on, passing left of two large grass 'traffic islands' to reach the A40 virtually opposite the 'King's Arms'.

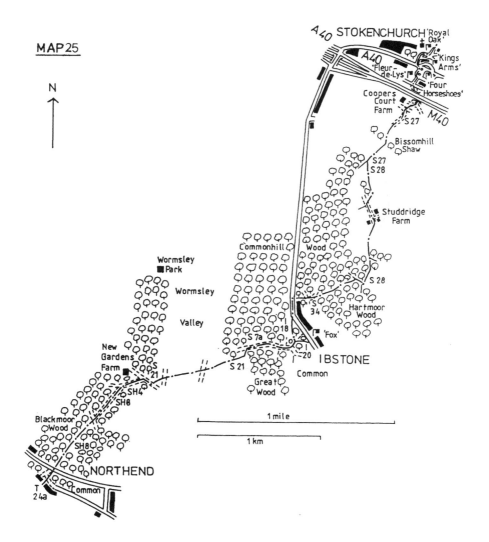

MAP 25

N

STOKENCHURCH 'Royal Oak'

A40

A40 'Kings Arms'

'Fleur-de-Lys' 'Four Horseshoes'

M40

Coopers Court Farm

S27

Bissomhill Shaw

S27
S28

Studdridge Farm

Wormsley Park

Commonhill Wood

Wormsley

S28

Valley

Hartmoor Wood

S 34 'Fox'

New Gardens Farm

18

S 7a

20 IBSTONE

S 21

S 21 Common

SH4

Great Wood

SH8

Blackmoor Wood

SH8

NORTHEND

T 24a Common

1 mile

1 km

145

Stokenchurch - Radnage (Map 26)

Maps
OS Landranger Sheet 165
OS Explorer Sheet 171 (or old Sheet 3)
Chiltern Society FP Maps Nos. 7 & 14

Parking
Large public car park outside the ´King's Arms Hotel`, Stokenchurch.

Stokenchurch, on the London-Oxford road on a ridgetop plateau about a mile from the escarpment and one of the highest major settlements in the Chilterns, has the unfortunate reputation of being ´the ugly duckling` of the Chilterns. This may arise from its former role as a centre of the Bucks furniture industry with its factories and timber yards or from the extent to which it has been developed for housing since the coming of the M40. Nevertheless the village, only transferred from Oxfordshire to Bucks in 1896, can boast extensive, attractive, well-maintained village greens where an annual horse fair used to be held on July 10th and 11th and a funfair is still held to this day. The twelfth-century parish church, hidden behind the ´King's Arms,` is quite sizeable when one considers that, until 1844, it was merely a chapel-of-ease for Aston Rowant and, despite many renovations, it is still worth a visit. This is also the burial place of Hannah Ball (1734-1792), a friend of John Wesley and founder of the first English Sunday school in High Wycombe in 1769. For the walker, however, the chief attraction of Stokenchurch is that it is an ideal centre for exploring some of the finest Chiltern countryside including the Wormsley Valley, Penley Bottom, Radnage and the escarpment.

Cross the A40 bearing slightly left and take Church Street, bearing right by Lloyds Bank and passing the church. At a crossroads by the ´Royal Oak`, turn left into Park Lane. Where the public road ends by the entrance to Longburrow Hall, take path S92 straight on along a private road past a sporadic line of ancient chestnut trees. At the far end of the trees, turn right through a kissing-gate by several gates onto path S79 beside a left-hand fence. Where the fence ends, follow a sporadic line of trees straight on to a kissing-gate, then bear half left, passing an electricity pole and aiming for a gate by the end of a hedge right of a bungalow. Here bear half right onto path S80 along a flint track. Where the track wiggles to the right and a left-hand hedge begins, turn left through a hedge gap then right and follow the hedge straight on through two fields with fine views ahead towards Bennett End in the valley and Bledlow Ridge beyond. At the far end of the second field, bear right through a hedge gap and descend some steps. Now bear left across a farm track and down more steps and aim for a signpost right of a line of four trees in the valley bottom. Here turn right onto bridleway S87, part of an ancient road to Oxford on the Bucks/Oxon boundary known as Colliers Lane, as it was, at one time, used by Welsh colliers to transport coal to London.

After 70 yards bear half left onto path CR10 crossing the corner of a field and entering the tip of a salient of Oxfordshire, soon crossing a stile and continuing to a second. Now bear right to reach a farm track, onto which you bear left. After 20 yards turn right through a concealed hedge gap into Grange Farm Road reentering Bucks. Now take path RA16 through a hedge gap opposite and bear half left up the field aiming for an electricity pole in the top hedge. Here turn left and follow the hedge uphill to a gap in the top corner where there is a fine view back towards Stokenchurch. Now go through the hedge gap and turn right through a gate, then follow the right-hand hedge uphill (soon on path RA15) to a field corner. Here turn right through two sets of gates, crossing one drive and reaching a second, then bear half right onto path RA13 along the macadam drive to Andridge Farm. At the first fork keep left, passing left of a bungalow, then, at a second, go straight on, soon entering a field. Here, if wishing to visit the `Three Horseshoes` at Bennett End, bear half right onto path RA14, at the bottom of which the pub is to your right. Otherwise, bear slightly left onto the continuation of path RA13, following a left-hand hedge downhill with a superb view ahead down Radnage Bottom towards West Wycombe Hill capped by St. Lawrence's Church, a thirteenth-century church extensively rebuilt in 1763 by Francis Lord le Despencer (formerly Sir Francis Dashwood of Hellfire Club fame) who added to its tower the golden ball for which it is famous.

At a corner of the field go through a hedge gap to cross a concealed stile and take the enclosed path downhill to Horseshoe Road. Turn left onto this downhill to a road junction in Radnage Town End, then turn left into Town End Road. At a left-hand bend turn right through a fence gap onto path RA5, following a left-hand hedge to cross a gravel drive and go through a gate, then keep straight on towards Radnage Church to a gate in a field corner. Now cross Church Lane and take the church drive straight on uphill. Where the drive bears left, take path RA6 straight on through an ornamental gate and up a path to the church door.

Radnage - Bledlow Ridge (Map 26)

Maps

OS Landranger Sheet 165
OS Explorer Sheet 171 (or old Sheet 3)
Chiltern Society FP Map No.7

Parking

Little parking is available on this section except at Bledlow Ridge (see below).

Radnage, whose name is a corruption of ´Radenach`, meaning ´red oak`, as it was recorded in the twelfth century, is a very scattered community comprising quite a number of separate hamlets, but the bulk of its population today lives on the ridge to the south of Radnage Bottom where the hamlets known as The City, Radnage Common and Green End have virtually been joined together by pre-war ribbon development of the type so deplored by the contemporary Chiltern writer, H.J. Massingham. Aerial photographs have, however, revealed that the eighteenth-century former rectory and the thirteenth-century church, notable for its unusual central tower, its Saxon font dug up in a nearby field and a thirteenth-century mural discovered beneath later murals during restoration work, once formed the nucleus of a larger settlement, but the reasons for its disappearance are unknown.

By the church door, take path RA6, bearing half right, passing a seat and continuing to the far side of the churchyard. Here cross a stone stile, then pass through a gate and bear half right across a field to another gate, where you continue across a further field to a set of gates. Now take path B66a bearing half left uphill to a gate in the top corner of the field by the edge of Yoesden Wood (the name of which is thought to be a corruption of ´yews-dene`), then keep right at a fork and follow a right-hand fence uphill. Where the fence bears right, follow it, then soon take a worn path bearing left and climbing steeply up the left side of a scrubby field, entering Yoesden Wood and continuing through a gate to reach a fork at the far side of the wood. Here turn left onto path B66 and follow it uphill between a hedge and a fence with fine views to your right in places, to reach Chinnor Road, the ridgetop spine road of Bledlow Ridge.

Bledlow Ridge - Wigan's Lane (Map 26)

Maps
OS Landranger Sheet 165
OS Explorer Sheet 171 (or old Sheets 2 & 3)
Chiltern Society FP Map No.7

Parking
Limited on-street parking is available in places at Bledlow Ridge and Rout's Green.

Bledlow Ridge village, most of which stretches along one and a half miles of the high steep-sided ridge of the same name, was described by the Chiltern writer, H.J. Massingham in 1940 as 'the bastard village' as he saw it as a particularly conspicuous manifestation of the pre-war ribbon development which was threatening to ruin the Chilterns. However, while there undoubtedly was a rash of pre-war building at Bledlow Ridge, the first edition Ordnance Survey map of 1822 already reveals clusters of scattered development along the ridge, which in 1868 was sufficient to justify the building of a church. Some of its cottages, indeed, even date from the seventeenth century, when a battle appears to have taken place here in 1643 during the Civil War as numerous weapons dating from that period have been found including a sword hidden in a chimney at Pankridge Farm.

Cross Chinnor Road and take path B62 straight on along a gravel lane, soon bearing left. Where the lane ends, bear slightly left along a path between a hedge and a fence to reach a gate and stiles. Here ignore the stile to your right and turn left, crossing a second stile. Now continue with a hedge to your left and fine views ahead towards Lodge Hill, a strange-looking single hill in the Saunderton valley where neolithic tools and bronze age burial mounds and pottery have been found, and to your right across the valley towards Whiteleaf Cross, a chalk cross carved into the hillside of unknown origin, Loosley Row and Lacey Green. On reaching Chapel Lane (path B61), take path B62 straight on through a gap between field gates, following a left-hand fence gently downhill through a scrubby field to a fence gap leading down to a kissing-gate. Now follow the right-hand fence, then the edge of a copse downhill and up again to cross a stile and follow an enclosed path to a road at the hamlet of Rout's Green (bridleway B57).
    Turn left onto this road, then, at a T-junction, turn right onto

bridleway B56. Where its macadam surface ends, bear left onto its stone continuation to reach the edge of Neighbour's Wood. Here continue into the wood and follow its inside edge straight on downhill. On leaving the wood, continue along an ancient green lane with close-up views of Lodge Hill to your right when the right-hand hedge becomes lower and finally peters out. On reaching a crossing track, turn left onto it, passing through a hedge gap, then immediately turn right onto a track passing Callow Down Farm to your right to reach its macadam drive. Now turn right crossing this drive and taking a concrete road towards black barns. Just past a metal gate to your left, turn left into a green lane, soon passing Old Callow Down Farm with its early seventeenth-century, half-timbered farmhouse with lattice windows. Just past the farm, join its drive and follow it straight on, soon bearing left and, now on path B84, continuing with fine views to your right towards Whiteleaf Cross and to your left over the remote country near Bledlow Great Wood, to reach Wigan's Lane.

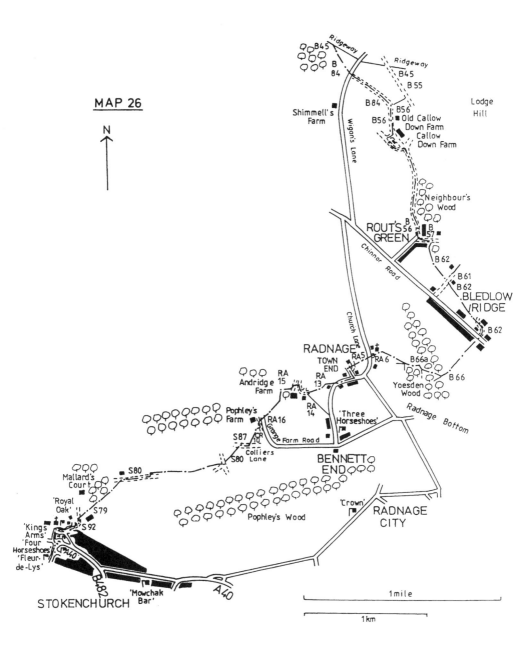

MAP 26

N

Ridgeway
B45
B 84
Ridgeway
B45
B 55
Shimmell's Farm
B 84
B56
B56
Old Callow Down Farm
Callow Down Farm
Lodge Hill
Wigan's Lane
Neighbour's Wood
ROUT'S GREEN
B56
B 57
Chinnor Road
B 62
B 61
B 62
BLEDLOW RIDGE
B 62
Church Lane
RADNAGE
RA5
RA 6
B66a
B 66
TOWN END
RA 13
Yoesden Wood
RA 15
Andridge Farm
RA 14
Radnage Bottom
Pophley's Farm
RA16
'Three Horseshoes'
Grange Farm Road
S87
CR
S80
Colliers Lane
BENNETT END
S80
Mallard's Court
S80
'Royal Oak'
S79
'Crown'
RADNAGE CITY
Pophley's Wood
'Kings Arms'
S 92
'Four Horseshoes'
'Fleur-de-Lys'
A40
B482
'Mowchak Bar'
A40
STOKENCHURCH

1 mile

1 km

151

Wigan's Lane - Bledlow (Map 27)

Maps
OS Landranger Sheet 165
OS Explorer Sheet 181 (or old Sheet 2)
Chiltern Society FP Maps Nos. 7 or 14

Parking
Parking is possible at a bend in Wigan's Lane a quarter mile north of where path B84 crosses it.

Cross Wigan's Lane and a stile opposite, then take path B84 bearing slightly right across a field to cross a stile in its far right-hand corner leading to the Ridgeway, where there are superb views ahead across Princes Risborough towards Whiteleaf Cross and to your right towards Loosley Row, Lacey Green and Lodge Hill. Now turn left onto path B45, briefly joining the Ridgeway, soon passing through a kissing-gate in the left-hand fence and continuing along the other side of the fence for 150 yards until you reach a stile in the fence. Leaving the Ridgeway, turn right over this and a second stile onto path B22, bearing half left downhill to a stile into a thicket. Go steeply uphill through the thicket to cross another stile, then keep straight on over a rise to reach a stile leading to the Upper Icknield Way. Cross this ancient green lane and a stile opposite, then follow a right-hand hedge straight on for over half a mile through two fields with views opening out ahead at the top of a rise towards Bledlow and the Vale of Aylesbury beyond. On reaching the backs of gardens at Bledlow, cross a stile and continue between fences to a village street called Church End.

Bledlow - Saunderton (Map 27)

Maps
OS Landranger Sheet 165
OS Explorer Sheet 181 (or old Sheet 2)
Chiltern Society FP Map No.7

Parking
Parking bay left of the telephone box in Church End, Bledlow between the church and the 'Lions'.

Bledlow, on the lower slopes of Wain Hill where the Risborough gap in the Chiltern Hills meets the Vale of Aylesbury, is now a picturesque Chiltern backwater, but it has an obviously strategic location and a history to match. Evidence of settlement in the Bronze Age has been found in nearby woods, but references to the village itself go back at least a thousand years. Its name, recorded in 1012 as 'Bleddanhlæw`, though undoubtedly of Anglo-Saxon origin, is variously said to mean 'Bledda's Hill` or 'Bloody Hill`, the latter interpretation being thought to refer to a battle near the village between the Saxons and the Vikings and in 1066, it is thought to have been visited and sacked by William the Conqueror's army. Bledlow today can boast a largely unaltered thirteenth-century church with a carved Norman font, fourteenth-century murals and heraldic glass and nearby are some attractive sixteenth-century timbered cottages with herringbone brickwork and the early eighteenth-century manor house which, since 1801, has belonged to the Carringtons.

Turn right into Church End and follow it past the cottages with herringbone brickwork, the church, a ravine containing a brook called The Lyde and the manor house to a T-junction opposite a former children's home. Here turn right, then, after 200 yards, just past the last left-hand house, turn left through a bridlegate onto bridleway B23, bearing slightly right across a field and heading towards an electricity pylon on the skyline, to reach a gap in the far hedge leading into Old Oddley Lane (byway B92), a green lane probably of Saxon origin following the ancient parish boundary between Bledlow and Saunderton. Turn right into this lane, then, after 70 yards, fork left over a stile onto path B35, bearing slightly right and following what is normally a crop break to the right-hand end of a hedge by a twin-poled pylon. Here bear slightly left, soon joining a farm road by Frogmore Farm with its fifteenth-century brick-and-timber farmhouse and following it straight on to a bend in a road called Oddley Lane. Now take this road straight on to a T-junction in Saunderton.

Saunderton - Lacey Green (Map 27)

Maps
OS Landranger Sheet 165
OS Explorer Sheet 181 (or old Sheet 2)
Chiltern Society FP Map No.7

Parking
Limited on-street parking is available at Saunderton and Loosley Row.

Saunderton comprises several small hamlets spread along the valley and for some strange reason, the original village with its church, where you now are, is much closer to Princes Risborough Station than to Saunderton Station, nearly three miles to the southeast! The thirteenth-century church, originally one of two suggesting that, in the Middle Ages, Saunderton was a place of some importance, was extensively restored in the nineteenth century, but retains its original font, an ancient brass and mediæval tiles, while nearby is the moat of a Norman castle and in a field to the east is the site of a Roman villa.

At the T-junction, turn left into Bledlow Road, then, by a postbox, turn right into Church Lane, passing two ornamental lakes. After 75 yards, virtually opposite the drive to Church Farm House, turn left onto path B83, following a concrete path to gates into the churchyard. Now take a grassy path straight on across the church-yard to a kissing-gate leading into marshy woodland concealing the old castle site. Here go straight on until you emerge into a field, then turn right onto path B37, following a right-hand hedge until a stile and flight of steps lead you to the Birmingham-bound track of the Chiltern Line on the course of the original single-tracked Wycombe Railway, extended in 1862 from High Wycombe to Thame. Cross the railway carefully, then descend its bank to cross another stile and follow the right-hand hedge, later a fence, then a garden hedge straight on to a gap leading to a road section of the ancient Upper Icknield Way (beware - poor visibility!)
    Cross this road and take path B37 straight on through the gates of

154

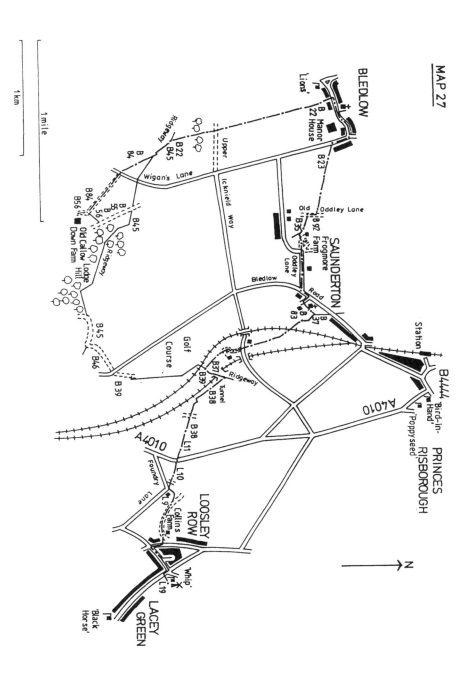

MAP 27

1 km
1 mile

BLEDLOW
'Lions'
Manor House
B 22
B 23

Ridgeway
Upper
B 22
B 45
Wigan's Lane
B 84
B 84
B 56
B 56
B 45
Old Callow Down Farm
Lodge Hill
Ridgeway
Icknield Way
Old Oddley Lane
B 92
B 35
Frogmore Farm
SAUNDERTON
Oddley Lane
Bledlow
B 45
B 46
Golf Course
B 39
Ridgeway
Bledlow Road
B 83
B 37
B 37
B 39
Tunnel
B 38
B 38
A4010
Station
B44444 'Bird-in-Hand'
'Poppyseed'
A4010 PRINCES RISBOROUGH
L11
L10
Foundry Lane
L9
Collins Farm
LOOSLEY ROW
'Whip'
L19
LACEY GREEN
'Black Horse'

N

155

The Old Rectory and along its drive, bearing right then left. Where the drive bears left again, leave it and follow the right-hand hedge straight on to a gate and stile into a field. Here bear slightly left over a slight rise, soon aiming for a clump of hawthorn trees ahead, where you turn left onto path B39, briefly joining the Ridgeway, passing right of a line of trees, then bearing slightly left uphill to a kissing-gate. Now go straight on through a belt of scrub above the mouth of a tunnel on the London-bound track of the Chiltern Line, built when the line became double-tracked and the direct line to Marylebone and Paddington opened in 1906. On reaching a small gate, go through it, then, leaving the Ridgeway, turn right onto path B38, following a right-hand hedge for 400 yards above the railway cutting with fine views to your left across the valley towards Whiteleaf Cross, Loosley Row and Lacey Green. Having wiggled to the left at one point, level with a twin-trunked oak tree in the sporadic hedge to your left, turn left across the field to this oak tree, where you cross a track and keep straight on across the next field (soon on path L11) to reach a kissing-gate in the far corner of the field leading to the A4010.

Before passing through the kissing-gate, turn round for a fine view back towards Lodge Hill and Wain Hill, then go through the gate, cross the main road and take path L10 straight on through a hedge gap opposite. Now follow a right-hand fence until you reach a crossing track. Here go straight on through a plantation to a hedge gap by some tall cypress trees leading to Foundry Lane. Do **not** go through this gap, but turn left onto path L9, following a right-hand hedge through scrubland. Where the hedge bears right, join a farm track and follow it gently uphill, soon enclosed by hedges and later fences. By some farm buildings, join a concrete road and follow it straight on uphill, soon bearing left. Before reaching a gate, fork right up a fenced path to reach a kissing-gate leading to Lower Road in Loosley Row.

Although it has sometimes been speculated that the name Loosley Row is an example of local humour referring to the straggling nature of the hamlet, experts believe it to come from the Saxon ´hlose-leah` meaning ´pigsty clearing`, suggesting what it may have been like a thousand years ago. Turn right onto this road, then, at a crossroads, turn left up Loosley Hill to reach a crossroads opposite the ´Whip Inn` at Lacey Green.

Lacey Green - Great Hampden (Map 28)

Maps
OS Landranger Sheet 165
OS Explorer Sheet 181 (or old Sheet 2)
Chiltern Society FP Maps Nos. 7 & 12

Parking
Limited on-street parking is available at Lacey Green.

Lacey Green, stretching along three-quarters of a mile of ridgetop above the Saunderton valley, was till the early twentieth century a hilltop hamlet of Princes Risborough, but the new parish, which had had its own church since 1822, has since expanded through pre-war ribbon development and post-war 'in-filling' into a sizeable village. Its windmill, the oldest surviving smock mill in the country, was originally built at Chesham in 1650, but was dismantled and rebuilt on its present site in 1821. After becoming disused in 1920, the mill became very dilapidated but was painstakingly restored to working order in the 1970s and 1980s by Chiltern Society volunteers.

At the crossroads by the 'Whip Inn', turn right into Main Road, then immediately left over a stile by an ornate bus shelter erected in 2002 to mark the Queen's Golden Jubilee onto path L19, following a left-hand hedge through three fields passing Lacey Green Windmill to your left. Where the hedge turns left in the third field, leave it and go straight on across the field to cross a stile under an oak tree, then bear half right across the next field to cross a stile in the far corner. Now take a fenced track straight on to a gate and stile into a field. Here follow the left-hand fence at first, then, where a hedge begins, leave it and go straight on across the field to cross a stile in its far hedge. Now bear half right across the next field to cross a stile into a belt of trees sheltering Grim's Ditch, an ancient earthwork of unknown origin believed, however, to date from before the Saxon period as 'Grim' is an alternative name for the Germanic god, Wodan, and they are unlikely to have attributed something to a god which they had built themselves. In the trees turn left onto bridleway L21, following Grim's Ditch to reach a road in Lily Bottom, where the 'Pink & Lily' pub, made famous by the poet Rupert Brooke, who frequented it before the First World War, is a third of a mile to your left.

Turn left onto this road, then immediately right onto bridleway G14, following a cottage drive at first, then keeping straight on into

Monkton Wood. At two forks take the left-hand option straight on, then go through a fence gap, keep left at a third fork and continue through a plantation, soon passing under a powerline, then bearing left and following the edge of a mature beechwood to a bridlegate and stile leading to a road junction. Here cross the major road and take the road to Redland End and Whiteleaf straight on through the tiny woodland hamlet of Redland End to reach a T-junction.

Here turn left, then, after about 20 yards, turn right over a stile onto path G29, following the bank of Grim's Ditch again through Kingsfield Wood until you reach a crossing track. Now bear right, following waymarks to a waymarked fork where you take the right-hand option (path G30) along a grassy track through Barnes's Grove. At a further fork, keep left and continue to follow the waymarks to enter a large parkland field. Now bear half right across the field, passing right of a tall lightning-damaged tree and through the middle of a large clump of trees, then keep straight on to the far corner of the field. Here cross a stone track and bear slightly right through gates onto bridleway G28, rejoining the course of Grim's Ditch with Hampden House coming into view ahead and follow this wide fenced track to a second set of gates at Great Hampden.

Great Hampden - Little Hampden (Map 28)

Maps
OS Landranger Sheet 165
OS Explorer Sheet 181 (or old Sheet 2)
Chiltern Society FP Maps Nos. 3 & 12

Parking
Limited parking is available where the Way crosses the road in Hampden Bottom.

Great Hampden is typical of many estate villages in having a church and manor house surrounded by a park and its village, called Hampden Row half a mile away on the edge of Hampden Common. Great Hampden was held by the Hampden family (later the Earls of Buckinghamshire) from before the Norman conquest, but the last Earl left Hampden House during the Second World War. The most famous Hampden was John Hampden (1594 - 1643), the leading Parliamentarian and soldier and cousin of Oliver Cromwell, whose refusal to pay Ship Money in 1635 led to a writ being served upon him at Hampden House and this was one of

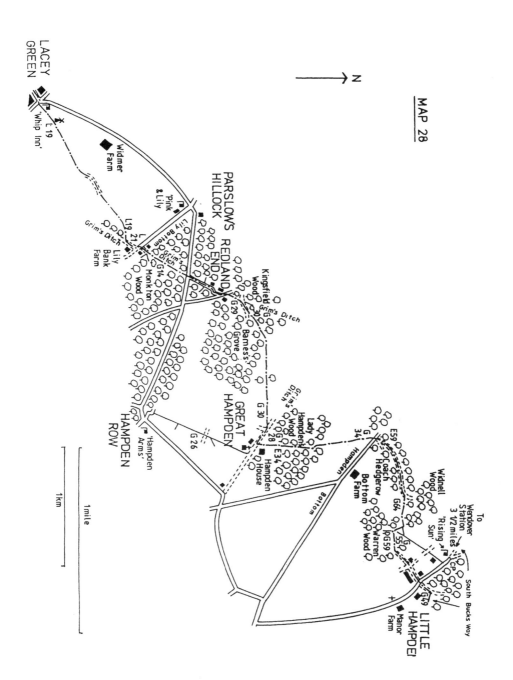

MAP 28

→ N

LACEY GREEN

'Whip Inn'

L 19

Widmer Farm

PARSLOW'S HILLOCK

'Pink & Lily'

Lily Bottom

REDLAND END

Kingsfield Wood

Grim's Ditch

L 19, 21

Grim's Ditch Lily Bank Farm

Monkton Wood

G 14

Grim's Ditch

G 29 G 30

Barnes' Grove

HAMPDEN ROW

'Hampden Arms'

GREAT HAMPDEN

G 30

Grim's Ditch Wood

Lady Hampden's Wood

28 G 31 E 34

Hampden House

G 26

G 34

G 64

Coach Hedgerow

Widnell Wood

E 59

G 59

Hampden Bottom

Bottom Farm

Warren Wood

G 59

G 55

To Wendover Station 3 1/2 miles

'Rising Sun'

Gcp

South Bucks Way

G 49

LITTLE HAMPDEN

Manor Farm

1km

1mile

159

the significant events leading to the Civil War. The battlemented fourteenth-century house was considerably altered both by John Hampden and again in the eighteenth century and has ceilings and fireplaces by Adam, while the thirteenth-century church, 120 yards ahead to your right, where John Hampden was buried in an unmarked grave after being mortally wounded at Chalgrove Field, contains various monuments to the Hampden family including one erected to John Hampden in 1743.

Just before the gates, turn left over a stile by double gates onto path G34, bearing slightly left across a field past the front of Hampden House to cross a stile into Lady Hampden's Wood. Now take a wide fenced path downhill through the wood to a gate and stile where fine views open out across Hampden Bottom, home of the late actor and country-lover, Sir Bernard Miles. Now go straight on to the far corner of the field where two tree belts meet. Here cross a stile by gates, the busy road and a stile by gates opposite into a tree belt called Coach Hedgerow noted for its bluebells and take path E59, following a timber track gently uphill through the tree belt. At the far end of the tree belt, where the track bears left into Widnell Wood, turn right onto a crossing track, leaving the wood. Now take path G64 bearing slightly right across the field, passing through one gate and reaching a second in the top hedge, then go straight on uphill through a plantation. On emerging into a field, turn right onto a permissive path kindly provided by the landowner and Chiltern Society President Emeritus, Sir Leonard Figg, following the edge of the plantation to a corner of the field, then turning left. After 30 yards, turn right onto path G55 into Warren Wood. Having crossed two boundary banks, turn left onto path G59, which leads you to a corner of the wood, then widens into a green lane. On reaching a crossways, take a rough lane straight on to reach a green and the village street at Little Hampden, where you join the South Bucks Way and the 'Rising Sun' is 350 yards to your left.

Here, if wishing to leave the Way for Wendover Station, turn left onto the South Bucks Way and follow it for nearly a mile to reach the Ridgeway, then turn right onto this and follow it for a further two and a half miles to reach the station.

Little Hampden - Lee Gate (Map 29)

Maps
OS Landranger Sheet 165
OS Explorer Sheet 181 (or old Sheet 2)
Chiltern Society FP Map No.3

Parking
There is a small car park on common land at Little Hampden opposite the ´Rising Sun` and a picnic area car park near the Way in Cockshoots Wood. There are also small laybys on the A413 at Wendover Dean.

Little Hampden, on a high ridge at the end of a long winding cul-de-sac lane, has often, with justification, been described as the remotest village in the Buckinghamshire Chilterns. For all this, an extensive network of inviting footpaths radiates from it. This tiny village with its small, rustic thirteenth-century church with its unusual two-storey fifteenth-century porch as well as thirteenth- and fifteenth-century murals, its picturesque old, but recently extended village pub and few farms and cottages was, till 1885, a separate parish. Since then, however, it has been merged with Great Hampden on the other side of Hampden Bottom to form the modern parish of Great and Little Hampden.

Joining the South Bucks Way, cross the road and take path G49 virtually opposite, following a grassy track to gates and a stile into woodland on Little Hampden Common. In the wood take the track straight on downhill, then, at a fork, bear right onto a waymarked path continuing downhill. On emerging into a field, bear left and follow a right-hand hedge downhill into the valley bottom, where you transfer to the other side of the hedge and continue uphill to a field corner. Here cross a stile into Hampdenleaf Wood, where you keep right at a fork and take the waymarked path steeply uphill, ignoring a crossing path near the top and continuing uphill to a stile into a field. Bear half right across this field to cross two stiles left of an electricity pole, then take bridleway G46, bearing slightly right and following a rough lane to Cobblershill Lane in the hilltop hamlet of Cobblers Hill.
    Cross this road and take bridleway W45 straight on. Just past a much-extended cottage to your right, leaving the South Bucks Way, turn left onto path W31b entering Cockshoots Wood. In the wood, keep left at a fork, following the left-hand edge of a plantation, then bear slightly right through mature woodland. On reaching a crossing

bridleway, bear half right, soon approaching a right-hand field, then follow the inside edge of the wood gently downhill. By a corner of the field, keep left at a fork, then, at a crossways, turn right onto a crossing track, bearing slightly left down a sunken way, eventually reaching the bottom edge of the wood. Here ignore a crossing path and go straight on into a green lane which continues downhill. Where this becomes a stone track, keep straight on (now on path W30), crossing a bridge over a railway, now part of the Chiltern Line, but originally built in 1892 as part of the Metropolitan Railway. Now, where the track turns left, leave it and go straight on through two gates into a parkland field. Here go straight on, diverging from the left-hand fence, but keeping just left of the parkland trees and passing Mayortorne Manor to your left, a late eighteenth-century house which, at one time, was home to the noted Chiltern writer, H.J. Massingham. Now cross a stile by a white gate and bear slightly right across two more fields to cross a stile into a belt of trees, then a second stile leading to the A413 at Wendover Dean, so called as the manor was once held by the Dean of Wendover.

Turn left onto this road, then, at a road junction, turn right into Bowood Lane and follow it for 300 yards to another junction by Wendover Dean Farm. Here bear slightly left onto path W36, passing through a hedge gap and crossing a stile by a gate, then go straight on up a field to cross a stile by a tall ash tree. Now cross the narrow lane to Durham Farm and a stile opposite and go straight on through a farm storage area and across a field to a gate and stile in the far hedge. Here bear slightly right up the next field to cross a stile in its top hedge, then take path L6, bearing half left up a field, heading just left of a long white cottage on the skyline when this comes into view to near the left-hand corner of its garage, where you should turn round for a fine view across the Wendover Gap before going straight on across a lawn to a garden gate into King's Lane.

Cross this road and a stile opposite and take path L6 straight on to a hedge gap right of a line of trees in the next hedge. Here bear slightly right across the next field, following what is normally a grass crop break, ignoring a crossing path right of a lightning-damaged tree, where you keep straight on to cross a stile in the far corner of the field. Now turn left and follow a left-hand hedge past derelict farm buildings, then join a drive and continue through a former pub car park to reach a road at Lee Gate.

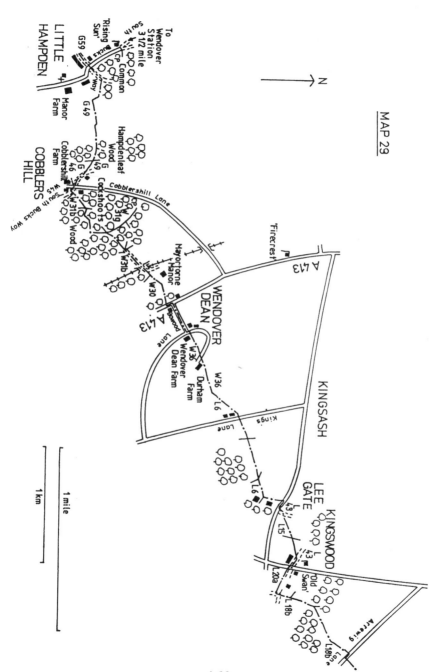

MAP 29

→ N

1 km
1 mile

163

Lee Gate - Arrewig Lane (Map 29)

Maps
OS Landranger Sheet 165
OS Explorer Sheet 181 (or old Sheet 2)
Chiltern Society FP Map No.8

Parking
There is very limited parking space on or around this section. Do **not** use the ´Old Swan` car park without the landlord's permission.

Lee Gate is one of several upland hamlets forming the parish of The Lee. The name Lee derives from the Saxon ´leah` meaning clearing and it is thought that this is the origin of at least the village called The Lee, three-quarters of a mile south of Lee Gate, where the original thirteenth-century church, its replacement built in 1868 and Church Farm stand within an ancient camp, a circular earthwork, where there is also evidence of a deserted village, and there is a picturesque village green surrounded by a pub, a manor house, a farm and old cottages which is frequently used as a film set. Other hamlets are frequently named after local features; in Lee Gate's case, the former inn which used to form its focal point.

By the former ´Gate Inn` turn right onto the road. After 70 yards, fork left into Furze Field Lane (byway L43). At a left-hand bend, leave it and take path L15 straight on through a hedge gap and across a field, heading just left of several cottages ahead to pass through a kissing-gate in the next hedge. Now bear half left across two paddocks, passing through a kissing-gate and two fence gaps to rejoin byway L43 and take this rough road to reach a road by the ´Old Swan` at Kingswood.

Turn right onto this road, then, after 20 yards, turn left over a concealed stile by a gate onto path L20a, following a left-hand fence, then keeping right of a line of trees straight on to cross a stile into a green lane. Now turn left, crossing a stile in metal rails ahead and taking path L18b beside a left-hand hedge through two fields, ignoring the stile of a branching path to your left. At the far end of the second field, cross a stile into a strip of woodland, then fork right crossing the wood diagonally and ignoring a crossing track. On leaving the wood, keep straight on over a rise to the point where three hedges meet in the next dip. Here go through a hedge gap and take the right-hand side of a hedge straight on uphill to a hedge gap leading to Arrewig Lane.

Arrewig Lane - St. Leonard's (Map 30)

Maps

OS Landranger Sheet 165
OS Explorer Sheet 181 (or old Sheet 2)
Chiltern Society FP Map No.8

Parking

There is very limited parking space on or around this section.

The unusual names of Arrewig Lane and nearby Erriwig Farm are often thought to be rustic corruptions of 'earwig', but, in fact, they are more likely to be of Saxon origin and to derive from the lane, (which probably dates from Saxon times as it follows the ancient parish boundary between the hillfoot strip parishes of Wendover and Aston Clinton and since 1932 between The Lee and Cholesbury-cum-St. Leonards), leading to traditionally arable fields and it thus means 'way to the arable fields'.

Turn right into Arrewig Lane, then, after 50 yards, turn left through a hedge gap onto path CY46, heading for the left-hand side of a clump of trees surrounding a pond. Now bear slightly right across the field to a hedge gap into a wood called Lady Grove. In the wood, ignore a crossing path and bear slightly left, soon going uphill, keeping left at a fork, passing right of a pond and continuing to another field. Go straight on across this field to enter the right-hand end of a wood called Ashen Grove where you soon reach crossing bridleway CY6, an ancient road called Broad Street Lane. Turn right onto this, leaving the wood and continuing along a green lane, eventually reaching a bend in a concrete farm road. Take this straight on, passing the moated Dundridge Manor to your right. There is thought to have been a manor house on this site since Saxon times and its name, which was documented in the thirteenth century as 'Dunrugge', derives from the Saxon 'Dun-hrycg' meaning 'bare ridge', but habitation of the area dates back even further as Iron Age pottery has been found here.

On passing some gates, you will see the drawbridge to your right. Now go straight on along a fine avenue of mature beeches, sycamores and oaks, keeping left at a fork to reach Oak Lane. Turn left onto this road, then, at a road junction, turn left again into Jenkins Lane and follow it for 100 yards to a left-hand bend by the 'White Lion' at St. Leonard's.

St. Leonard's - Buckland Common (Map 30)

Maps
OS Landranger Sheet 165
OS Explorer Sheet 181 (or old Sheet 2)
Chiltern Society FP Map No.8

Parking
There is very limited parking space on or around this section. Do not use the 'White Lion` car park without the landlord's permission.

St. Leonard's, a scattered, remote Chiltern hamlet some 700 feet above sea level, was, till 1932, an upland hamlet of the seven-mile-long strip parish of Aston Clinton. Despite this, however, due to its remoteness from the mother church nearly four miles away at the foot of the escarpment, St. Leonard's has had its own chapel-of-ease since at least the thirteenth century and the present picturesque building dates from the fifteenth century.

On reaching the 'White Lion`, turn right onto path CY11, passing through the pub car park and two fence gaps, then go straight on downhill, passing right of two clumps of bushes to cross a stile by a gate into Bottom Road. Now cross a stile by a gate opposite and bear half right across the next field to cross a stile by a gate onto Little Twye Road at Buckland Common.

Buckland Common - Wigginton (Map 30)

Maps
OS Landranger Sheet 165
OS Explorer Sheet 181 (or old Sheet 2)
Chiltern Society FP Map No.8

Parking
There is limited parking space on verges at Buckland Common.

Until 1932, Buckland Common was another upland hamlet of a hillfoot strip parish, in this case, as its name suggests, Buckland, but this settlement is thought to be more recent and an example of unauthorised encroachment on a remote common.

166

MAP 30

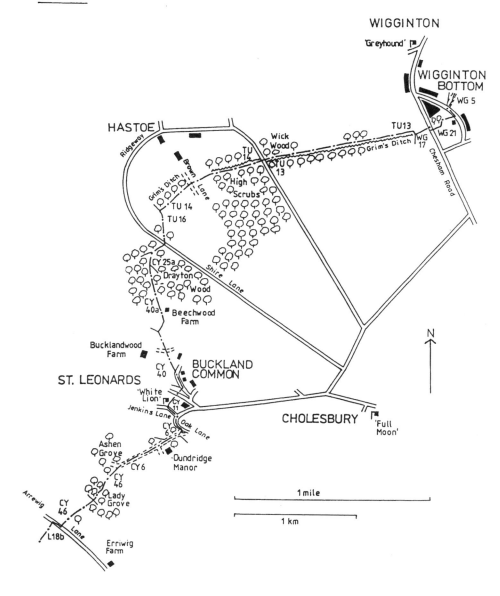

Turn left onto Little Twye Road, passing a large cream cottage, the former ´Boot & Slipper` pub. At a right-hand bend, fork left through gates onto path CY40, bearing half right across a field towards a group of trees left of a garden shed, to reach a gap in the far hedge leading to a farm road. Cross this road and go through a kissing-gate opposite, then follow a right-hand hedge to a kissing-gate in the far corner of the field. Now turn right onto path CY40a, following a right-hand hedge to cross a stile, then taking a fenced path straight on past paddocks (containing young llamas in 2009) to a stile into Drayton Wood, whose name reminds us that this wood was formerly part of yet another hillfoot strip parish, Drayton Beauchamp, which till mediæval times, also included Cholesbury. In the wood, follow an obvious winding path generally straight on. At a waymarked junction, take path CY25a, bearing slightly left and keeping right at a further waymarked junction to leave the wood by a stile and take a fenced path to a stile into Shire Lane, so called as it marks the ancient county boundary between Buckinghamshire and Hertfordshire.

Now in Hertfordshire, take path TU16 opposite, bearing half left through a strip of woodland to enter a field. Here bear half left across the field to the corner of a hedge, then bear half left again and follow the hedge to a field corner. Now turn right onto path TU14, following the outside edge of a tree belt shading another section of Grim's Ditch, an ancient earthwork of unknown origin believed, however, to date from before the Saxon period as ´Grim` is an alternative name for the Germanic god, Wodan, and they are unlikely to have attributed something to a god which they had built themselves. At the far end of the tree belt, go straight on through a hedge gap into Brown's Lane, an ancient green lane, where Hastoe, at 770 feet the highest village in Hertfordshire (no pub) and the Ridgeway are a third of a mile to your left.

Here take path TU14 straight on through a hedge gap opposite and continue to a corner of a wood called High Scrubs. Now enter the wood and keep straight on for over a quarter mile, following another surviving section of Grim's Ditch and eventually reaching a road. Cross this road and take path TU13 straight on over a stile opposite, following Grim's Ditch through Wick Wood, then generally along the edge of a tree belt. Where the trees peter out, take a grassy track straight on until you reach a hedge, then turn right and follow it for 35 yards. Now turn left through a kissing-gate onto path WG17 and go straight across a field to a kissing-gate onto Chesham Road on the edge of Wigginton, where the ´Greyhound` is a third of a mile to your left.

Wigginton - Aldbury (Map 31)

Maps
OS Landranger Sheet 165
OS Explorer Sheet 181 (or old Sheet 2)
Chiltern Society FP Map Nos. 8 or 18 & 19

Parking
On-street parking is possible at Wigginton and there is a small car park on Tom's Hill Road east of Aldbury.

Wigginton, a hilltop Chiltern village above Tring with superb views in places across the surrounding countryside, was, at one time, very much an estate village housing workers from Lord Rothschild's estate at Tring Park and many of its sturdy nineteenth-century cottages were, indeed, originally built by this benevolent estate. Just to the south is the well-known health farm of Champneys in a house which also dates from this period, while the mediæval parish church was largely rebuilt in 1881, but retains the fifteenth-century West Chamber. Like many other villages in the northern Chilterns, Wigginton was, in the nineteenth century, also a centre for straw-plaiting which supplied the hat-making industry of Luton and Dunstable.

Turn right into Chesham Road. After 20 yards, turn left through a kissing-gate onto path WG21 through a copse, then between a hedge and a fence eventually reaching a road at Wigginton Bottom. Turn left onto this road, then in the bottom of a dip, turn right onto path WG5 along a short lane into a field, then taking the right-hand grassy track uphill beside a right-hand hedge then a fence, then keep straight on to rejoin the right-hand hedge by some ash trees. Now follow it, bearing right into a green lane, along which you continue until you reach a stile by gates into Lower Wood. Here keep right at a fork and take path WG6 generally straight on through the wood, eventually descending into a valley bottom. At a T-junction, turn right onto path WG8, soon leaving the wood by a kissing-gate and following a left-hand fence straight on to a gate and kissing-gate at the far end of the field. Now go straight on across the next field to a kissing-gate into a green lane (path WG11). Turn right into this lane, soon becoming a concrete road and bearing right beside the A41 Berkhamsted Bypass, then dropping to reach Bottom House Lane.

Turn left onto this road, passing under the A41 bridge, then, by a large house called Tinker's Lodge, turn right onto byway WG10, following its drive at first, then continuing along a rough lane. After this bears left, ignore a branching path to your right and keep straight on for a third of a mile, eventually reaching the A4251 at Cow Roast by the 'Cow Roast Inn`. The inn, after which the hamlet is named, is thought originally to have been called the 'Cow Rest` and to have been a resting place for cattle drovers on their way along the main road to London.

Turn right onto the A4251, then, just past the inn, turn left onto a narrow road, crossing a bridge over the Grand Union Canal by Cow Roast Lock. Here, if wishing to leave the Way for Tring Station, turn left down a ramp onto the towpath and follow it for 1.4 miles to the second crossing road bridge where the station is to your right. Otherwise, continue along the lane, bearing right, then, after 150 yards, turn left over a concealed stile onto path NC29, bearing slightly right across a field to cross a high footbridge over the former L&NWR Euston-Birmingham main line built in 1838, the height of which was raised when what is now known as the West Coast main line was electrified in the 1960s. Now keep straight on across the next field to pass through a hedge gap. Here turn right onto restricted byway NC30, a fenced grassy track, then, at a T-junction, turn left onto the continuation of path NC29, soon passing through a gate and bearing slightly right to reach the drive to Norcott Court Farm.

Turn sharp left onto this, crossing a stile by a gate, then turn right over another stile by a gate into a field. Here bear half left, crossing the field diagonally with fine views across the Tring Gap in the Chiltern escarpment to your left including the spectacular sloping footbridge carrying the Ridgeway over the A41. At the far corner of the field, cross a stile by a gate and follow a deer fence across the next field to the corner of a hedge. Keep left of this hedge and follow it to a field corner. Here bear half right through the thick hedge and up a bank to cross a stile, then take path AB3, bearing half left over a rise to cross a stile in the far corner of the field. Now follow the edge of a wood called The Hangings for 50 yards, looking out for a gate into it. Turn right through this onto byway AB1, taking a track gently uphill through the wood. After passing through a gate, take a stony track straight on past an industrial site to join a macadam road at Tom's Hill with a view of Tom's Hill House to your right.

Follow this road straight on, keeping left by Rose Cottage and then ignoring branching paths to left and right. On reaching a T-junction at a hairpin bend in Tom's Hill Road, fork left onto the major road. Where its left-hand crash-barrier ends, fork left again onto path AB39, taking a terraced woodland path steeply downhill to reach the end of a village street in Aldbury called Malting Lane.

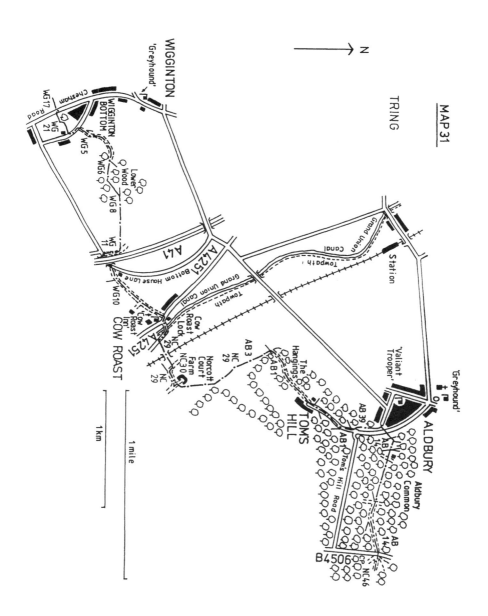

MAP 31

171

Aldbury - Berkhamsted Common (Map 31)

Maps
OS Landranger Sheet 165
OS Explorer Sheet 181 (or old Sheet 2)
Chiltern Society FP Map No.19

Parking
On-street parking is possible in Aldbury village, but can be very difficult at weekends and bank holidays. There are small car parks on Tom's Hill Road and where the Way crosses the B4506.

Aldbury is a renowned picture-postcard village with a green with a duckpond, stocks and a whipping-post surrounded by attractive sixteenth- and seventeenth-century cottages and a seventeenth-century manor house. The nearby church, of thirteenth-century origin but now mainly fourteenth-century with a fifteenth-century tower, is noted for its monuments to the Duncombe family who held Stocks Manor for 500 years and the Pendley Chapel with its monuments to the Whittingham and Verney families and a fine stone screen, which were moved to the church from the former Ashridge Monastery in 1575. Buried in the churchyard is Mrs. Humphrey Ward (1851-1920), a grand-daughter of Dr. Arnold of Rugby School and niece of the poet Matthew Arnold and a popular novelist of her day, whose husband bought Stocks in the 1890s and who was visited there by her son-in-law, the historian Dr. G.M. Trevelyan and the playwright George Bernard Shaw.

Do **not** continue into Malting Lane, but turn sharp right onto bridleway AB14, taking a sunken way steeply uphill through woodland on Aldbury Common, much of which, since the sale of the Ashridge Estate in 1929, has been owned by the National Trust. You soon cross Tom's Hill Road and then, at a five-way junction, bear half left up a steep gravel path. Near the top, fork right, continuing uphill to follow the right-hand edge of a clearing, at the top of which there are fine views to your left towards Aldbury Nowers and Pitstone Hill. Now ignore branching bridleways to left and right and keep straight on along a gravel path, passing under a powerline, soon crossing a drive by a lodge and taking the main track straight on for half a mile, ignoring all branching or crossing paths or tracks to cross the B4506 by a corner of a field to your left onto Berkhamsted Common.

Berkhamsted Common - Little Gaddesden (Map 32)

Maps

OS Landranger Sheet 165
OS Explorer Sheet 181 (or old Sheet 2)
Chiltern Society FP Map No.19

Parking

There is a small car park where the Way crosses the B4506.

Berkhamsted Common with its extensive woodland is today taken for granted as a place where local people and Londoners can go for fresh air and exercise, but few of its many visitors realise that in 1866 it was all but lost to land enclosure. In that year, 400 acres of the Common, which had, in mediæval times, formed part of the park of Berkhamsted's Norman castle, were enclosed by the lord of the manor, Lord Brownlow of Ashridge Park, with a high iron fence. This might easily have led to the land being split into fields and brought into agricultural use, but Augustus Smith, owner of the nearby Ashlyns Estate and one of the enraged Berkhamsted commoners, supported by Lord Eversley, chairman of the newly-founded Commons Preservation Society (now the Open Spaces Society), assembled a gang of 100 London labourers and chartered a special train to bring them by dead of night to Berkhamsted Common. By 6 a.m. the fence had been completely dismantled and four years of litigation followed, but finally, in 1870, Augustus Smith won, with an injunction being granted forbidding enclosure and defining the rights of common. The judgment did not, of course, give public access but preserved the rights of common, so that, when the Law of Property Act 1925 granted public access to urban commons, Berkhamsted Common was able to qualify, subject to certain limitations to protect the golf course.

From the B4506, take bridleway NC46 straight on eastwards for a quarter mile along an avenue of ancient beech and oak trees with a pronounced boundary bank to your left. By the corner of a field to your left, turn left onto path LG5, following the inside edge of the wood. Where the field fence turns away to your right, go straight on, soon wiggling to your right, passing right of a pond and joining a track which merges from your left. On reaching a bend in a macadam private road, join it and follow it straight on, soon crossing a grassy avenue called Prince's Riding, where Ashridge House can be seen two-thirds of a mile to your right and the Bridgewater Monument is nearly a mile to your left.

Ashridge House, which has been variously described as being 'like a snowman, built up by sticking on lumps instead of having good bones inside it' and by the Chiltern writer, H.J. Massingham as being 'like a gigantic wedding cake' and 'hideous but ... also comic', was commissioned by the third Duke of Bridgewater before his death in 1803 to replace a mediæval house, which had passed to his family in 1604 and had formerly been a monastery. Designed in the neo-Gothic style by James Wyatt and his nephew, Sir Jeffry Wyatville, it was eventually completed in about 1820. At the other end of the Riding, which forms part of the landscaping carried out by Capability Brown in about 1767, is the Bridgewater Monument, a tall Doric column also designed by Sir Jeffry Wyatville and erected in 1832 in memory of the third Duke, who is noted as 'the Father of British Inland Navigation'.

On emerging from the woods onto Ashridge Golf Course, keep straight on past Old Park Lodge. Where the macadam surface ends, fork right onto a waymarked path, passing right of a barn and continuing downhill through woodland to emerge onto another part of the golf course. Now keep straight on, passing right of a green and left of the clubhouse, then take a waymarked path through a copse to join a macadam drive and follow it straight on to a T-junction. Here, leaving the drive, bear half right through the trees, crossing another drive and taking a fenced track (still path LG5) straight on between gardens into woodland. On reemerging onto the golf course, ignore a crossing golfers' path and go straight on downhill between tees and through woodland to the bottom of a dip known as Witchcraft Bottom. Here take a fenced path straight on between gardens, soon crossing a drive and continuing uphill to a private road. Cross this and take the fenced path straight on uphill to enter the 'Bridgewater Arms' car park and reach the road through Little Gaddesden.

Little Gaddesden - Studham (Map 32)

Maps

OS Landranger Sheets 165 & 166
OS Explorer Sheet 181
Chiltern Society FP Maps Nos. 19 & 20

Parking

There is a small car park in Church Road, Little Gaddesden. Do **not** use the ´Bridgewater Arms` car park without the landlord's permission.

Little Gaddesden, a long straggling village, most of which is on one side of the Ringshall - Nettleden road with Ashridge Park on the other, can boast an attractive village green by which is a timber-framed cottage with an overhanging upper floor called John o'Gaddesden's House, which was reputedly home to this fourteenth-century doctor to Edward II and Edward III, who died in 1361, but is thought more likely to date from the fifteenth century. The stone-built manor house also dates from 1576, while the fifteenth-century parish church, which stands in splendid isolation in fields at the end of a cul-de-sac lane, is principally notable for the wealth of memorials it contains to members of the Egerton family, the Earls and Dukes of Bridgewater, who held nearby Ashridge from 1604 to 1849.

Turn right onto the road, then, after 50 yards, turn left through a kissing-gate onto path LG12, following a fenced path between paddocks, glimpsing the church through a gap in the trees ahead and ignoring a branching path to your right. Having passed through another kissing-gate, you emerge into a meadow where you bear half right, passing the corner of a fenced garden to reach a kissing-gate in the far corner of the field leading to Church Road. Turn left onto this road, then immediately right through a kissing-gate and bear half left across a paddock with fine views of the church to your left. Having passed through another kissing-gate, bear half left across the next field to the left-hand of two kissing-gates in the next fence. Now bear half left again across a prairie field, heading for a large oak tree some way left of a distant cottage, eventually passing the oak tree to reach the far corner of the field. Here ignore a kissing-gate on a crossing path and bear half left through a hedge gap, following a right-hand hedge downhill with fine views opening out across the Gade Valley ahead, eventually passing a copse and reaching a gap in the bottom hedge. Now ignore a bridlegate to your right and join bridleway LG11, following a grassy track straight on downhill beside a right-hand hedge, soon crossing the Bedfordshire boundary and continuing along bridleway ST33 to the A4146 in the valley bottom.

Cross this road and take bridleway ST25 straight on, passing through a gap left of a padlocked gate and following a left-hand hedge uphill. Soon after the hedge bears right, pass through a hedge gap, then go straight on uphill between a hedge and a deer fence protecting a young plantation, passing a copse to your right and eventually entering Ravensdell Wood. Keep straight on through this wood to a gate into a field, then follow a grassy track beside a right-hand hedge straight on. After 50 yards, turn right through a kissing-gate onto path ST26 and bear half left across a field, aiming just left of a line of three trees and a cottage with white window frames at Studham beyond and eventually reaching a kissing-gate. Now go straight on, passing left of a lightning-damaged ash tree to a kissing-gate by a gate left of the cottage, then follow a short drive to a gate and stile onto Common Road on the edge of Studham.

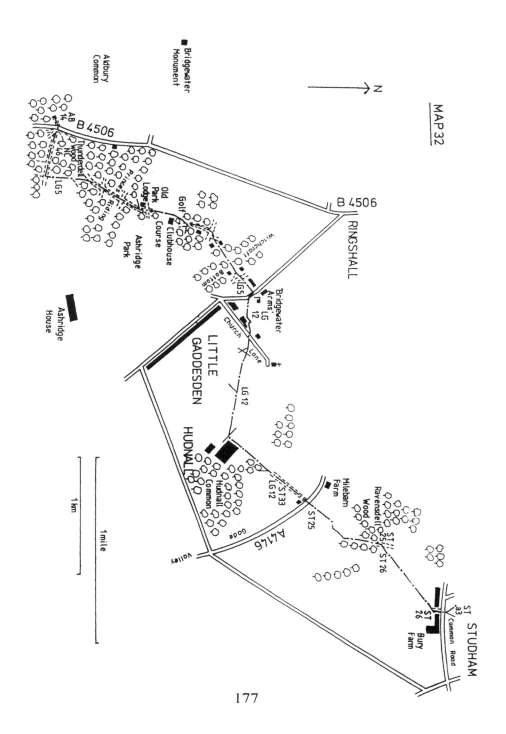

MAP 32

177

Studham - Whipsnade (Map 33)

Maps
OS Landranger Sheet 166
OS Explorer Sheets 181 or 182
Chiltern Society FP Maps Nos. 20 & 21

Parking
There is a small car park at Studham Church, but avoid using it when there are church services.

Studham, the southernmost village in Bedfordshire, nestles in a hollow in the backland of the Dunstable Downs, surrounded by an extensive upland plateau. Until 1897, the village, which was once a centre of the straw-plait industry and was one of the early strongholds of Nonconformity, in fact, straddled the Hertfordshire boundary and it was only then that the southern half of its extensive common and many of its scattered farms and cottages were transferred to the same county as the church and village centre. The cement-rendered thirteenth-century church, which is somewhat isolated and hidden at the end of its cul-de-sac lane, has a surprisingly beautiful interior with fine carved stone capitals and an unusual carved Norman font predating the present building.

Bear slightly right across Common Road and go through a hedge gap, then bear half left onto path STa3, heading for the bottom left-hand corner of the field. Here go through a hedge gap, cross Valley Road and take path ST23 through another gap opposite, following the right-hand hedge through two fields. In the second field, turn right over a stile by a gate onto path ST20, going straight uphill to a corner of a wood called Castle Grove, then follow its edge uphill to a stile leading to bridleway ST6 (where the road to the church is a short distance to your right).

Here ignore a blue-green gate to your left and turn left onto fenced bridleway ST6, soon entering a wood called Church Grove. Just inside the wood, disregard a branching path to your left and follow the inside edge of the wood straight on for a quarter mile, ignoring a signposted crossing path and two branching paths to your left. On emerging from the wood into a field corner, disregard a branching track to your right and take a grassy track beside a right-hand hedge straight on through two fields. At the far end of the second field, go straight on into a copse, then, at a fork, take the right-hand option straight on, soon reaching the perimeter fence of

Whipsnade Wild Animal Park. Now keep straight on between this fence and a tree belt for over a quarter mile to reach Studham Lane. Turn left into this narrow road closed to through-traffic and follow it for a quarter mile. Where the lane forks, keep right, then immediately turn right through a kissing-gate onto path ST10, following a left-hand hedge to pass through a kissing-gate at the far side of the field. Now turn left through gates onto path WP8 and follow a right-hand hedge towards Whipsnade Church. At the far side of the field, go through a kissing-gate into the churchyard and pass left of the church to reach gates leading out to Whipsnade Green.

Whipsnade - Dunstable Downs (Map 33)

Maps
OS Landranger Sheet 166
OS Explorer Sheets 181 or 182
Chiltern Society FP Map No.21

Parking
There are car parks at Whipsnade Tree Cathedral and just off the B4540 at Whipsnade Down.

Whipsnade village is notable for the extensive green, around which its scattered cottages are situated, and being the highest village in Bedfordshire. Its unusual brick-built church has a sixteenth-century tower and an eighteenth-century nave but incorporates details of an earlier building, while at the back of the village is the Tree Cathedral planted in the 1930s by Edmund Kell Blyth in memory of friends killed in the First World War and now looked after by the National Trust. However what Whipsnade is best known for is the Wild Animal Park, which was opened by the Royal Zoological Society in 1931 to exhibit and breed its hardier animals in natural surroundings. The Wild Animal Park in its scenically spectacular setting can be toured by a steam railway which you may have heard while skirting the Park's perimeter on bridleway ST6.

At the church gates, turn left and follow the back of the green at first. Having crossed the drive to Church Farm, keep straight on to a road junction left of a former chapel. Here cross the B4540 and take the road signposted to the 'Tree Cathedral'. At a fork, keep right, then immediately bear right again through a gap by a padlocked gate onto bridleway WP4, following a green lane past the Tree Cathedral. On reaching a kissing-gate into the Tree Cathedral to your left, bear right to pass through a fence gap onto a private road.

Turn left onto this road, then, after 70 yards, fork right, following a right-hand hedge through scrubland, part of the Sallow Springs Nature Reserve, then along the edge of two meadows. At the far end of the second meadow, turn left and follow a right-hand fence to rejoin the private road. Turn right onto this, ignoring a branching path to your left and the entrance to a luxury housing development to your right and soon entering Sallowspring Wood. At the far side of the wood, by a telecommunications mast, fork right, joining bridleway WP1 which follows a green lane along the edge of the wood. On emerging onto another private road, take a sunken way straight on along the edge of the wood to reach a bridlegate leading to Whipsnade Down, where superb panoramic views open out with a glider airfield below you, Dunstable Downs to your right, Totternhoe Knolls ahead and the Vale of Aylesbury beyond. Here turn right onto a National Trust permissive bridleway, following the top hedge of the Down for 250 yards to reach a bridlegate. Go through this, then follow a right-hand hedge straight on. Where the hedge ends, bear slightly right to reach the corner of a macadam path by a large metal artwork, where the new Dunstable Downs Visitors' Centre is to your right. Here take the macadam path straight on over a slight rise, where a superb view along the Dunstable Downs opens out ahead, to reach the main car park.

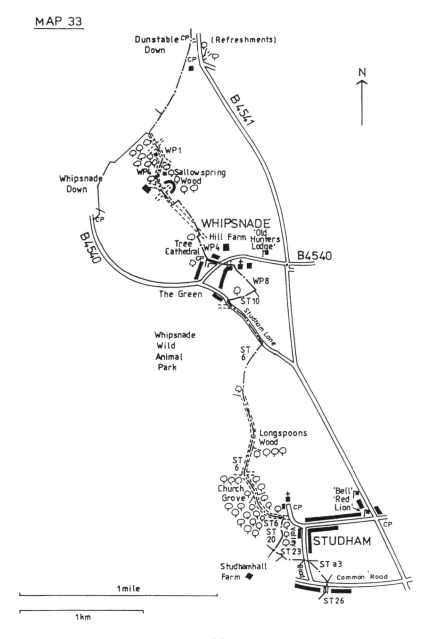

MAP 33

Dunstable CP (Refreshments)
Down
CP

N

B4541

WP1
WP4 Sallow spring
Wood
Whipsnade
Down
CP

B4540

WHIPSNADE
'Old
Hill Farm Hunters
Tree Lodge'
Cathedral WP4 B4540
CP
WP8
The Green ST10

Whipsnade
Wild Studham Lane
Animal ST
Park 6

Longspoons
Wood
ST
6
Church
Grove
'Bell'
'Red
CP Lion'
ST6 CP
ST
20 STUDHAM
ST23
Studhamhall ST a3
Farm Common Road

1mile

1km

ST26

181

Dunstable Downs - Dunstable (Map 34)

Maps
OS Landranger Sheet 166
OS Explorer Sheets 181 or 182 & 193
Chiltern Society FP Map No.21

Parking
There are car parks at Dunstable Downs.

The Dunstable Downs, with their spectacular views along the Chilterns to Ivinghoe Beacon and out over the Vale of Aylesbury towards Oxfordshire and the Cotswolds, are today a real ´honeypot` for people from Dunstable, Luton and farther afield, for picnics and walks with superb views and ample parking. Four thousand years ago, these hills must also have been frequented, as, at the northern end of the Downs, are the Five Knolls, five huge Neolithic or Bronze Age barrows, where excavations have not only revealed remains from this period, but also a large number of skeletons originating from the fifth century AD, some of which had injured bones or their hands tied behind their backs, suggesting that they were the victims of some battle or massacre.

By the main car park, follow the macadam path straight on, bearing left then right and continuing to an overflow car park, now with additional views behind you towards Ivinghoe Beacon. Now take the macadam path straight on parallel to the B4541 to your right towards Five Knolls Hill for half a mile, passing the top of a deep, steep-sided coombe called Pascomb Pit, with further views briefly opening out to your right across Dunstable, Houghton Regis and Luton with Blows Down to your right. On approaching Five Knolls Hill, where the macadam path passes through a fence gap, fork left to its summit, where you have panoramic views in all directions. Here bear half right, passing left of four of the Five Knolls and then descending through a kissing-gate and joining path D23 to reach mown parkland at the bottom of the slope. Now follow a right-hand line of trees, bearing left when nearing the B4541, to reach a roundabout on the edge of Dunstable at the junction of the B489 and B4541.

Dunstable - Chalk Hill (Map 34)

Maps
OS Landranger Sheets 165 & 166
OS Explorer Sheets 192 & 193
Chiltern Society FP Map No.23

Parking
On-street parking is possible in residential roads near the Way on the outskirts of Dunstable.

Dunstable, the centre of which is three-quarters of a mile to your right, is situated at the crossroads of the prehistoric Icknield Way (now the B489) and Watling Street, a Roman road from Dover via London to Holyhead (now the A5). The area is believed to have been inhabited since the Stone Age, as archæologists have made finds dating from various ages in close proximity to the town. Although a Roman staging post known as Durocobrivæ was recorded, it is believed not to have been very large and it was only in 1131, when King Henry I founded an Augustinian priory and constructed a royal lodge known as Kingsbury, that Dunestaple` (as it was then known) became a place of any size. Originally the Priory was of vast proportions, being 320 feet long and having transepts 150 feet wide, but the west towers collapsed in a storm in 1222 and the transepts, central tower, long choir and monastic buildings were, at some stage, demolished to leave the present parish church with its massive Norman columns, round arches and fifteenth-century north tower. In 1533, the Priory was also the scene of a major historical event, as it was here that Thomas Cranmer, the then Archbishop of Canterbury, pronounced the annulment of the marriage of Henry VIII and Catherine of Aragon, which led to the English Reformation. In the eighteenth century, improved road communications caused Dunstable to become an important port of call for stagecoaches and so the town's inns flourished, as did the local straw-hat industry, but it has only been in the last century that Dunstable has mushroomed into the large industrial town it is today.

Now cross the B489 (Tring Road) left of the roundabout, passing the left-hand end of metal railings, then bear half right, passing through a squeeze-stile beside a gate and taking byway D4 along the surprisingly rural, wide, tree-lined Green Lane between housing estates, ignoring a crossing macadam path. Soon on byway D-TT12, (becoming TT12), continue for a further third of a mile, ignoring all branching or crossing paths or tracks, later with fine views through gaps in the left-hand hedge along the Chiltern escarpment including the Dunstable Downs, Whipsnade Down with its white lion cut in the chalk hillside in 1933 as an advertisement for the newly-opened zoo, Ivinghoe Beacon, Aston Hill and more hills beyond. Some 250 yards beyond the end of the right-hand tree belt, where the macadam cycle track and footpath bear right, turn right onto bridleway HR35, following the tarmac track beside a left-hand hedge with views ahead towards Houghton Regis with its prominent fifteenth-century church tower. Where the hedge and track bear left, follow them, looking out through gaps in the left-hand hedge for a circular earthwork capped by a hedge called Maiden Bower, a large Iron Age plateau-fort built on the site of Neolithic causewayed enclosures. Near this, the track becomes enclosed in a green lane and starts to descend, soon bearing left and following Sewell Cutting to your right, part of the former Dunstable Branch of the London & North Western Railway, closed in 1962, now part of a long-distance cycle-track, where Roman pottery was found during construction of the railway in 1859 and a nature reserve noted for its chalkland flowers.

At the bottom of the hill, where old chalk quarry faces can be seen to your left and the former railway is on a low embankment, turn right under a wooden cycle bridge spanning the old railway bridge abutments into Sewell Lane. Now follow this road through the picturesque hamlet of Sewell for nearly a quarter mile. Just past the drive to Sewell Manor, turn left through a squeeze-stile onto path HR24 (still on the Icknield Way long-distance path), following a fenced path downhill, then bearing right, eventually crossing a stile into a field. Bear slightly left across this field to cross a stile under a tall sycamore tree, then turn left onto a sometimes overgrown path through a tree belt, eventually emerging over a footbridge into a field. Now turn right and follow this ditch and a sporadic hedge until you reach a tree belt covering the embankment of the A5. Here turn right onto path HR31, following the edge of the tree belt until a marker post indicates a hedge gap leading to a steep flight of steps up the embankment to a stile onto the A5 at Chalk Hill.

MAP 34

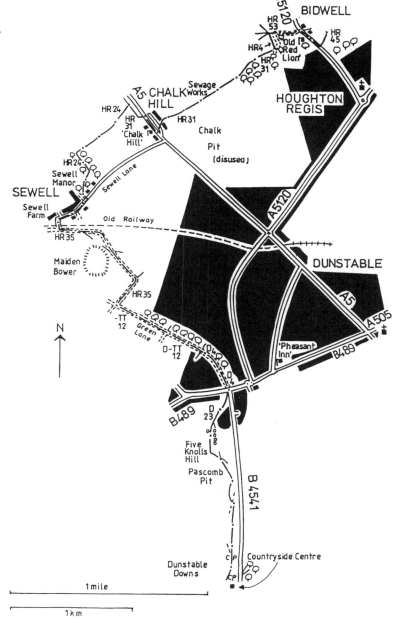

BIDWELL

HR 53

HR4

Old
Red
Lion

HR 45

HR 31

A5120

CHALK HILL

Sewage Works

HOUGHTON REGIS

HR 24

HR 31

HR 31

'Chalk Hill'

Chalk Pit (disused)

A5

HR 24

Sewell Manor

Sewell Lane

A5120

SEWELL

Sewell Farm

Old Railway

DUNSTABLE

HR 35

Maiden Bower

HR 35

A5

A505

N

-TT 12

Green Lane

D-TT 12

'Pheasant Inn'

B489

B489

D 23

Five Knolls Hill

Pascomb Pit

B4541

Dunstable Downs

C P

Countryside Centre

C P

1 mile

1 km

185

Chalk Hill - Bidwell (Map 34)

Maps
OS Landranger Sheet 166
OS Explorer Sheet 193
Chiltern Society FP Map No.23

Parking
On-street parking is possible in residential roads off the A5 on the outskirts of Dunstable.

Chalk Hill, on the A5 just northwest of Dunstable, must have once been a very steep and dangerous hill for stagecoaches to negotiate, no doubt exacerbated by the slippery nature of chalk surfaces in wet weather, as, in 1837, just before the dawning railway age ruined the financial viability of the turnpikes, the responsible turnpike trust went to the considerable expense of excavating a cutting and creating an embankment to reduce its gradient and produce the long gradual incline we know today.

Cross the main road carefully and turn right onto its footway, passing a filling station, then, just before the ´Chalk Hill` inn, by a traffic island, turn left onto the continuation of path HR31, descending a flight of steps to the old road. Turn left onto this, then, just past a timber-framed cottage, turn right onto an enclosed path (still HR31) and follow it to enter a field. Now follow its left-hand hedge straight on for half a mile, passing Houghton Regis Sewage Works to your left and eventually reaching the corner of a copse concealing an old chalkpit. Here go straight on, passing left of a small fenced compound, entering a green lane and continuing for a quarter mile until you emerge onto a concrete road. Turn left onto this, then, where it immediately bears right, leave it and take path HR4 straight on through a squeeze-stile and across a field to the left-hand end of a hedge. Here, leaving the Icknield Way long-distance path, turn sharp right onto path HR53, following the near side of the hedge to pass through a squeeze-stile in the field corner. Now bear left onto a concrete road and follow it to the A5120 at Bidwell.

Bidwell - Chalton (Map 35)

Maps
OS Landranger Sheet 166
OS Explorer Sheet 193
Chiltern Society FP Map No.23

Parking
On-street parking is possible in residential roads off the A5120 on the outskirts of Houghton Regis.

Bidwell, an attractive hamlet of Houghton Regis at the foot of the hill on the Bedford road with an inn and half-timbered farmhouses and cottages, has today almost been swallowed up by its larger neighbour, which has expanded to a mere 100 yards from the hamlet. The mother ´village,` with its fine fourteenth-century church with a fifteenth-century tower and clerestory, its large village green and some thatched cottages, must once also have been picturesque, but, since the 1960s, it has been swamped with modern housing and commercial development, which have made its character suburban. The name Houghton Regis is of Saxon origin, its first part meaning ´settlement on a hill´ and its second denoting that it was a royal manor and it was this which saved the village from being sacked when visited by William the Conqueror soon after the Battle of Hastings. This was also the reason for nearby Dunstable (which then belonged to the manor) being chosen as the site for Henry I's palace and priory, of which Dunstable's present magnificent church was only a small part. In more recent times, the chalk, on which the village is built, brought it renewed prosperity, as the straw-plait made from the white straw which grew on it, was valuable to Luton's straw-hat industry, while the chalk itself was quarried for making cement.

Turn right onto the A5120, passing the ´Old Red Lion`, then, after 250 yards, turn left through a kissing-gate onto path HR45. Now walk round the end of a ditch sometimes obscured by nettles and bear half left over a rise to reach the corner of a fence, then bear half left again and follow it to a kissing-gate. Here go straight on, following a left-hand hedge at first. Where the hedge turns left, bear slightly right across the field to pass through a gap in the corner of a hedge and follow the left-hand field boundary to the far end of the field. Here cross a footbridge and stile and turn right onto path HR14, following the right-hand hedge and stream, soon crossing another footbridge.

Now continue to follow the right-hand stream and an increasingly sporadic hedge through four more fields, until you reach a crossing powerline. Here turn left onto bridleway HR22, following a grassy track beside a left-hand hedge and the powerline to Grove Farm, then continuing straight on. On nearing a corner of Grove Spinney, turn right onto a fenced path beside a left-hand hedge uphill, entering a green lane.

At the top of the low ridge, where views open out towards the Sundon Hills ahead and Toddington to your left, turn right onto byway HR43, following a green lane uphill and continue along the ridge (later on byway CT9) for three-quarters of a mile with fine views to right and left for much of the way. 120 yards after a crossing powerline, turn left over a footbridge and through a hedge gap onto path CT5, then bear slightly left across a field to enter an alleyway just right of the tallest house on the edge of Chalton and emerge at a road junction. Go straight on downhill, then, at a right-hand bend, opposite a bungalow called 'Drumlin`, turn left onto the continuation of path CT5, following an enclosed path through what, at the time of writing, is a construction site, eventually crossing a macadam drive into a children's playground, then bear right, following its right-hand edge to enter a macadamed alleyway which leads you out to the B579 opposite the 'Star`.

Chalton - Upper Sundon (Map 35)

Maps
OS Landranger Sheet 166
OS Explorer Sheet 193
Chiltern Society FP Maps Nos. 23 & 25

Parking
On-street parking is possible in residential roads off the B579 in Chalton. Do not use the pub car park without the landlord's permission.

Chalton is today best known for its large electricity sub-station, which together with the sewage works and nearby quarries and landfill sites, disfigures what must once have been a highly attractive area. Traditionally a remote hamlet of Toddington on the Luton road with some attractive cottages, Chalton, which has grown due to postwar housing developments, has recently become an independent parish.

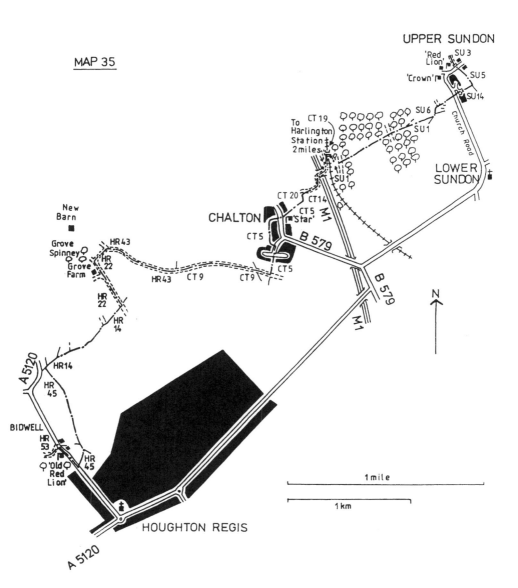

MAP 35

UPPER SUNDON

Cross the B579 and bear slightly left, passing the left-hand corner of the 'Star' to reach a kissing-gate in the back left-hand corner of its car park. Now take path CT5 straight on, keeping right of a line of trees and following them through scrub to cross a farm bridge, then turn left onto path CT20 beside the stream to a field corner. Here turn right onto path CT14, following a left-hand hedge to join a farm road. Take this road straight on, soon bearing left then right over a bridge over the M1, then bear left again. After 120 yards fork right onto path CT19 to cross a high new footbridge over the St. Pancras main railway line.

At the far side of the railway take path SU1 bearing half left across a field to a yellow-capped marker post in a line of poplar trees. Here bear left crossing a concrete road, then bear slightly left across a field, passing right of a pylon to reach the far left-hand corner of the field. Now go straight on into scrubland, where you cross a chalky track and continue beneath a powerline. At a fork ignore a branching path to your right and continue uphill through scrub, disregarding a branching path to your left. Just before leaving the scrub, fork right through a kissing-gate and follow a left-hand hedge straight on for 200 yards, until you reach a marker post, where there are views to your right across Luton towards Blows Down. Here turn left through a kissing-gate and take path SU6, descending a flight of steps to the floor of an old chalkpit, soon climbing another flight of steps to a hedge gap leading to a private road. Cross this road and go through a hedge gap opposite, then bear slightly right across a field to a kissing-gate right of a gap in the houses at Upper Sundon leading to Church Road.

Now go straight on through an alleyway into a small estate, then continue to the end of the cul-de-sac. Here go through a concealed kissing-gate and take path SU14 (the line of which is under review, so please heed the waymarks!), currently following a right-hand fence along the edge of a recreation ground to reach a kissing-gate in it. Here turn left onto path SU5, heading for the right-hand end of the 'Red Lion' to reach a kissing-gate. Now continue past a pond, then bear slightly left across the green to cross Harlington Road right of the 'Red Lion'.

Upper Sundon - Sundon Hills Country Park (Map 36)

Maps
OS Landranger Sheet 166
OS Explorer Sheet 193
Chiltern Society FP Map No.25

Parking
There is a car park at Sundon Hills Country Park and limited on-street parking is also possible in Upper Sundon.

Upper Sundon on a plateau half a mile north of Lower Sundon in its hollow above the source of the River Lea, is the much larger of the two hamlets. As Lower Sundon is the location of the parish church and manor house, this suggests that it was the site of the original settlement, but that it became a 'closed village` to escape the cost of the Poor Law and its displaced population instead settled in Upper Sundon which was probably an upland common. Sundon's large thirteenth-century church is notable for its mediæval murals and stone seats around its walls for the elderly and infirm from before the introduction of pews (from which the phrase 'the weak go to the wall` derives). In 1653 this church briefly gained historical significance, as it was the setting of the wedding of William Foster, a persecutor of the non-conformist author and preacher, John Bunyan, and Anne Wingate, sister of the magistrate, who later imprisoned Bunyan in Bedford Gaol.

Take bridleway SU3 straight on past the right-hand side of the 'Red Lion` and along a rough lane to enter a field, then continue downhill to the gates of a sewage works. Here fork right through gates into a field and bear slightly left across it to a bridlegate left of its far corner. Do **not** go through this, but, rejoining the Icknield Way long-distance path, turn right onto path SU20 through a hedge gap in the field corner, where fine views open out ahead towards Harlington and Ampthill beyond. Here turn right and follow the hedge uphill to a field corner, then turn left beside the top hedge with superb views across Bedfordshire to your left, now including Toddington over your left shoulder. At the far side of the field, go straight on through a gap by a gate onto Harlington Road, where you turn right, then, after 50 yards, turn left through a kissing-gate into the Sundon Hills Country Park car park.

Sundon Hills Country Park - Sharpenhoe Clappers (Map 36)

Maps
OS Landranger Sheet 166
OS Explorer Sheet 193
Chiltern Society FP Map No.25

Parking
There is a car park at Sundon Hills Country Park.

Sundon Hills Country Park with its chalk downland rich in flora and superb views towards Sharpenhoe Clappers and across the Bedfordshire lowlands to the north is today a justifiably popular destination for visitors from nearby towns, to which public access was gained only thanks to its purchase by the former Bedfordshire County Council. In the seventeenth century the surrounding countryside was, however, the scene of critical events in the life of John Bunyan, who was arrested at Lower Samshill in 1660. Bunyan subsequently appeared before the magistrate, Francis Wingate, at his sixteenth-century manor house in Harlington before being incarcerated for twelve years in Bedford Gaol where he wrote his `Pilgrim's Progress`, for which he is still famous today. Indeed, it is thought that these hills and the Barton Hills to the east were the inspiration for his reference there to `the Delectable Mountains` and this is why they form part of the John Bunyan Trail, with which this section of the Chiltern Way coincides.

Now bear right across grassland to a wooden kissing-gate, then continue in your previous direction to the top hedge of this large downland field. Here turn left and follow this hedge with fine views ahead towards Sharpenhoe Clappers and to your left across the Bedfordshire lowlands. At the far end of the field, go through a kissing-gate, then bear right onto a grassy track, following a right-hand fence round the rim of a steep-sided coombe, then uphill and bearing right.
　　Now fork right through a kissing-gate onto path SU19, following a left-hand hedge gently uphill with fine views behind you. At the far side of the field, turn left through a hedge gap onto path SU4, following the outside edge of Holt Wood straight on, then, at the far end of the wood, bear half left onto a farm track leading to a corner of Fernhill Wood. Here bear half left again with fine views ahead towards Harlington. At the next corner of this wood, turn right,

leaving the track, and follow the outside edge of the wood to the far side of the field. Here ignore a path into the wood and turn left, still following the outside edge of the wood. After 120 yards, by a marker post, you finally enter the wood and bear left to reach a waymarked junction at the top of some steps. Here turn right onto path SL15 and follow it straight on for 350 yards, ignoring branching paths to right and left and soon skirting the top edge of a deep coombe. At a fork, where gates can be seen to your right, fork right towards the gates, then, by the gates, fork left onto a fenced track along the outside edge of the wood. Where this track bears right, leave it and go straight on through a kissing-gate by a gate. Now, diverging from the wood edge, keep straight on across the field with fine views opening out ahead towards Sharpenhoe, Pulloxhill and Ampthill beyond and later to your left towards Harlington, to reach a kissing-gate in the far hedge. Go through this and descend some steps to Sharpenhoe Road opposite the entrance to Sharpenhoe Clappers Car Park.

Sharpenhoe Clappers - Streatley (Beds.) (Map 36)

Maps
OS Landranger Sheet 166
OS Explorer Sheet 193
Chiltern Society FP Map No.25

Parking
There is a car park on Sharpenhoe Road near Sharpenhoe Clappers

The name Sharpenhoe Clappers is of mixed origin, as the village name of Sharpenhoe is Saxon, meaning ´sharp spur of land`, while Clappers comes from Norman French meaning ´rabbit warren`. While the village at the foot of the hill, which unusually has always been a hamlet of the hilltop village of Streatley, may therefore have originated in Saxon times, the hill shows much earlier signs of habitation, as it is capped by an Iron Age hill fort and both Iron Age and Roman pottery have been found there, but the Normans adapted it for breeding rabbits and thus arose the second part of its name. Clappers Wood within the earthworks, though ancient in appearance, was, in fact, only planted between 1834 and 1844 and a painting from 1815 shows it completely bare. In the wood is an obelisk erected by W.A. Robertson in memory of his two brothers who were killed in the First World War and this was also his reason for donating the Clappers to the National Trust in 1939. The former moated manor near Bury Farm just north of the village below was home to both the leading seventeenth-century mathematician, Edmund Wingate and Thomas Norton (1532 - 1584), the Calvinist zealot, who was both Solicitor General to Elizabeth I, nicknamed 'Rackmaster General' due to his ready use of torture against Roman Catholics, and a poet and playwright credited with being the forerunner of and model for Shakespeare and Marlowe.

Cross Sharpenhoe Road and take path SL14 straight on through the car park and a gap by a gate. Here take a macadam track straight on, ignoring a crossing bridleway and passing through further gates, then, at a three-way fork, turn left onto a grassy path into woodland and follow it straight on, later through scrub. On emerging from the scrub, where a superb view opens out to your left towards Toddington, Harlington and Sharpenhoe, keep left at a fork following a left-hand fence to reach the near left-hand corner of the mature beech copse within the ancient earthworks on Sharpenhoe Clappers known as Clappers Wood. Now continue between the fence and the earthwork to the far end of Clappers Wood where the **Chiltern Way Extension** takes path SL14 straight on downhill (now see Map 39).

The **original Chiltern Way** forks right onto a permissive path, immediately bearing right to join a parallel path within the copse, which you follow round the inside edge of two further sides of the mature beechwood, then fork left down a steep bank and take a path straight on through scrubland. On reaching a kissing-gate, go through it, turn left through a second kissing-gate and follow a worn winding path across open downland with superb views to your left across Barton-le-Clay and the Barton Hills, ignoring a crossing path.

Having rejoined the Icknield Way long-distance path, another kissing-gate eventually leads you onto a fenced track where you turn left and follow the track to a transverse hedge. Here turn left through a kissing-gate, then, having passed through a hedge gap, take fenced bridleway SL42 straight on along the edge of scrubland and woodland for over three-quarters of a mile, ignoring several gates and kissing-gates to your left, then turning right, rounding the top of a steep wooded coombe called Watergutter Hole and later turning sharp right by a corner of the field to reach the end of a belt of tall beech trees. Now turn left through the hedge and follow the edge of the tree belt to a hedge high above the A6 Barton Hill Cutting. Here the track turns right and you follow this hedge, then, at the far side of the field, it turns right then immediately left and continues between fences through allotments to a car park off Church Road, Streatley. Now turn right onto a macadam path, soon joining the road and following it into the village to reach a T-junction near the 'Chequers'.

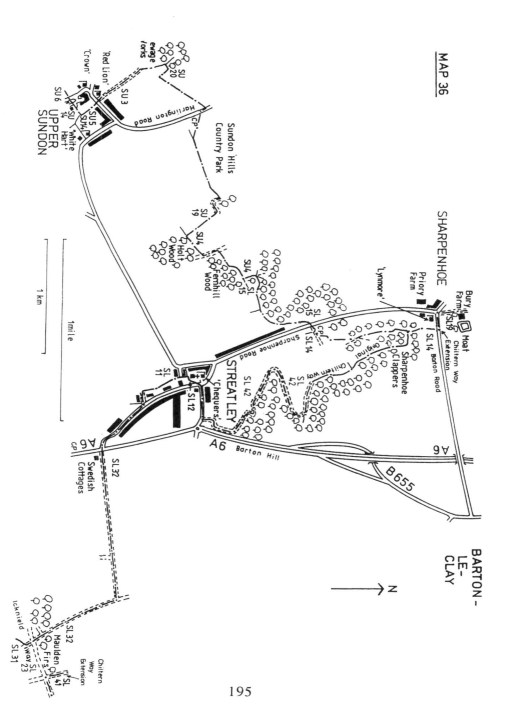

MAP 36

Streatley (Beds.) - Icknield Way (Maulden Firs) (Map 36)

Maps

OS Landranger Sheet 166
OS Explorer Sheet 193
Chiltern Society FP Map No.25

Parking

There is a small car park by the allotments in Church Road, Streatley, limited on-street parking is possible in the village and there is a northbound layby on the A6 south of Swedish Cottages.

Streatley (pronounced 'Strettley' unlike its more famous Berkshire cousin and meaning 'clearing by the road'), once comprised just a few cottages and only in the last century did it start to grow into the medium-sized village we find today. For this reason, in the early twentieth century, its fourteenth-century church with its earlier font, fifteenth-century tower and mediæval wall painting of St. Catherine, was in ruins. It was only in 1938 that the church, where Thomas Norton was buried in 1584, was restored by Sir Albert Richardson.

At the T-junction, turn left into Sharpenhoe Road, then immediately right up a drive, passing left of the 'Chequers' to go through gates into the churchyard. Now take path SL12, forking left to pass left of the church and reach a wrought-iron gate into an alleyway. Fork left into this, taking path SL11, soon passing the end of Churchill Close and crossing a stile into a field. Now follow the left-hand hedge straight on downhill into a dip, where you go through a kissing-gate and turn left through another kissing-gate into Bury Lane, which leads you out to Sharpenhoe Road. Turn right onto this and follow it out of Streatley with views opening out ahead towards Galley Hill, Warden Hill and Luton, eventually reaching the A6.

Cross this road carefully and take bridleway SL32 straight on along a farm track for three-quarters of a mile with views to your right towards Galley Hill, Warden Hill and Luton, passing Swedish Cottages and later ignoring a branching track to your right. At a junction of tracks by a large metal pylon, turn right (still on bridleway SL32), following a grassy track beside a left-hand hedge towards Galley Hill. At the edge of a wood called Maulden Firs, ignore a branching track to your right and go straight on through the wood to reach the ancient Icknield Way.

Icknield Way (Maulden Firs) - Lilley (Map 37)

Maps
OS Landranger Sheet 166
OS Explorer Sheet 193
(part only) Chiltern Society FP Map No.25

Parking
Limited parking is possible in Butterfield Green Road leading to Whitehill Farm and there is a car park at its junction with the A505 at Stopsley.

The Icknield Way, possibly the most ancient road in Britain, which generally follows the foot of the escarpment of the Wessex Downs and Chilterns from Wiltshire to East Anglia, unusually between Dunstable and Hitchin, crosses the hills to avoid the detour to pass north of the Sundon and Barton Hills. The Way, which is believed either to have been named after Boadicea's people, the Iceni, or to be a corruption of ´ychen`, a Celtic word for cattle which may have been driven along it, is thought originally to have consisted of a number of parallel routes, of which the one or, in some places, two routes shown on modern maps are merely the survivors. The modern Icknield Way long-distance path with its various alternative routes is therefore very much in the tradition of its ancient namesake.

Galley Hill, which you are about to climb, has an equally long history as one of the ancient barrows scattered across it was found to contain both fourth-century and neolithic corpses. Its name, however, is a corruption of ´Gallows Hill`, as, in addition to these ancient burials, the barrow also contained the remains of fifteenth-century gallows victims.

At the crossways, **if wishing to link to the Chiltern Way Extension,** turn left onto the Icknield Way (bridleway SL23) to join it in 350 yards (see Map 40). **Otherwise,** take bridleway SL31 straight on, following a grassy track at first. After 60 yards, at the far side of the second hedge gap to your right, bear half right off the track and follow the edge of a left-hand belt of scrub, then keep straight on across a golf course fairway (beware of golfers driving from your left!) to a bridlegate into scrubby downland. Here take the worn path straight on up Galley Hill. At the top, where superb panoramic views open out over Luton and Streatley to your right and the hills on the North Hertfordshire border to your left, keep straight on, soon passing through a bridlegate and following a right-hand fence towards Warden Hill ahead. At a field corner, where a kissing-gate and stile lead back onto the downland, do **not** use these, but turn left and continue to follow the right-hand fence until you reach crossing bridleway SL27. Turn right onto this, entering a sunken way. After 120 yards, where a left-hand fence begins, turn left through a kissing-gate and take a permissive path, bearing half left up Warden Hill. At the top of the ridge by a marker post, joining path SL28, bear slightly left, keeping left at a fork and climbing to a kissing-gate at a junction of fences. Now follow a left-hand fence straight on along the top of the ridge with superb views to your right across Luton. Near the far end of the ridge, where the fence turns left, leave it and go straight on across open downland, aiming towards a yellow-capped marker post and a church with a pointed steeple on the skyline at Stopsley beyond, passing left of some earthworks, then continuing downhill past another yellow-capped marker post to reach a path leading down through hillside scrub, ignoring one crossing path and reaching another crossing path (SL26) by the bottom fence.

Turn left onto this and on emerging from the scrub, turn right through a kissing-gate and follow the left-hand side of a winding sporadic hedge with more views to your right across Luton. On reaching a farm road, turn right onto it, rejoining bridleway SL31, and follow it beside a right-hand hedge with fine views to your left towards Telegraph Hill, until you reach a crossing farm road. Here go straight on between large concrete blocks and follow a farm road straight on for half a mile, passing Whitehill Wood to your left and reaching the end of Butterfield Green Road by the entrance to Whitehill Farm.

Take this road straight on. After 50 yards by a telephone pole, turn left over a concealed stile onto path LU26, bearing half left across a field and soon becoming path SL34. In the far corner of the field, cross a stile and bear slightly left across the next field, passing just right of an oak tree to reach a gap in the bottom hedge with fine views ahead in mid-field across Lilley Bottom and Lilley towards Great Offley on the next ridge. Go straight on through a gap in the bottom hedge and, now in North Hertfordshire, take path LL3, following a left-hand hedge, then the edge of Lilley Park Wood straight on. At the far end of the wood, now on path LL2, continue along a green lane, eventually emerging into the car park of the Cassel Memorial Hall in Lilley. Go straight on through this car park to reach the village street, then turn left onto its footway.

Lilley - Mangrove Green (Map 37)

Maps
OS Landranger Sheet 166
OS Explorer Sheet 193

Parking
There is a large car park by the Cassel Memorial Hall in Lilley and limited on-street parking is also possible in the cul-de-sac village streets leading to the 'Silver Lion` and 'Lilley Arms` and in Lilley Hoo Lane to the east.

Lilley, situated just off the A505 (Luton - Hitchin main road), is clearly recognisable as an old estate village with a large number of its cottages bearing the rampant silver lion crest of the Docwra (pronounced 'Dockray`) and later the Sowerby families, both of Cumbrian origin, who, at various times, owned nearby Putteridge Bury. The former twelfth-century church was almost entirely rebuilt by Thomas Jekyll in 1870, but retains the Norman chancel arch and fifteenth-century font of the original building. In the seventeenth century, Lilley was a centre of non-conformity, being home to the religious writer, James Janeway, and it is believed that John Bunyan, author of 'Pilgrim's Progress`, secretly preached in the cellar of one of the village cottages. An infamous later resident of the village was the nineteenth-century alchemist, Johann Kellermann, who disappeared from Lilley as suddenly as he came.

After 60 yards, opposite the near corner of Lilley churchyard, turn right onto enclosed path LL4, soon reaching a kissing-gate into a field. Here go straight on, following a left-hand fence at first, then continuing across the field to a kissing-gate left of an oak tree. Now bear half right across the next field to a kissing-gate in the far corner. Here bear left, keeping right of a hedge and following it over the Lilley Hoo ridge, at the top of which was once open downland with an eighteenth-century racecourse where the Prince Regent (later King George IV) raced his horses. At the top of the ridge, fine views open out towards Great Offley ahead and down Lilley Bottom to your right. Now follow the hedge downhill to reach Lilley Hoo Lane near Lilley Hoo Farm. Turn right onto this cul-de-sac road and follow it for a quarter mile, passing through a tunnel under the A505 to reach a T-junction with the old main road at the foot of Hollybush Hill, where the **Chiltern Way Extension** and Great Offley are one third of a mile and two thirds of a mile to your left respectively (see Map 41).

Here the **original Chiltern Way** turns left, then, after 100 yards, turns right into Glebe Farm, immediately forking right onto byway OF51, a green lane right of the buildings. Now continue for over half a mile to a road called Luton White Hill, part of an ancient route from Luton via Putteridge Bury to Great Offley and Hitchin. Turn right onto this, then, at a crossways in Lilley Bottom, take byway OF20 straight on for a third of a mile. Just before reaching the park wall of Putteridge Bury near East Lodge, fork left through a gap onto path OF8, following the left side of the wall uphill for two-thirds of a mile. At the far end of the second field, by the corner of a hedge, leave the wall and bear slightly left onto path OF50, following a left-hand hedge to a gate and kissing-gate. Go through the kissing-gate, pass Mangrove Hall to your left and take its macadam drive straight on to reach the end of a public road by the 'King William' at Mangrove Green.

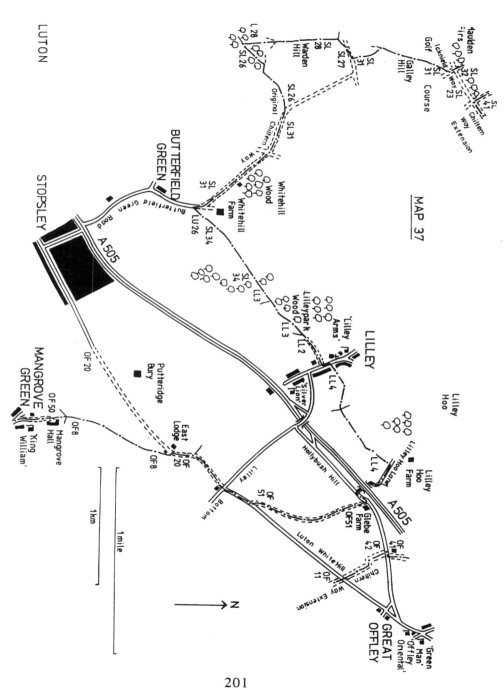

MAP 37

LUTON

STOPSLEY

BUTTERFIELD GREEN

MANGROVE GREEN

LILLEY

GREAT OFFLEY

201

Mangrove Green - Breachwood Green (Map 38)

Maps
OS Landranger Sheet 166
OS Explorer Sheet 193

Parking
On-street parking is possible at Mangrove Green and Cockernhoe.

The twin hamlets of Mangrove Green and Cockernhoe with their greens and scattered cottages give a deceptively rural impression, which belies the fact that both are now less than half a mile from the edge of Luton with its voracious appetite for building land. It is largely the existence of the county boundary which they have to thank for so far being spared the fate of nearby Stopsley, which has long been swamped by urban development.

Take this road straight on across the green and down a lane to reach Cockernhoe Green. Here, at a three-way fork, take the central option straight on, then, by a bus stop, join the priority road and follow it straight on towards Luton. Just past the last house in the village, where the edge of Luton can be seen a field's length ahead, turn left over a stile by a gate onto path OF2, ignoring a grassy track to your right and taking a path between a hedge and a fence straight on through scrub. On emerging at the edge of Brickkiln Wood, turn right into a field and then left, following the edge of the wood with views to your right towards Luton and Luton Airport, soon forking left onto a fenced path through the wood. By the corner of a left-hand field, bear right, soon emerging into the corner of a right-hand field. Here turn left, then, after 15 yards, bear left again onto a fenced path into a tree belt, soon bearing right and later bearing right again to enter a field. Now turn left and follow a left-hand hedge with more views of Luton and its airport. At the far end of the field, take a short green lane straight on, passing some cottages and following their drive straight on to a road junction by Wandon End Farm.

Here bear half right across a traffic island and the priority road to pass the left-hand end of a wooden fence and enter a field. Now turn left onto path KW41, following the edge of the field parallel to the road for 200 yards. By a slight left-hand bend in the road, bear slightly right across the field, passing Wandon End to your left to rejoin the field edge by an oak tree and follow it to rejoin the road at a road junction. Here take the Darley Hall, Breachwood Green and King's Walden road straight on. At a left-hand bend, leave the road and take bridleway KW52, following a winding grassy track straight on for 300 yards to reach the corner of a hedge. Now go through a hedge gap and follow a sporadic left-hand hedge uphill. At the next hedgeline, leave the bridleway and take path KW6, bearing slightly right across a field towards a severely lightning-damaged oak tree left of and beyond a pair of oak trees, joining the top of a grass bank left of the pair of oak trees. Now follow this bank past the lightning-damaged oak tree and a second, then, just past this, bear slightly right, descending the bank and crossing a field corner to the corner of a fence. Here follow this fence straight on at first, then, where it turns left, continue along a grass path past a large oak tree. Some 30 yards beyond this tree, bear half left across the field to a kissing-gate onto Chapel Road on the edge of Breachwood Green.

Breachwood Green - Peter's Green (Map 38)

Maps
OS Landranger Sheet 166
OS Explorer Sheets 182 & 193

Parking
On-street parking is possible at Breachwood Green.

Breachwood Green, a hamlet of King's Walden parish on a ridgetop above Lilley Bottom, would seem a very remote location when approached through the maze of lanes between Luton and Stevenage and indeed the history and appearance of the surrounding countryside would tend to confirm this, but it will not be long before you realise that the village is beneath the flightpath of the approach to Luton Airport. Despite this, however, Breachwood Green, whose name derives from the Ancient British chief Breah and whose Edwardian baptist church can boast a pulpit used by the non-conformist preacher and author, John Bunyan at nearby Bendish in 1658, makes a good centre for exploring the rolling hills around Lilley Bottom which is reminiscent of Hampden Bottom in the Chiltern heartlands but far less well-known.

Turn right onto Chapel Road, then, at a road junction, go straight on down Lye Hill. After 250 yards, at a right-hand bend, fork left onto path KW3 up a slight slope into a field. Here bear right and follow the right-hand hedge downhill. Where the hedge ends, leave it and go straight on downhill to a hedge gap in Whiteway Bottom. Do **not** go through this, but turn left onto path KW51, following the field edge, later a right-hand hedge to a corner of the field. Here turn right through a hedge gap onto path KW4, going straight uphill to the corner of a hedge, then following this right-hand hedge straight on to a gap by a corner of a wood called Sellbarn's Dell. Go through this and follow the edge of the wood straight on. Where it bears left, leave it and keep straight on across the field, passing just left of an electricity pole to cross a stile by gates in the far hedge. Here take a grassy track straight on beside a right-hand fence across the next field to cross a stile by gates into Wandon Green Farm. Now go straight on, passing right of a barn and left of the farmhouse to reach a road.

Turn left onto this road, then, at a junction, turn right onto the road to Peter's Green. Take this road straight on for a mile, ignoring a turning to your left, then looking out for views of Lawrence End Park to your right and eventually reaching Peter's Green. Here, at a fork, keep right to reach a T-junction where you turn right, **rejoining the Chiltern Way Extension**. Now turn to look at Map 44 for the continuation.

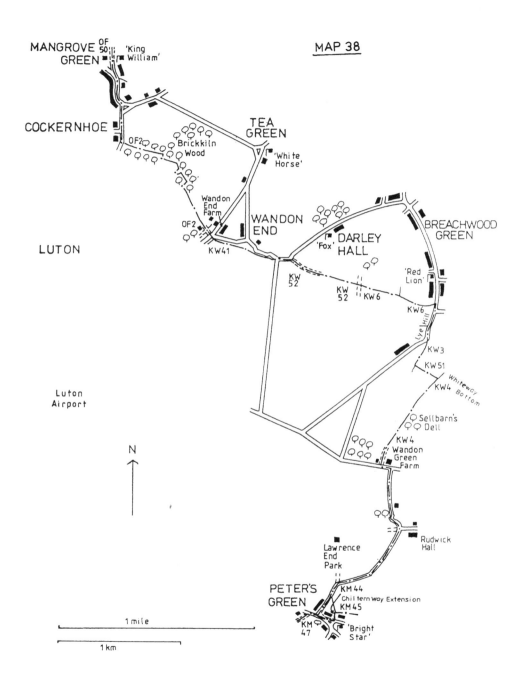

MAP 38

MANGROVE GREEN
OF 50
'King William'

COCKERNHOE

OF2
Brickkiln Wood

TEA GREEN

'White Horse'

Wandon End Farm

OF 2

LUTON

WANDON END

KW41

'Fox'

DARLEY HALL

BREACHWOOD GREEN

'Red Lion'

KW 52

KW 52   KW 6

KW 6

Lye Hill

KW3

KW 51

KW4

Whiteway Bottom

Luton Airport

N

Sellbarn's Dell

KW 4
Wandon Green Farm

Rudwick Hall

Lawrence End Park

PETER'S GREEN

KM 44
Chiltern Way Extension

KM 45

KM 47

'Bright Star'

1 mile

1 km

205

Sharpenhoe Clappers - Barton-le-Clay (Map 39)

Maps
OS Landranger Sheet 166
OS Explorer Sheet 193
Chiltern Society FP Map No.25

Parking
There is a car park on Sharpenhoe Road near Sharpenhoe Clappers and a large layby in Barton Road, Sharpenhoe.

Notes
The section between Sharpenhoe village and the A6 may be heavy-going during or after very wet weather. In such conditions, you may prefer to turn right at Sharpenhoe onto Barton Road and follow it to rejoin the Chiltern Way Extension by the 'Royal Oak' in Barton-le-Clay.

The **Chiltern Way Extension** now takes path SL14 straight on downhill, soon descending a long flight of steps through scrubland to enter a field. Here follow a left-hand hedge straight on to reach Barton Road on the edge of Sharpenhoe.

Turn left onto this road, then, at a junction by the 'Lynmore', turn right onto bridleway SL19, following the drive to Sharpenhoe Bury. At Bury Farm bear right across a concrete yard to the end of a brick wall, then bear left, passing left of some large barns. Now take a rough track straight on towards Pulloxhill Water Tower, ignoring two branching tracks and a sleeper bridge to your left.

Having passed through a hedge gap, turn right onto path BC11, following a right-hand hedge at first, then bearing slightly right across the field with panoramic views towards the Barton Hills ahead, Sharpenhoe Clappers to your right and Pulloxhill to your left, to reach a gap by the tallest tree in the far hedge. Here cross a footbridge and go through a hedge gap, then turn right onto a grassy track following the right-hand hedge along the edge of a plantation. On reaching a powerline, turn left and follow it, soon walking between hedges and passing two World War II concrete 'pillboxes' (on which anti-aircraft guns were mounted). Eventually you cross a stile and bear left into a green lane, immediately forking right over a stile. Now cross the next field diagonally to a gate and stile under the powerline, then follow a left-hand fence beneath the powerline to a stile and footbridge leading into a spinney. Keep straight on through this, then, on entering a field, follow a right-hand hedge straight on still beneath the powerline. At the far end of the field, bear left to a kissing-gate into the car park of a weatherboarded watermill on the edge of Barton-le-Clay built in about 1790.

Now go straight on across the car park, an island of grass, a gravel track and a rose border and take a gravel track straight on, soon bearing right to cross a stile leading to the A6. Here bear left to reach steps up to the road, then cross it via a staggered gap in the central-reservation crash-barrier. Now take macadam path BC33 straight on, passing a redundant stile and continuing along an alleyway, soon joining a macadam drive. Having crossed an estate road, take path BC33 straight on along a bollarded disused road to a road junction. Now keep straight on along Mill Lane to the B655 (Bedford Road) in the centre of Barton-le-Clay.

Barton-le-Clay - Icknield Way (Maulden Firs) (Map 39)

Maps
OS Landranger Sheet 166
OS Explorer Sheet 193
Chiltern Society FP Map No.25

Parking
On-street parking is possible in many places in Barton-le-Clay.

Barton-le-Clay, formerly known as Barton-in-the-Clay meaning 'barley farm in the clay land`, sits astride the old route of the A6 from London to Bedford and Carlisle at the foot of the Chiltern escarpment where the clay land to the north, from which its name derives, gives way to Chiltern chalk. As such, in the days of the stagecoach, Barton was a place of busy coaching inns, but earlier its history was marked by less peaceful pursuits as in 54BC the nearby 22-acre Iron Age hill fort of Cassivellaunus, dating from about 550BC and now known as Ravensburgh Castle, was attacked by Julius Cæsar, while the village itself was the scene of a ninth-century battle between Saxons and Danes.

Despite Barton being swamped with modern housing since the

Second World War, the vicinity of its church with its picturesque cottages remains an area of rural tranquillity and beauty. The church itself dates from 1180, but was much enlarged in the thirteenth century, while its tower is of fifteenth-century origin and it can also boast a finely-carved roof depicting eagles, saints and apostles. Its moated timber-framed rectory dates from about 1550 and is said to be the second oldest parsonage in England still serving its original purpose. It is also said to be haunted by ´a beautiful grey lady` called Anne Humphreys, the wife of the contemporary rector, who is believed to have died in childbirth in 1700 and is said to be searching for her lost love following her husband's subsequent remarriage.

For the walker, however, Barton's principal attraction is as a centre for walks with spectacular views of and from the range of hills which bears its name and represents the northern-most ridge in the Chilterns and it is these hills which are thought to have been the inspiration for John Bunyan´s ´delectable mountains` in his ´Pilgrim's Progress`.

Turn right into Bedford Road passing the ´Bull`. At a mini-round-about by the ´Royal Oak`, fork left into a side road, part of the ancient London road, passing a half-timbered cottage and the ´Coach & Horses`, then take Hexton Road (B655) straight on. At a left-hand bend, fork right into Old Road, which is so named as it formed part of the ancient London road until it was rerouted in 1832 in order to lessen the gradient of Barton Hill. Just past its junction with Washbrook Close, turn left through gates onto path BC4 across a recreation ground, heading just right of the church and tennis courts to reach a kissing-gate. Now take a fenced path to Church Road opposite the church.

Here turn right, passing the rectory to your left. After 100 yards, near the end of the lane, turn left onto fenced bridleway BC26, following a left-hand hedge past a paddock and an arable field. By an iron gate, bear right to a fork. Here ignore a green lane to your left and take a permissive path straight on up steps and through a kissing-gate into the Barton Hills Nature Reserve. Traditionally glebe land with customary public access, the Barton Hills in the nineteenth century became the subject of a conflict between successive rectors, who sought to restrict access, and local people who jealously guarded what they saw to be their rights, but, in 1894, agreement was reached and in 1965 the hills became a national nature reserve.

Now continue steeply uphill through scrubland, soon climbing steps, then bear half right, climbing two more flights of steps to reach a gate. Do **not** use this, but turn left and follow a right-hand fence up

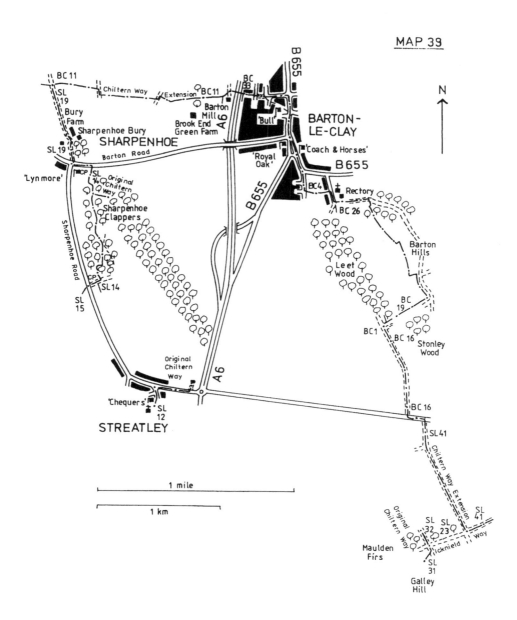

MAP 39

N

further steps to a kissing-gate at the end of a ridge where you should turn round for a panoramic view with Sharpenhoe Clappers to your left, Barton-le-Clay and Pulloxhill ahead and Shillington with its prominent church to your right.

Now resume your previous direction, following a left-hand fence straight on across downland, eventually passing through another kissing-gate and reaching a corner of the fence at the rim of a deep coombe formed 10,000 years ago by the melting of a glacier at the end of the last Ice Age. Here turn left and follow the fence to a stile. Do **not** cross this, but turn right beside the fence, passing the top of the coombe with the hill-fort called Ravensburgh Castle in woodland to your left. By a gate and stile, turn right, joining path BC19 and following a left-hand hedge above the coombe with fine views to your right and, at one point, across the hills ahead towards Streatley, Luton and the Dunstable Downs, eventually passing through a kissing-gate into a belt of scrub. Now go straight on through the scrub, keeping left at a fork to reach a kissing-gate into a field. Here turn left onto path BC1, a grassy track along the edge of the scrub. On leaving the scrub behind, take bridleway BC16 straight on along the grassy track for half a mile, soon with views of Galley Hill and Warden Hill slightly to your right, eventually reaching a gate and motorcycle-trap, then turning left onto a road.

After 150 yards, turn right through a gap left of a bund onto bridleway SL41 along a grassy track by a left-hand hedge. After 250 yards, ignore a branching track to your right and bear slightly left, still following the left-hand hedge, now with fine views to your right towards Galley Hill and across Luton towards the distant Blows Down and Dunstable Downs, eventually passing the left-hand end of Maulden Firs and reaching the ancient Icknield Way.

Icknield Way (Maulden Firs) - Pegsdon (Map 40)

Maps
OS Landranger Sheet 166
OS Explorer Sheet 193
Chiltern Society FP Map No.26

Parking
There is very limited parking space on or around this section.

The Icknield Way, possibly the most ancient road in Britain, which generally follows the foot of the escarpment of the Wessex Downs and Chilterns from Wiltshire to East Anglia, unusually between Dunstable and Hitchin crosses the hills to avoid the detour to pass north of the Sundon and Barton Hills. The Way, which is believed either to have been named after Boadicea's people, the Iceni, or to be a corruption of ´ychen`, a Celtic word for cattle which may have been driven along it, is thought originally to have consisted of a number of parallel routes, of which the one or, in some places, two routes shown on modern maps are merely the survivors.

Galley Hill, to your right, has an equally long history as one of the ancient barrows scattered across it was found to contain both fourth-century and neolithic corpses. Its name, however, is a corruption of ´Gallows Hill`, as, in addition to these ancient burials, the barrow also contained the remains of fifteenth-century gallows victims.

At the crossways, **if wishing to rejoin the original Chiltern Way**, turn right onto the ancient Icknield Way (bridleway SL23), then, in 350 yards, turn left onto crossing bridleway SL31. Now see Map 37. **Otherwise**, turn left onto the ancient Icknield Way (still on bridleway SL41) and follow this green road for two-thirds of a mile, soon passing a gate at the Hertfordshire county boundary then continuing on byway HX8/LL23 to a gate and motorcycle trap leading to a bend in the Lilley-Hexton road. Still on the ancient Icknield Way, take this road straight on for a third of a mile, then, at a sharp left-hand bend, leave it and take byway HX10/LL24 straight on. Still on the ancient Icknield Way, take a grassy track straight on for over half a mile, following a left-hand hedge towards Telegraph Hill, later becoming enclosed by trees. On reaching a fork by the Hertfordshire & Middlesex Wildlife Trust noticeboard about Telegraph Hill, leaving the Icknield Way, keep right. At a second fork, take a grassy permissive track straight on up

Telegraph Hill to its top where there are fine views to your left towards the Barton Hills and Pulloxhill and behind you towards Warden and Galley Hills.

Telegraph Hill, at 184 metres (602 feet) the highest point in North Hertfordshire District, is so named as it was used during the Napoleonic Wars as a semaphore and heliograph signalling station. Previously known as Pegsdon Beacon, it is thought to have been used in 1588 for one of a chain of beacons warning of the approach of the Spanish Armada and again in the Civil War in 1643 to warn of Prince Rupert's advance on Dunstable.

Now ignore a branching track to your right and keep straight on, soon following the edge of a large upland field called Lilley Hoo, where horse-racing took place in the eighteenth century and the Prince Regent (later King George IV) raced his horses. At the far side of this field, bear left through a hedge gap to rejoin the Icknield Way (now byway SH61/OF53 straddling the Bedfordshire boundary). Turn right onto this, then, after 50 yards, reentering Bedfordshire, turn left through a kissing-gate onto path SH17, crossing a field to a corner of a fence. Now follow this fence straight on, ignoring a stile in it, eventually with views to your right towards Pegsdon, Shillington and a water tower near Stondon. On passing through a kissing-gate, keep straight on above a deep coombe known as Barn Hole, soon with superb panoramic views across lowland Bedfordshire, gradually descending and passing through another kissing-gate. Now once again follow a right-hand fence, ignoring all stiles and gates in it. Where the fence makes a right-angle turn to the right, leave it and take a grassy track straight on downhill towards distant Clophill, eventually reaching a kissing-gate onto the B655 at Pegsdon.

Pegsdon - Clouds Hill (Map 40)

Maps
OS Landranger Sheet 166
OS Explorer Sheet 193
Chiltern Society FP Map No.26

Parking
Cul-de-sac road off Shillington road at Pegsdon and a layby on the B655 at its junction with the Icknield Way east of Deacon Hill.

Pegsdon, a tiny village with a green and a pub at the foot of the Chiltern escarpment below Deacon Hill, has always been a hamlet of the Bedfordshire parish of Shillington surrounded on three sides by Hertfordshire. To the east of the village is a hill called Knocking Hoe capped by a Neolithic long barrow known as Knocking Knoll. Legend has it that the ghostly knocking sounds said to emanate from inside giving it its name are made by an Ancient British chieftain guarding a great chest of treasure against tomb raiders. On the sides of steep-sided coombes between Knocking Hoe and Deacon Hill to the south, are mediæval ´strip lynchets` (terraces cut into the hillside to enable steeply-sloping ground to be ploughed) giving evidence of early cultivation of what would appear to be a rather infertile terrain.

Now cross the B655 and a strip of verge opposite, then continue along a cul-de-sac road to a T-junction. Here turn left onto the Shillington road, then, at a left-hand bend, turn right into Pegsdon Way and follow it through the village passing the ´Live and Let Live`. Now, at a right-hand bend near its junction with the B655, turn left onto path SH16, following a private road towards Pegsdon Common Farm for over a quarter mile, bearing right then left with fine views of Deacon Hill to your right. On rounding a left-hand bend, by a signpost turn right onto a grass crop-break across a field to reach a flight of steps, now additionally with fine views towards Knocking Hoe to your left. Climb the steps then ignore a crossing track and climb a second flight. Now continue uphill with a plantation to your left and a fenced coombe to your right. After leaving the plantation behind, follow the top edge of the coombe straight on for 150 yards until you reach a marker post, then turn left and follow the left-hand side of a sporadic hedge with superb panoramic views towards Knocking Hoe and a water tower near Stondon ahead, Pulloxhill with its prominent water tower, Higham Gobion and Shillington to your left and Deacon Hill behind you. At the far end of the field, turn right onto a sunken track, climbing gently with a deep coombe with strip lynchets and a close-up view of Knocking Hoe to your left, to reach gates and a gap with a low rail at the top of the hill by the corner of Tingley Field Plantation, (a Viking name meaning ´meeting-place in a clearing`) where it is worth turning round for a superb view towards Sharpenhoe Clappers, Pulloxhill, Shillington and beyond.

Now go through the gap and turn left onto bridleway SH2, which is enclosed by a right-hand fence at first, but is later open to your right. At the far side of the right-hand field, crossing again into Hertfordshire, turn left onto bridleway PI8, following a wide green lane known as Wood Lane gently downhill for nearly half a mile, with a brief view at one point through a gap in the right-hand hedge towards Letchworth. Now, just after a left-hand bend and seat, turn right through a hedge gap between beech trees onto path PI9, following a grassy track beside a left-hand hedge downhill and up again, with views through gaps in the hedge towards Pirton and Letchworth. On reaching a corner of Tingley Wood, take the grassy track straight on along its outside edge, with High Down House coming into view to your left and views over your left shoulder towards Pirton, the water tower near Stondon, Holwell and Letchworth.

High Down House, unusually for this part of the country, a stone house with twisted chimney stacks and mullioned windows, was built in 1612 by Thomas Docwra (pronounced ´Dockray`), a descendant of Sir Thomas Docwra, Lord Grand Prior in England of the Knights of St. John in Jerusalem, in an imposing position previously occupied by an earlier house. In 1648 the house is said to have been the scene of the murder of a cavalier named Goring, who had been hiding here from Parliamentarian troops, and his headless ghost is said to ride to Hitchin Priory on a white horse once a year.

On entering a second field, by a large oak tree, leave the edge of the wood and bear slightly left across the field to the right-hand of two gaps in the far hedge at the top of High Down. Here take path PI7 straight on through a kissing-gate, then follow the left-hand side of a hedge downhill and up again to a gap in a belt of trees concealing a section of the B655 which follows the ancient Icknield Way. In this gap, fork left onto a permissive path between fences at first within the tree belt to emerge onto the B655 opposite your continuation.

Cross this road and take path OF37 straight on through a hedge gap opposite, then bear slightly right across the field to pass the right-hand side of a clump of trees on the skyline concealing an old pond.

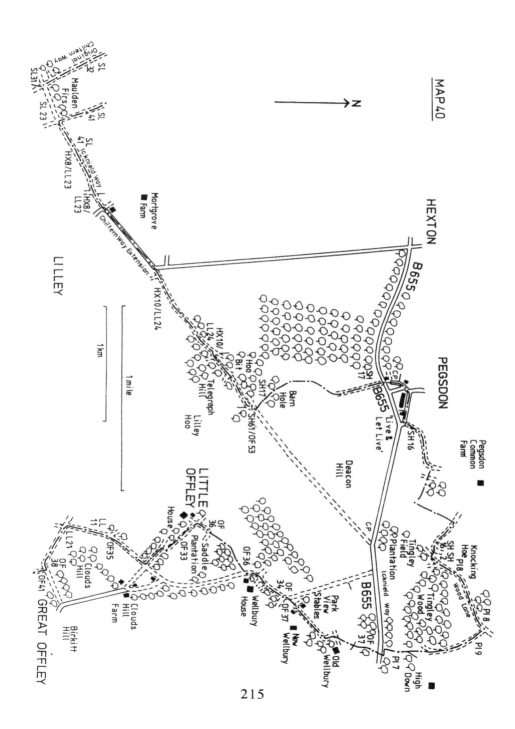

MAP 40

→N

HEXTON

B 655

PEGSDON

LILLEY

Mortgrove Farm

Maulden Firs

SL 32
SL 31
Original Chiltern Way
SL 41
SL 23
SL 41
Icknield Way
HX8/LL23
HX8/LL23
Chiltern Way Extension
HX10/LL24

1km
1mile

HX10/LL24
HX10/LL24
Hoo Bit
Telegraph Hill
Lilley Hoo
SH17
SH61/OF53
Barn Hole
SH17

'Live & Let Live'
B655
CP
SH16

Pegsdon Common Farm

Knocking Hoe
PI8
SH SH 16 12
Tingley Wood
Wood Lane
PI8
PI9

Deacon Hill

Tingley Field
Plantation
Icknield Way
CP

High Down

PI7

Old Wellbury

New Wellbury

Park View Stables
OF OF 37
OF 34

Wellbury House

OF 36
OF 34

OF 36
Saddle Plantation
OF 33

LITTLE OFFLEY
House

Clouds Hill

Clouds Hill Farm

Birkitt Hill

GREAT OFFLEY

LL 21
OF 35
OF 38
OF 41
LL 11

B655
OF 37

Now bear slightly left to reach a marker post by a large treestump where there are fine views to your left towards Hitchin. Here disregard a crossing path and bear slightly right to reach a kissing-gate in the far corner of the field. Ignoring a crossing track, go through the kissing-gate. Now disregard a stile to your right and follow a wide enclosed grassy track bearing left then right, then ignore two branching tracks to your left and continue to Park View Stables. Here keep straight on, by the house following a left-hand wall to a kissing-gate into a belt of trees, through which you continue to a macadam private road (bridleway OF34).

Turn left onto this road, immediately forking right onto a rough road. Now follow this road for a quarter mile, ignoring branching drives to your left leading to Wellbury House and passing through trees. Where another field opens out to your right and the road is once again macadamed, follow it straight on. Just past a speed hump, turn right onto bridleway OF36, crossing a field to the bottom corner of a copse called Saddle Plantation. Here bear slightly left, following its outside edge. At its far end, keep straight on uphill to pass right of the end of a hedge and join a grassy farm track leading straight on towards Little Offley. On approaching Little Offley Farm, by a clump of young trees to your right, turn left onto bridleway OF33, following a grassy track beside a right-hand hedge. Where this hedge ends, bear slightly right through the trees to reach the drive to Little Offley House, a fine late Tudor brick manor house set in parkland.

Turn left onto this drive within an avenue of lime trees, looking out for a fine view of Little Offley House over your right shoulder. Where the avenue of lime trees ends, turn right onto crossing bridleway OF35, following a rough track beside a right-hand hedge. Near the far side of the field, ignore a branching track to your right, then go straight on through a hedge gap and take bridleway LL11, following a grassy track straight on. At the next hedge, go through a hedge gap, then turn left onto bridleway LL21, taking a grassy track up Clouds Hill beside a left-hand hedge with fine views to your right across Lilley Bottom towards Putteridge Bury. At the top of Clouds Hill (now on bridleway OF38), follow the track bearing left to reach a bend in a green lane called Honeysuckle Lane (bridleway OF41).

Clouds Hill - Great Offley (Map 41)

Maps
OS Landranger Sheet 166
OS Explorer Sheet 193

Parking
On-street parking is possible at Great Offley, which is circled by this section of the Chiltern Way Extension and can be reached via various crossing or branching roads and paths.

At the top of Clouds Hill, turn right into Honeysuckle Lane (bridleway OF41) and follow this green lane to cross the A505. On the far side of this dual-carriageway, turn right onto the continuation of bridleway OF41, entering a green lane which bears left and leads you to Luton Road (the old route of the A505) (where the **original Chiltern Way** is a third of a mile to your right) (see Map 37). Turn right onto its footway, then immediately left onto bridleway OF42, following a grassy track beside a left-hand hedge uphill, wiggling left at one point and continuing with more fine views across Lilley Bottom to your right, to reach a road called Luton White Hill, part of an ancient route from Luton via Putteridge Bury to Great Offley and Hitchin.

Cross this road and take path OF11 straight on along a macadam drive, then pass left of a padlocked gate and take a grassy track beside a left-hand hedge straight on through two fields. Near the far side of the second field at a waymarked junction, turn left through a hedge gap onto fenced path OF13, following a left-hand hedge. At the next corner of the field, fork left through the hedge and a kissing-gate and follow a left-hand hedge to the far end of the next field. Here go through a kissing-gate and bear half right to pass just left of a group of small lime trees screening Offley Pumping Station, then, just past the pumping station, turn right then left to join its concrete drive and follow it to gates out onto King's Walden Road, Great Offley opposite the ´Red Lion`.

Great Offley - Preston (Map 41)

Maps
OS Landranger Sheet 166
OS Explorer Sheet 193
(parts only) Chiltern Society FP Map No.29

Parking
On-street parking is possible in various places in Great Offley.

Great Offley, on the old Luton-Hitchin road at the top of the Chiltern escarpment, was once an important stopping point for travellers weary from the steep climb and is still today character-ised by its old coaching inns. Its location also makes it an ideal centre for walking as, not only does Great Offley give access to the escarpment with its steep slopes and spectacular views, but, in addition, it offers walks in the quiet and beautiful Chiltern uplands around Lilley Bottom and King's Walden. It is therefore hardly surprising that two leading twentieth-century walkers, Don Gresswell MBE, for more than 50 years active in walking and path protection groups and founder of the Chiltern Society's Rights of Way Group, and Ron Pigram, well-known author of London Transport walks books, chose to live here.

The village also has a long history; its name (recorded as 'Offanlege` as early as 944A.D.) deriving from King Offa II of Mercia, a warrior king who built Offa's Dyke and expanded his kingdom at the expense of his Saxon neighbours and who is believed to have had a palace here and died here in 796A.D. In the eighteenth century, Offley Place, a late Elizabethan house built by Sir Richard Spencer in 1600 on the site where legend has it that Offa's palace stood, was home to Sir Thomas Salusbury, Judge of the High Court of Admiralty, and was often visited by his niece, Hester Thrale as a child, who later came to prominence as a friend of Dr. Johnson. As well as rebuilding much of Offley Place (except for one wing of the old house which still survives), Sir Thomas rebuilt the chancel of the thirteenth-century parish church with its beautiful fourteenth-century font, eighteenth-century monuments by Sir Robert Taylor and Nollekens and an early nineteenth-century brick tower.

Opposite the 'Red Lion', turn left into King's Walden Road. After 50 yards, turn right through a kissing-gate onto hedged path OF14, passing Great Offley churchyard to your left, then ignoring a branching path to your left and soon entering a field. Here follow the outside edge of a wood called Botany Bay Plantation straight on, then, at the far end of the field, take a fenced track straight on through Aldwick's Plantation to a kissing-gate where a fine view opens out ahead across Hitchin. Now follow the outside edge of the wood straight on downhill. At the far end of the wood, keep straight on across a field corner to a kissing-gate by the right-hand corner of Minsbury Plantation. Go through this, turn left and take a fenced path along the outside edge of the wood. By its far end, bear left through a hedge gap and follow a right-hand hedge straight on, bearing right where the hedge does to reach a bend in a green lane. Turn left into this lane, then, after 400 yards at a T-junction of old lanes, turn right and follow a grassy track beside a right-hand hedge through two fields to reach a green lane called Hoar's Lane (byway H28) at the Hitchin boundary.

Turn right into this lane and follow it downhill for a quarter mile to the crossways with an unmade road called Chalk Hill near Temple End. Here take the continuation of Hoar's Lane, also an unmade public road, straight on through a hedge gap and beside a right-hand hedge, soon entering a green lane. Where its hedges end, take a grassy track straight on, soon entering another section of green lane, then passing a copse to reach a bend in a narrow road.

Here turn right onto bridleway PR6, following a grassy track through a gate into a field where views of Offleyholes Farm soon open out to your left. Where the track bears left through a gate, leave it and follow the left-hand fence straight on to a bridlegate into Pinnaclehill Plantation. Keep straight on through this copse to a gate into another field, then follow the left-hand fence straight on, ignoring a gate and stiles in it and reaching a bridlegate into West Wood. Go straight on through the corner of this wood, climbing steeply into a field. Now take a grassy track along the outside edge of the wood for 350 yards. Having passed an old overgrown gate into the wood, by a marker post where the track bears right, leave it and bear slightly left across the field to a gap in the far hedge. Now take bridleway KW28 straight on through the gap and beside a left-hand hedge to gates and a gap leading to a bend in a green lane (restricted byway KW47), which you follow straight on to the end of the road in the tiny hamlet of Austage End.

Some 25 yards along this road, turn left onto enclosed path KW37, following a right-hand hedge, soon with a fence to your left. On emerging into a field, follow a left-hand hedge, later the edge of a plantation, straight on to a large oak tree. Now bear slightly right across the field to a hedge gap with a marker post midway between trees flanking a green lane (byway KW46). Turn left into this lane, then, after 100 yards at the far end of a long gap in the right-hand hedge by a marker post and a hollybush, turn right onto the continuation of path KW37, climbing a steep bank and crossing a field to a gap in the trees on the skyline left of a group of larger trees, where you reach a track junction. Here ignore the first right-hand track and take the second (byway KW48), entering a wide green lane called Dead Woman's Lane. After 300 yards, just past a left-hand bend and a large oak tree to your right, turn left through a concealed kissing-gate onto path PR5, following a left-hand hedge to a gate and stile. Now keep straight on to the right-hand side of a gap between farm buildings, then bear half right across a field towards a tall fir tree right of a yellow-painted house at Preston to reach a kissing-gate into Butcher's Lane. Turn left onto this narrow road, then, just before a left-hand bend by the end of the right-hand houses, turn right onto enclosed path PR4 leading to Church Meadow, a small millennium green. Follow its left-hand edge straight on to enter another enclosed path between hedges leading to Chequers Lane. Turn right onto this road and follow it to a T-junction where you turn right into Hitchin Road to reach Preston's picturesque village green.

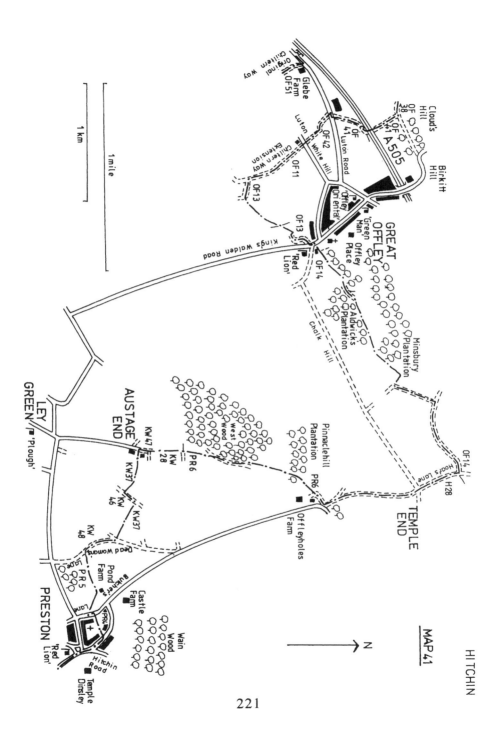

MAP 41

→ N

221

Preston - St. Paul's Walden (Map 42)

Maps

OS Landranger Sheet 166
OS Explorer Sheet 193
Chiltern Society FP Map No.29

Parking

On-street parking is possible in the side roads around Preston village green and elsewhere in the village, but do **not** use the 'Red Lion` car park without the landlord's permission. There is also a small car park off the B651 just west of Langley End.

Preston, with its leafy green with an attractive well and pub, is the epitome of the English village. Like most villages, it has a long history, its manor of 'Deneslai` being listed in the Domesday Book. In 1147, the manor was given to the Knights Templar, an order of warrior-monks, who held it till their suppression in 1312, and thus it became known as Temple Dinsley. Subsequently the manor was held by another monastic order called the Knights Hospitaller before it fell to the Crown in the Reformation. The present house called Temple Dinsley, built in 1714 and greatly enlarged by Sir Edwin Lutyens in 1908, is now a private girls' school called the Princess Helena College, but the fact that it is on the site of the ancient monastery was proved in 1902 when a thirteenth-century stone coffin lid bearing the emblem of the Knights Templar was unearthed in the gardens and this is now preserved in the parish church built in 1900. The vicinity of Preston, however, also has other religious associations as nearby Wain Wood was the scene of secret midnight services with massive congregations held by the Puritan writer and preacher John Bunyan, author of 'Pilgrim's Progress`, while Castle Farm stands on the site of Hunsdon House, whose non-conformist occupants also suffered seventeenth-century religious persecution. This same house was converted in the 1760s to resemble a castle (hence the name of the farm) by Captain Robert Hinde, an eccentric retired army officer, whom the contemporary author, Laurence Sterne took as the model for his Uncle Toby in his 'Tristram Shandy`.

At the village green, take School Lane straight on past the 'Red Lion' towards St. Paul's Walden and Whitwell and follow it for half a mile, passing the gates of Temple Dinsley to reach a T-junction with a road called St. Alban's Highway. Here turn left towards Gosmore and Hitchin, then, after about 70 yards, turn right through a hedge gap onto path PR2, following this fenced path past an underground reservoir. On emerging into a field, follow a right-hand hedge straight on, turning left at a corner of the field and continuing until you reach a gap in the hedge. Here transfer to the other side of the hedge and take path LA1, still following the hedge to Poynders End Farm with its fine wooden barns and timber-framed farmhouse. Go straight on past the farm, then take a grassy track beside a left-hand hedge. Where the hedge turns left, follow the grassy track straight on with wide views across the valley towards Hitchin to your left and Stevenage beyond the next rise. Eventually the track joins a right-hand hedge, which you follow to the B656 at Chapelfoot.

Turn right onto this road and follow it past the 'Royal Oak', part of which dates from the seventeenth century. At the far end of the pub garden, before reaching a black wooden barn, turn right onto bridleway LA2, joining the Hertfordshire Way, passing the end of the pub and turning left by a large chestnut tree into a fenced path. On emerging into a field, follow the left-hand hedge straight on, gently climbing. Where the hedge ends, bear slightly left, heading just left of the ruins of Minsden Chapel to reach the corner of Minsden Chapel Plantation near the chapel ruins.

Built in the fourteenth century, Minsden Chapel was a chapel-of-ease of Hitchin parish serving the lost hamlet of 'Minlesden' referred to in the Domesday Book. By 1650 the hamlet would seem to have disappeared as the chapel was already reported to be in a decayed state and during the last recorded service at the chapel, the wedding of Enoch West and Mary Horn in 1738, the curate is believed to have narrowly missed being struck by falling masonry. In the early twentieth century, the noted local historian, Reginald Hine, who was fascinated by these allegedly haunted ruins, leased them from the Church of England and was subsequently buried here in 1949.

Now follow the outside edge of the wood straight on downhill. At its far end, bear slightly left across the field, then right to follow the field side of a roadside hedge to a hedge gap leading to the B651. Turn right onto this road, then fork immediately left onto bridleway LA17, climbing gently through hillside scrubland. At a T-junction of tracks, bear left, climbing more steeply to reach the end of a macadam road by Hill End Farm at Langley End.

Take this road straight on, then, at a left-hand bend, fork right onto path LA16, passing through a copse to cross a stile. Now, with views towards Stevenage to your left, take a track beside a right-hand hedge straight on. At the far end of the field, bear right between hedges, then, where the track bears left into another field, fork right into a narrow green lane. Now follow its winding course, eventually entering a copse where you keep right at a fork and continue to Langley Lane. Turn left onto this narrow road, then immediately right onto path LA3, leaving the wood and heading for the right-hand end of a coniferous plantation to pass through a fence gap. Now go straight on, at first skirting the conifers, then continuing ahead to join a track straight on through a copse called Hitch Spring to reach the B651, onto which you turn left, passing the lodge gates of Stagenhoe Park surmounted by a stag and wrought-ironwork.

Mentioned in the Domesday Book, Stagenhoe Park's present house was built in 1737 and is now a Sue Ryder Home. In the 1880s it was occupied by Sir Arthur Sullivan, who composed ˝The Mikado˝ here and outraged local people by his life-style.

On rounding a left-hand bend, turn right through a hedge gap onto path PW7, bearing left along the left-hand edge of the field. On nearing a cottage, bear slightly left into a path between a hedge and a fence leading to a narrow road at St. Paul's Walden.

St. Paul's Walden - Whitwell (Map 42)

Maps
OS Landranger Sheet 166
OS Explorer Sheet 193
Chiltern Society FP Map No.29

Parking
There is a small car park by the southern entrance to St. Paul's Walden churchyard, but avoid parking here during church services.

St. Paul's Walden, set in hillside parkland above the Mimram valley in the far north-east corner of the Chilterns, is probably best known for its disputed claim to have been the birthplace in 1900 of the late Queen Mother, daughter of the Earl and Countess of Strathmore, whose family, the Bowes-Lyons (formerly Bowes), have owned St. Paul's Waldenbury for more than 200 years. The present house, which can be seen from path PW3, was built in 1767 and considerably extended in 1887. The parish church, where the Queen Mother was christened and which she attended as a child,

MAP 42

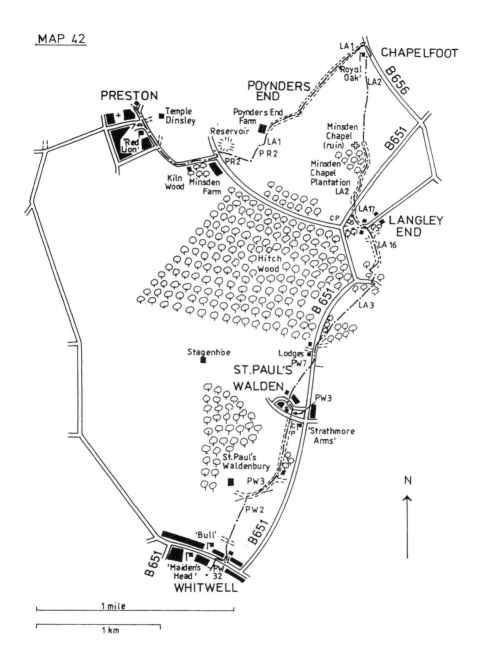

dates from the fourteenth century and has a chancel rebuilt by Edward Gilbert in 1727. When this church was built, however, the village had another name as it was then called Abbot's Walden because the manor belonged to St. Alban's Abbey, but during the Reformation the manor passed to St. Paul's Cathedral and so was renamed St. Paul's Walden in 1544. The royal wedding in 1923 did not, however, create the village's first royal connection as there is a memorial in the church to Henry Stapleford, who died in 1631 at the age of 76 having acted as a servant to three very different monarchs, Elizabeth I, James I and Charles I.

Turn left into St. Paul's Walden village street, passing the White House, then, at a left-hand bend, fork right onto path PW3, passing through the churchyard to reach gates onto another road. Now cross this road and take a fenced track (still path PW3) straight on, descending gently for a quarter mile through old parkland. By a cottage called The Garden House, take a macadam drive straight on, ignoring a branching drive to the left and continuing uphill to cross an avenue of trees where you can obtain a view of St. Paul's Waldenbury to your right. Now ignore a kissing-gate to your left and on rounding a right-hand bend, fork left through a kissing-gate by a field gate, then fork left again onto fenced path PW2, which later starts to descend with views of Whitwell in the Mimram valley opening out ahead and reaches a crossing farm road. Here keep straight on to a gate and kissing-gate leading to a footbridge over the River Mimram (until recent years often given the alternative name of Maran). Cross this bridge and bear slightly left across a field to a gate and kissing-gate, then follow a rough drive bearing right to reach the B651, Whitwell High Street.

Whitwell - Peter's Green (Map 43)

Maps
OS Landranger Sheet 166
OS Explorer Sheets 182 & 193
(part only) Chiltern Society FP Map No.29

Parking
On-street parking is available in the modern residential side-streets of Whitwell and there is a car park off Bradway near the recreation ground.

Whitwell, locally pronounced 'Whi'll', in the picturesque Mimram valley has long been famous for its watercress and was, at one time, also a centre of straw plaiting for the Luton hat-making industry. Though always a hamlet of St. Paul's Walden parish without its own church, Whitwell appears both to be an ancient settlement and to have long been larger than the mother village as the vicinity of its narrow High Street can boast a fascinating collection of half-timbered cottages and inns, dating back in at least the case of the 'Bull' to the sixteenth century, as well as some fine Georgian houses. This suggests that practical and economic factors such as a convenient water supply and its location on an ancient valley bottom road from Hatfield towards Bedford and not just a displacement of population to create the park at St. Paul's Waldenbury may be the reason for its size.

Turn right onto the B651 (Whitwell High Street), then, after 90 yards, turn left onto path PW32, following a grassy sunken way, which soon becomes enclosed between hedges and fences, uphill, ignoring a branching path to your right and eventually emerging into a field. Here, leaving the Hertfordshire Way, turn right onto bridleway PW34, following the right-hand hedge and later ignoring a crossing path and reaching a corner of the field. Now keep straight on along a green lane to reach the car park off Bradway. At its far side, turn left onto enclosed macadam path PW28, soon passing a recreation ground to your left and the end of a residential cul-de-sac to your right. At the far end of the recreation ground, the path becomes enclosed by hedges and bears right then left to meet a road called Hill View, onto which you turn right to reach the B651, Horn Hill.

Turn left onto this road, leaving Whitwell, soon with fine views to your right up Lilley Bottom. Just past a water tower, at a sharp left-hand bend, leave the B651 and take Long Lane, the left-hand of two green lanes, bearing slightly right. Now follow this unmade public road for one mile, enclosed by hedges at first, then passing a wood called Rose Grove to your left before becoming open and continuing, ignoring all branching or crossing tracks or paths, finally keeping left at a fork to enter a sunken lane. On reemerging into a field, go straight on, keeping right of the hedge ahead and following it then a line of trees along the valley bottom to a gap in a transverse hedge. Now bear slightly left and take a grassy track downhill and up again to a hedge gap leading to Whitewaybottom Lane.

Cross this road and take path KM54 straight on through a gap by a gate opposite, then gently uphill beside a right-hand hedge. At the far end of the field turn left and follow the right-hand hedge uphill. At the top of the hill, where the hedge bears left, turn right through a hedge gap and bear right across the next field, with views towards Breachwood Green over your right shoulder, to reach a gap in the far hedge leading to a narrow road.

Turn left onto this road, then, after nearly 300 yards, at a slight left-hand bend by the far side of a copse called Long Tom's Spring, turn right through a gap by a gate and take path KM43, following the right-hand side of a hedge with views towards Peter's Green on the ridgetop ahead. On reaching a scrubby copse called Bilmore Dell, bear half left and follow its outside edge downhill into a valley bottom. Here turn right onto bridleway KM51, taking a grassy track beside the nearside of the bottom hedge for over half a mile, ignoring a branching path to your left and later climbing towards Peter's Green. At the far end of the field, turn right onto path KM45, following a left-hand hedge to a field corner, then go through a hedge gap and bear slightly left, following a left-hand fence or hedge for 250 yards. On reaching a powerline, bear left into a field corner, then turn left along fenced path KM44 between gardens to reach Kimpton Road at Peter's Green opposite the ʹBright Starʹ.

Turn right onto this road and follow it across the green, ignoring turnings to your left and then passing a triangular grass traffic island to your right and rejoining the **original Chiltern Way**.

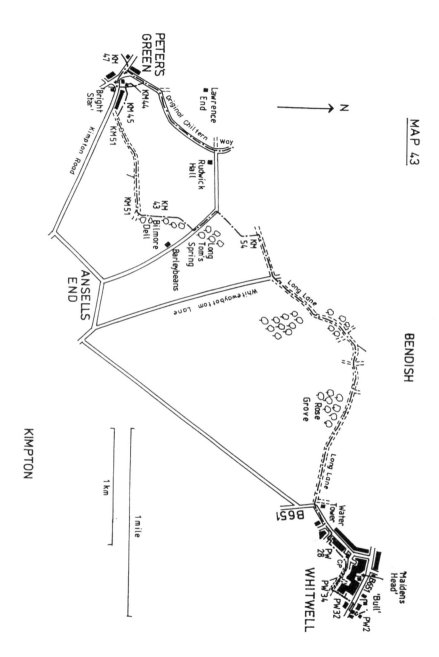

MAP 43

PETERS GREEN

KM 47

Bright Star'

KM 44

KM 45

KM 51

Kimpton Road

Lawrence End

original Chiltern Way

Rudwick Hall

KM 43

Bilmore Dell

Long Tom's Spring

Barleybeans

KM 51

KM 54

ANSELLS END

Whitewaybottom Lane

Long Lane

BENDISH

Rose Grove

Long Lane

Water Tower

B651

Pw 28

CP

WHITWELL

'Bull'

B651

PW 34

PW 32

PW 2

'Maidens Head'

KIMPTON

1 km

1 mile

N

229

Peter's Green - East Hyde (Map 44)

Maps
OS Landranger Sheet 166
OS Explorer Sheet 182

Parking
On-street parking is possible at Peter's Green.

Peter's Green is a typical remote North Hertfordshire hamlet with a picturesque green flanked by a pub and cottages reached by a network of tortuous narrow lanes. Such settlements would seem to have been established through unauthorised encroachment on remote commons near parish boundaries by country people displaced from their home villages by landowners trying to minimise the financial effects of the Poor Law if empty houses attracted an increased population. In this, Peter's Green is typical, being more than two miles from the mother village of Kimpton and on both the county boundary with Bedfordshire and the parish boundary with King's Walden.

After 30 yards, the **reunited Chiltern Way** forks left through a hedge gap onto path KM47, following a grassy track across a field towards a tall ash tree at the southern tip of Chiltern Green, an even smaller hamlet similar to Peter's Green on the Bedfordshire side of the boundary. Reentering Bedfordshire, bear slightly right across the green, then cross a gravel track and a stile and take path HY9, following a left-hand fence to cross another stile, then continuing to a third. Now follow the left side of a field boundary straight on for two-thirds of a mile with views of Luton Hoo to your right and The Hyde to your left opening out at the top of a rise.

    Luton Hoo, in its extensive park laid out by Capability Brown, was originally designed in 1767 by Robert Adam for the third Earl of Bute, George III's first prime minister and a keen botanist, who was instrumental in the establishment of Kew Gardens. Following two extensive fires, however, it had to be remodelled in 1903, while an earlier house on the same site is said to have been the birthplace in 1507 of Anne Boleyn, one of the six ill-fated queens of Henry VIII. The Hyde, though less pretentious in scale, is also of Georgian origin.

    On reaching a large clump of trees to your left, go past its right-hand end to reach a junction of tracks, then turn left onto path HY7, following a grassy track past the back of the clump. After 300 yards,

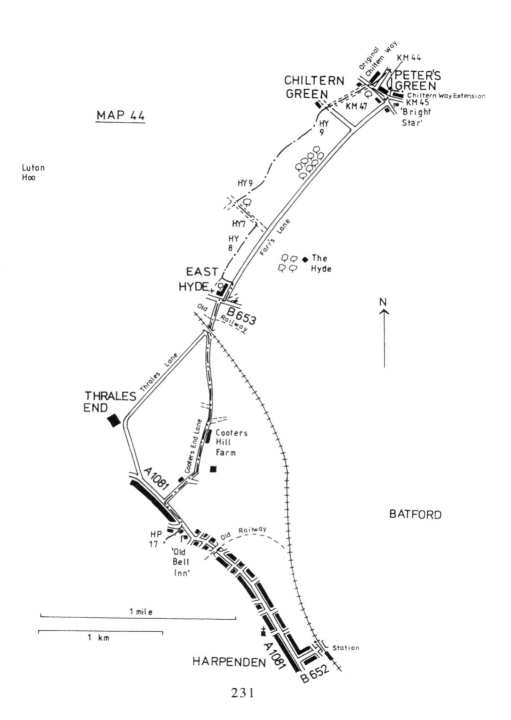

MAP 44

Luton
Hoo

CHILTERN
GREEN

PETER'S
GREEN

Original
Chiltern Way

KM 44

KM 47

Chiltern Way Extension
KM 45
'Bright
Star'

HY
9

HY 9

HY 7

HY
8

Farr's Lane

The
Hyde

EAST
HYDE

B 653

Old Railway

THRALES
END

Thrales Lane

Cooters End Lane

Cooters
Hill
Farm

A 1081

BATFORD

HP
17

'Old
Bell
Inn'

Old Railway

Station

N

1 mile

1 km

HARPENDEN

A 1081

B 652

231

turn right onto path HY8, following a grassy track downhill towards the turret of East Hyde's red-brick Italianate church in the Lea valley, built by Ferrey in 1841, eventually reaching a hedge at the edge of the village by a tall oak tree. Here turn left and follow the hedge to Farr's Lane, then turn right down it to reach a staggered crossroads with the B653.

East Hyde - Harpenden (Map 44)

Maps
OS Landranger Sheet 166
OS Explorer Sheet 182

Parking
Limited on-street parking is available at East Hyde.

The village of East Hyde, extending along the B653 in the Lea valley, barely existed in the early nineteenth century, but the coming of the railways with no fewer than two railway stations would seem to have led to its expansion. First the Great Northern Railway built a branch line from Welwyn Garden City up the Lea valley to Luton and Dunstable in 1860 with a station at East Hyde known as Luton Hoo and then, in 1868, the Midland Railway built their St. Pancras - Bedford main line, nicknamed the 'Bed-Pan Line' with a station at East Hyde known as Chiltern Green. While the old GNR branch line with Luton Hoo Station was closed by Dr. Beeching in 1962, the Midland Railway station had already been closed and so all that now remains is one main line with no station, but much of the old branch line has since become part of the Lea Valley Walk.

Turn right onto the B653, then left into Thrales End Lane, crossing a bridge over the River Lea and the old GNR line (now part of the Lea Valley Walk), then passing under a railway bridge carrying the St. Pancras main line. Now turn left into Cooters End Lane and, back in Hertfordshire, follow this quiet single-track road for a mile, at first climbing with views to your left towards Batford, then passing Cooters Hill Farm and descending, ignoring a turning to your left and eventually reaching the A1081 (formerly part of the A6 London-Manchester main road) on the edge of Harpenden.

Harpenden - Flamstead (Map 45)

Maps
OS Landranger Sheet 166
OS Explorer Sheet 182
(part only) Chiltern Society FP Map No.27

Parking
On-street parking is available in Harpenden.

Harpenden, whose name is said to mean `valley of the nightin-gales`, is today a small Hertfordshire town with some 30,000 inhabitants, but local people still refer to it as `the village`. This is, indeed, indicative of the fact that, 100 years ago, it still was a small village, which, till 1859, had been merely a hamlet of nearby Wheathampstead parish, but the coming of the railways - first the Great Northern Railway Dunstable branch in 1860 with a station at nearby Batford and then the Midland Railway main line in 1868 with a station near the village centre and its branch to Hemel Hempstead, known as the `Nicky Line` - brought Harpenden within easy reach of London and so, by 1900, well-to-do commuters were starting to colonise the village. The preservation of its large common, which extends into its centre, has, however, enabled the retention of its rural atmosphere, which belies the spread of suburban villas in all directions.

Turn left onto the A1081, which is said to be of Roman origin (where Harpenden Station can be reached by continuing for 1 mile and then turning left onto the B652). After 250 yards, just before the `Old Bell Inn`, turn right into Roundwood Lane, immediately forking left onto path HP17, following a macadam path past a small factory, then continuing along a fenced path to a recreation ground. Bear half right across this to its far corner to enter a fenced path between allotments, which you follow gently uphill, crossing two roads, passing the end of a third and crossing a fourth. Now ignore the entrances to a school and its playing fields and continue until you emerge into the corner of a field. Here follow a left-hand hedge straight on, soon bearing left and later entering a short green lane. Now on path HR11, by the corner of a right-hand hedge, bear half left and follow a left-hand hedge to a gap leading to the former Midland Railway Hemel Hempstead Branch. Known as the `Nicky Line`, it was closed to passenger traffic in 1947, but remained in use for goods trains till the 1970s and has now become a foot and cycle path from Harpenden to Hemel Hempstead.

Turn right onto the old railway, where several sleepers have been retained in its surface to show its origin, passing between safety barriers and continuing for over a quarter mile. At the end of a short macadamed section by a seat, turn right onto a crossing path, rejoining path HR11, passing through a hedge gap and following the edge of a wood to a squeeze-stile leading onto a golf course. Now bear left and follow the edge of the wood along the edge of the golf course until a marker post directs you to enter the wood. Take the obvious path through it, eventually emerging through a kissing-gate into a field. Here turn right and pass through an outcrop of scrub, then follow a right-hand fence and sporadic hedge, ignoring a stile in the fence provided for golfers to retrieve lost balls. Eventually you pass through another kissing-gate and bear left to reach a kissing-gate into a fenced lane (bridleway HR1). Take this straight on downhill past Harpenden Bury Farm, then, at a junction of tracks, turn right onto a wide gravel track, soon crossing the golf course and passing cottages and later stables to your right to reach Kinsbourne Green Lane.

Cross this road and take path HR16 straight on through a hedge gap opposite, bearing slightly right across a large field to a prominent hedge gap in its far left-hand corner. Here go straight on, keeping left of a hedge and following it until it bears right, then go straight on across the field, heading for a house at Verlam End ahead to cross a stile in a post-and-rail fence. Now on path HR18, bear slightly left across a paddock to pass through three gates, crossing the drive to Verlam End, then turn left onto a track crossing a bridge over the River Ver.

The name Verlam End is interesting as it recalls the old name 'Verlamstead', of which Flamstead is a corruption and although the River Ver now forms the boundary here between Harpenden Rural and Redbourn parishes, it suggests that Flamstead parish must once have extended to this point.

Now turn right onto path RB6, heading for the right-hand end of Whitehill Wood on the hillock ahead, to reach a small gate leading to the A5183 (formerly the A5, following the course of the Roman road from Dover, via London, St. Alban's and Dunstable to Holyhead known as Watling Street) near Junction 9 of the M1. Turn right onto its footway and at a roundabout, cross the sliproads of the M1 and take the A5 footway straight on under the motorway bridge. At a second roundabout, cross the Kinsbourne Green road, then follow the road side of the crash-barrier until you have sufficient visibility to cross the A5 dual-carriageway. Now bear left to reach a concrete field entrance leading off the roundabout, where you turn right through a

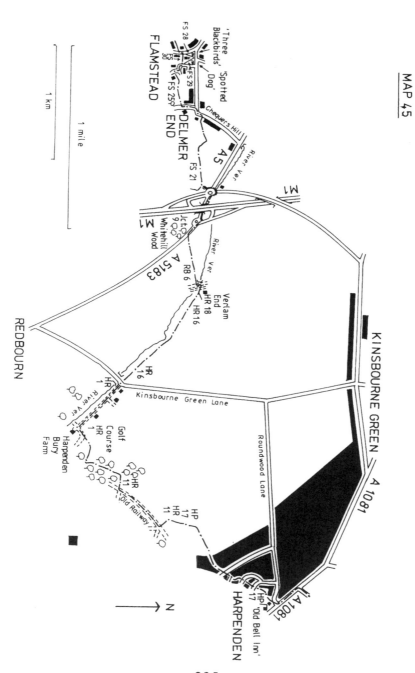

MAP 45

gap by gates and take path FS21, bearing half right up a field to the corner of a hedge on the hillside. (NB At the time of writing, this field is being used as a construction depot for work to widen the M1, but presumably it will eventually be restored to agriculture. In the meantime it may be necessary to take a slight detour). At the hedge corner, turn right and follow the hedge to a field corner, where you bear left into a path between the hedge and a fence, later between hedges, to reach a gate onto a road called Chequers Hill at Delmer End.

Turn left onto its footway, going round a right-hand bend, then, at a road junction, turn left into Delmerend Lane. Having rounded a left-hand bend, turn right onto path FS25, taking a short green lane to a squeeze-stile into a field, then follow the right-hand hedge straight on to a kissing-gate into an alleyway leading to a road in Flamstead called Pie Garden. Turn right onto this road and follow it round left- and right-hand bends, then turn left through a kissing-gate into Flamstead churchyard.

Flamstead - Gaddesden Row (Map 46)

Maps
OS Landranger Sheet 166
OS Explorer Sheet 182
Chiltern Society FP Maps Nos. 20 & 27

Parking
Limited on-street parking is available in Flamstead.

Flamstead, a corruption of 'Verlamstead', on its hilltop above the Ver valley, has an attractive village centre with half-timbered and flint cottages and a row of almshouses dating from 1669, but is dominated, when seen from afar, by its magnificent twelfth-century church with a massive tower incorporating Roman bricks and a small mediæval spire known as a 'Hertfordshire spike'. The church also boasts some of the finest mediæval murals in Hertfordshire, which were only rediscovered in about 1930, as well as exquisite seventeenth- and eighteenth-century marble monuments by Stanton and Flaxman and is the burial place of the founder of the renowned transport firm, Thomas Pickford, who died in 1811. Despite being less than a mile from both the M1 and the A5, Flamstead has remained a remarkably quiet, rural village and, with its open, hilly surroundings, offers a selection of pleasant walks with fine views.

In the churchyard, if wishing to visit one of the pubs or the attractive village centre, fork right onto path FS29, passing right of the church. Otherwise, take path FS30, the left-hand of the three paths through the churchyard, straight on to gates and a kissing-gate leading to Trowley Hill Road. Turn left onto this road, then immediately right onto path FS32, a fenced alleyway leading you out past a housing estate into a field. Now go straight on across the field, passing an electricity pole and then heading for a hedge gap left of an ash tree in tall bushes ahead. Go through this gap and turn left onto a narrow road called Pietley Hill. At a left-hand bend, turn right through a hedge gap onto path FS37 downhill to pass through a fence gap at the bottom, then bear slightly right uphill to reach the top hedge, where you turn right and follow the near side of the hedge to a gap in a field corner leading to Wood End Lane where there is a fine view behind you back across the valley to Flamstead.

Go through this gap, then turn right into Wood End Lane. Just after Scratch Wood begins to your left, turn right through a gap by a gate and take path FS45, bearing slightly left across a field to the near corner of a wood called Yewtree Spring. Here keep right of the wood and follow its outside edge to a waymarked fenced gap leading into it. Turn left through this and take the waymarked path through the wood, which is carpeted with bluebells in April and May, to reach a fence gap at the far corner into a field. Here bear slightly right across the field, with views ahead across these remote hills towards the distant Bedfordshire village of Studham, to the corner of a hedge. Now bear left and follow it to cross a stile in it, then follow the other side of the hedge. On nearing Little Woodend Cottages, where the left-hand fence diverges from the hedge, cross a stile in the fence and keep left of a shed to join a drive by the cottages. Take this drive straight on to reach Puddephat's Lane.

Turn left onto this road and follow it through Newland's Wood. Just after a slight left-hand bend, where the right-hand wood ends, turn right over a stile by a gate onto path FS46, following a left-hand fence to a kissing-gate into a field, then bearing slightly left across the field, passing the corner of a copse called Abel's Grove to reach a gate and kissing-gate in the far corner of the field. Go through this and turn left into a green lane. Where the lane forks, bear half right, taking path GG28 along its continuation, eventually passing a school to your right to reach a road at Gaddesden Row.

Gaddesden Row - Gaddesden Place (Map 46)

Maps
OS Landranger Sheet 166
OS Explorer Sheet 182
Chiltern Society FP Map No.20

Parking
There is a small car park at the end of path GG28 opposite Gaddesden Row School.

Gaddesden Row is an unusual settlement, largely comprising a series of isolated farms and cottages ranged along a two-mile-long ridgetop road with the hamlet of Jockey End at its northwest end. Despite its scattered nature, Gaddesden Row would, however, seem to have been populated since the Stone Age, as Stone Age flints, tools and weapons have been found here.

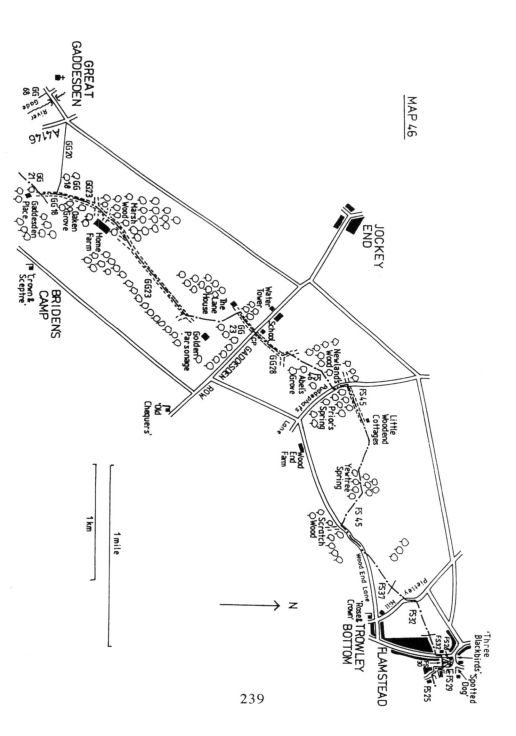

MAP 46

GREAT GADDESDEN

JOCKEY END

BRIDEN'S CAMP

FLAMSTEAD

TROWLEY BOTTOM

1 km

1 mile

N

239

By the school, cross the road and take path GG23 straight on along the drive to The Lane House. On reaching a gate and kissing-gate, turn left and follow a right-hand hedge to a field corner, where you turn right through a hedge gap and go through a kissing-gate to enter a parkland field with a view ahead of the Golden Parsonage, the original home of the Halseys, who have held land in Great Gaddesden since 1512, of which only a wing built in 1705 remains. Now bear half right across two fields, later with fine views of the Golden Parsonage to your left, to reach a gap in the far hedge at a junction of farm tracks. Here bear half right onto a track, following a right-hand hedge at first, then continuing between a fence and a belt of trees to reach a corner of Marsh Wood.

Now fork right onto a track into the wood and follow it straight on, ignoring a branching track to your right, passing Home Farm to your left and then disregarding a crossing track, to reach a gate into a field. Here take a rough track straight on, passing left of a dying oak tree, then continuing with views to your right across the Gade valley. Soon on path GG18, cross a stile left of a gate in a slight dip and follow a right-hand fence uphill until you reach a small gate in the fence. Turn right through this onto path GG21, bearing half left and passing just left of a cattle trough to reach a gate in the next fence. Now bear slightly right, aiming for a cream cottage with a gable at Water End in the Gade valley when this comes into view, with Gaddesden Place emerging from the trees to your left. Eventually you cross a stile in the left-hand fence near the bottom left-hand corner of the field with superb views across the picturesque hamlet of Water End with its seventeenth-century brick-and-timber cottages below you and towards Great Gaddesden with its prominent church to your right.

Gaddesden Place - Potten End (Map 47)

Maps
OS Landranger Sheet 166
OS Explorer Sheet 182
Chiltern Society FP Map No.20

Parking
Limited on-street parking is available in Great Gaddesden village.

Great Gaddesden, which, like so many ´great` villages, is smaller than its ´little` namesake, is set in an idyllic location in the Gade valley, but the picturesque cluster of church, farm, school and cottages is marred by an insensitive council house development tacked onto it. In the past, Great Gaddesden was very much the estate village of the Halseys, who have lived here since 1512, still have a large estate here and continue to live at Gaddesden Place. This Palladian mansion was built for the Halseys between 1768 and 1773 by James Wyatt, designer of Ashridge, to replace their previous house, the Golden Parsonage, of which only a wing from 1705 remains, while the church contains the eighteenth-century Halsey Chapel with over twenty monuments to family members including examples of the work of Rysbrack and Flaxman. The twelfth-century church is also noted for the use of Roman bricks from a nearby villa in its construction and its massive fifteenth-century tower with some fearsome gargoyles.

Having crossed the stile, continue downhill on path GG21, crossing another stile and bearing slightly left to reach the near left-hand corner of the cream cottage at Water End. Now follow its fence to a stile and gate onto the A4146. Cross this with great care (beware of the blind bend to your left!), then turn right onto its footway. After 10 yards, turn left onto path GG66 down an alleyway to a kissing-gate into a riverside meadow. Here bear half right, following a right-hand fence at first to a footbridge over the Gade, then turn left over another footbridge and a stile by an electricity pole. Now, bear slightly right, heading for a hawthorn bush on a rise, where you join a right-hand fence and follow it, ignoring a stile in it and eventually crossing a stile by a gate to reach gates onto Nettleden Road.

Turn right onto this, then, after 90 yards, turn left through a kissing-gate onto path GG63 straight uphill, passing left of a large treestump to enter Heizdin's Wood. Here turn round for a fine view back across Water End towards Gaddesden Place, then, in the wood, take a wide terraced track, bearing half right, climbing gently and ignoring a crossing path. On leaving the wood, turn right through a hedge gap and head for the left-hand of two oak trees. Now bear half left, with fine views to your right across Nettleden in its peaceful valley towards Ashridge on the skyline, to reach the near end of a hedge. Here turn left onto path GG62 along the near side of the hedge to a kissing-gate in a field corner leading to a bend in a track. Bear right then left onto this track and follow it along a lane to a road called Potten End Hill on the edge of Potten End.

Potten End - Hemel Hempstead Station (Map 47)

Maps
OS Landranger Sheet 166
OS Explorer Sheet 182
Chiltern Society FP Maps Nos. 5 & 20

Parking
Limited on-street parking is available in Potten End village, some distance from the Way and on-street parking is also possible in the suburbs of Hemel Hempstead.

Potten End, with its picturesque green surrounded by its church, a pub, the village hall and cottages, would seem the epitome of the English village, but a brief glance at a map of 1834 reveals that, in contrast to most villages which were established in Saxon times, Potten End then comprised little more than a few scattered cottages on the edge of Berkhamsted Common. Indeed, its church is Victorian and most of its houses and cottages are of even later origin and so it is really a suburban settlement which grew up when the coming of the railways and later the motor car provided easy access to London. Its name, which is shown on the 1834 map and is often the butt of jokes and the subject of speculation, probably arises from the presence of hilltop clay, which may have been used for pottery.

Turn right onto this road, then, at a right-hand bend, turn left through a bridlegate onto narrow fenced path GG59 and continue to a stile into a field. Now follow the right-hand fence straight on, passing a tall oak tree, then continuing between the fence and a left-hand hedge to a stile in the valley bottom. Here turn left onto path HH17, following a fenced cattle track, soon turning right over a stile by a gate and

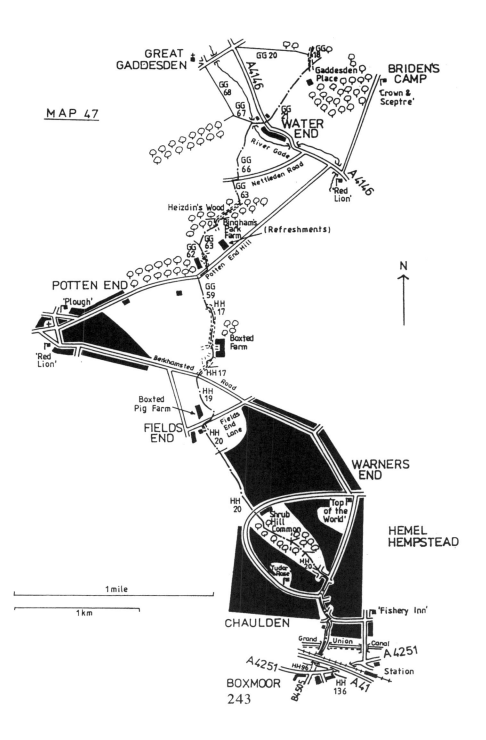

MAP 47

GREAT GADDESDEN

GG 20

GG 18

Gaddesden Place

BRIDEN'S CAMP

'Crown & Sceptre'

A4146

GG 68

GG 67

GG

WATER END

River Gade

GG 66

Nettleden Road

GG 63

'Red Lion'

A4146

Heizdin's Wood

Bingham's Park Farm

(Refreshments)

GG 62

GG 63

Potten End Hill

GG 59

POTTEN END

'Plough'

HH 17

Boxted Farm

'Red Lion'

Berkhamsted

HH 17

Road

Boxted Pig Farm

HH 19

FIELDS END

Fields End Lane

HH 20

WARNERS END

HH 20

'Top of the World'

Shrub Hill Common

HEMEL HEMPSTEAD

Tudor Rose

HH 20

N

1 mile

1 km

CHAULDEN

'Fishery Inn'

Grand Union Canal

A4251

Station

A4251

HH 96

A4251

A41

BOXMOOR

B4505

HH 136

243

taking the track uphill to gates near Boxted Farm. Now follow a left-hand fence straight on, crossing two fenced drives, then bear right and follow the left-hand fence to another stile. Here turn left onto a drive, immediately bearing right and following it to Berkhamsted Road, then take path HH19 through a kissing-gate by a gate opposite and bear half left across a field to a corner of a fence left of Boxted Pig Farm. Now follow this fence straight on to cross a stile into an area of scrub, through which you keep straight on. Under a powerline, bear right between hedges to reach a squeeze-stile leading to Fields End Lane at Fields End.

Turn right onto this road. After 100 yards, just before a pair of cottages to your left, turn left onto path HH20, following a macadam drive at first. then continuing between hedges for over half a mile, ignoring all hedge gaps and branching or crossing paths, soon skirting Hemel Hempstead and eventually reaching a crossing road called Long Chaulden. Cross this, bearing slightly right and continue on path HH20, passing between safety barriers, then lined by hedges, soon entering woodland on Shrub Hill Common. After a quarter mile at a major crossways in a clearing with a rough meadow to your left and a mown recreation ground to your right, bear half right onto the second crossing path (still HH20), following the inside edge of the wood. On eventually emerging onto the recreation ground, keep straight on, passing left of a children's playground, then bear slightly right to reach a road junction.

Here join the major road (Jocketts Road) and follow it uphill to a mini-roundabout. Now turn right and take Northridge Way downhill, going straight on at the first mini-roundabout, then turning right at the second into Chaulden Lane, immediately forking left into Old Fishery Lane. Take this quiet cul-de-sac downhill, crossing a bridge over the picturesque Grand Union Canal. At the end of the road, go straight on through gates and under the West Coast main line and A41. At the far end of the tunnel. go through gates, then turn left through a kissing-gate onto path HH96. following a left-hand fence to a kissing-gate onto the A4251. Turn left onto its footway, then, **if wishing to continue southwards on the Chiltern Way**, just before a series of bridges, cross the A4251 and take fenced path HH136 leading off the end of a short cul-de-sac opposite. Now turn back to p.25 for the continuation. **Otherwise, for Hemel Hempstead Station**, continue under the bridges to a roundabout, then turn right for the station.

INDEX OF PLACE NAMES

245

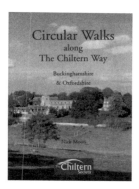
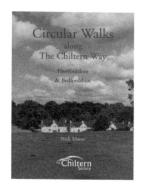

CIRCULAR WALKS ALONG
THE CHILTERN WAY

Volume One Buckinghamshire and Oxfordshire
Volume Two Hertfordshire and Bedfordshire

Nick Moon

A two volume series with special maps provided for each walk. The walks range from 4.3 to 8.5 miles which makes for a comfortable half day or a leisurely full day walk. In addition, details of several possible combinations of walks of up to 22 miles are provided for those who would like a longer, more challenging walk.

Each walk gives details of nearby places of interest and is accompanied by a specially drawn map of the route which also indicates local pubs and a skeleton road network.

Book Castle
PUBLISHING

CHILTERN WALKS
Hertfordshire, Bedfordshire and North Buckinghamshire

CHILTERN WALKS
Buckinghamshire

CHILTERN WALKS
Oxfordshire and West Buckinghamshire

Nick Moon

A series of three books providing a comprehensive coverage of walks throughout the whole of the Chiltern area (as defined by the Chiltern Society). The walks included vary in length from 3.0 to 10.9 miles, but are mainly in the 5-7 mile range popular for half-day walks, although suggestions of possible combinations of walks are given for those preferring a full day's walk.

Each walk gives details of nearby places of interest and is accompanied by a specially drawn map of the route which also indicates local pubs and a skeleton road network.

Book Castle
PUBLISHING

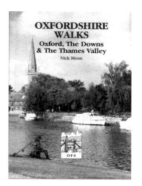

OXFORDSHIRE WALKS VOLUME 1
Oxford, The Cotswolds & The Cherwell Valley

OXFORDSHIRE WALKS VOLUME 2
Oxford, The Downs & The Thames Valley

Nick Moon

Two titles each containing thirty circular walks. The two titles together provide comprehensive coverage of walks throughout the whole of Oxfordshire (except the Chiltern part already covered in "Chiltern Walks: Oxfordshire and West Buckinghamshire" by the same author). The walks vary in length from 3.3 to 12.0 miles, but the majority are in, or have options in, the 5 to 7 miles range, popular for half-day walks, although suggestions of possible combinations of walks are given for those preferring a full day's walk.

Each walk gives details of nearby places of interest and is accompanied by a specially drawn map of the route, which also indicates local pubs and a skeleton road network.

Book Castle PUBLISHING

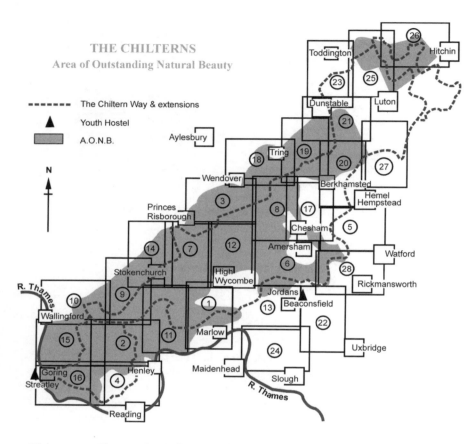

THE CHILTERNS
Area of Outstanding Natural Beauty

- - - - - - - The Chiltern Way & extensions

▲ Youth Hostel

A.O.N.B.

This expanding series of currently 28 maps at a scale of 2½ inches to the mile depicts footpaths, bridleways and other routes available to walkers, riders and cyclists across the Chilterns, as well as pubs, railway stations, car parking facilities and other features of interest. Several suggested walks also appear on the back of each map. New titles appear regularly and will extend coverage of the area.

Book
Castle
PUBLISHING

COMPLETE LIST OF CHILTERN SOCIETY FOOTPATH MAPS

1. High Wycombe & Marlow
2. Henley & Nettlebed
3. Wendover & Princes Risborough
4. Henley and Caversham
5. Bovingdon and Abbot's Langley
6. Amersham & Penn Country
7. West Wycombe & Princes Risborough
8. Chartridge & Cholesbury
9. The Oxfordshire Escarpment

10. Wallingford & Watlington
11. The Hambleden Valley
12. Hughenden Valley & Gt. Missenden
13. Beaconsfield & District
14. Stokenchurch & Chinnor
15. Crowmarsh & Nuffield
16. Goring & Mapledurham
17. Chesham & Berkhamsted
18. Tring & Wendover
19. Ivinghoe & Ashridge

20. Hemel Hempstead & the Gade Valley
21. Dunstable Downs & Caddington
22. Gerrards Cross & Chalfont St. Peter
23. Toddington & Houghton Regis
24. Burnham Beeches & Stoke Poges
25. Sundon & the Barton Hills
26. Hitchin & Hexton
27. Flamstead & Redbourn
28. Rickmansworth & Chenies

Book Castle
PUBLISHING

FAVOURITE WALKS
in and around Bedfordshire

Ivel Valley Walkers

The Ivel Valley Walkers were founded 25 years ago, and for most of that time has been a group within the Ramblers.

To celebrate our anniversary, we asked our members to contribute their 25 favourite walks in and around Bedfordshire. The result is this book, which covers virtually every area of the county, offers walks from 4 to 16 miles long, and will allow you to fully explore the delights of this under appreciated area.

Most of the walks are circular. Although primarily country walks, three do include some of the historic and recreational areas of Bedford, the town at the heart of our area. The two linear walks have reasonable bus services between the start and end.

So, put your boots on, get out and enjoy the Bedfordshire countryside.

Book
Castle
PUBLISHING

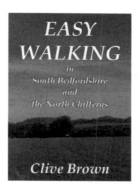

EASY WALKING
in South Bedfordshire and the North Chilterns

Clive Brown

The Northern Chilterns and the southern part of Bedfordshire are a well kept secret. While other areas and regions of this country have a deserved reputation for being excellent walking country, this part of the world has hidden away, guarding its beauty and its diversity. Thick wooded slopes, rolling chalk downland, steep hillsides with terrific views at the top. Tranquil towpaths alongside canals with the occasional narrowboat chugging past. Peaceful undulating farmland and sleepy picturesque villages. The book presents a comprehensive guide to the best walks in this locality; the routes use paths, bridleways, rights of way, National Trails and canal towpaths. Some background information and nature notes are included after the walk directions. All the walks are circular; some are in areas already popular with walkers, others are in areas less popular and perhaps less accessible.

The area covered in this book is dominated by the chalk ridge escarpment of the Chiltern Hills. Not particularly high in comparison to other ranges of hills in this country, they nevertheless tower over the flatter land to the north and the lower south eastern end of the Greensand Ridge around Woburn.

Book Castle PUBLISHING

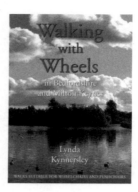

WALKING WITH WHEELS
in Bedfordshire and Milton Keynes

Lynda Kynnersley

The walks have all been chosen for their ease of access with as much information as possible about the physical features of the route, to enable people with limited mobility to decide for themselves whether a particular walk is within their ability. Some walks are on trails that have been specially adapted to make them more accessible but others are on country paths, which have reasonably flat, smooth and hard surfaces.

The walks vary in length from a mile and a half up to seven miles, with the possibility of extending them to up to fourteen miles. The majority of the walks are designed to be circular with different outward and return routes, but in a few cases there are no suitable return routes and the directions will say to retrace your steps to the start point.

Details of how to get to the start point, where to park and where to find refreshments are all included, as well as general information of interest about the area and what wildlife you may see - everything in fact for a good trip out.

Book
Castle
PUBLISHING